BROKEN JOURNEY

A true story of courage and survival

Dedication

To Simon, Justin, Suzanna and Christy
– and to Colin to whom I owe my life

BROKEN JOURNEY

A true story of courage and survival

Jennifer Murray

Polar First
One Onslow Gardens
London, SW7 3LX
jeffasolo@aol.com
www.polarfirst.com

Copyright © Jennifer Murray 2006

A catalogue record for this book is available from the British Library
ISBN 10: 1-903872-189
ISBN 13: 978-1903-872185

The author and publishers have made every effort to ensure the accuracy of the information in this book at the time of going to press. However, they cannot accept any responsibility for any loss, injury or inconvenience resulting from the use
of information contained in this guide.

All rights reserved. No part of this publication may be reproduced, stored in a retrieval system, or transmitted, in any form or by any means, electronic or mechanical, including photocopying and recording, or by any information storage and retrieval system except as may be expressly permitted by the UK 1988 Copyright Design & Patents Act and the USA 1976 Copyright Act or in writing from the publisher. Requests for permission should be addressed to Polar First, One Onslow Gardens, London, SW7 3LX

Cover photographs: © Mike Sharp
Additional photographs courtesy of Martin Hartley, Mike Sharp and Colin Bodill
Cover design: Catherine Ames
Editor: Susannah Wight

Produced for Polar First by
Navigator Guides
info@navigatorguides.com
www.navigatorguides.com

Printed in Great Britain by Biddles Ltd

Contents

6365

The Route

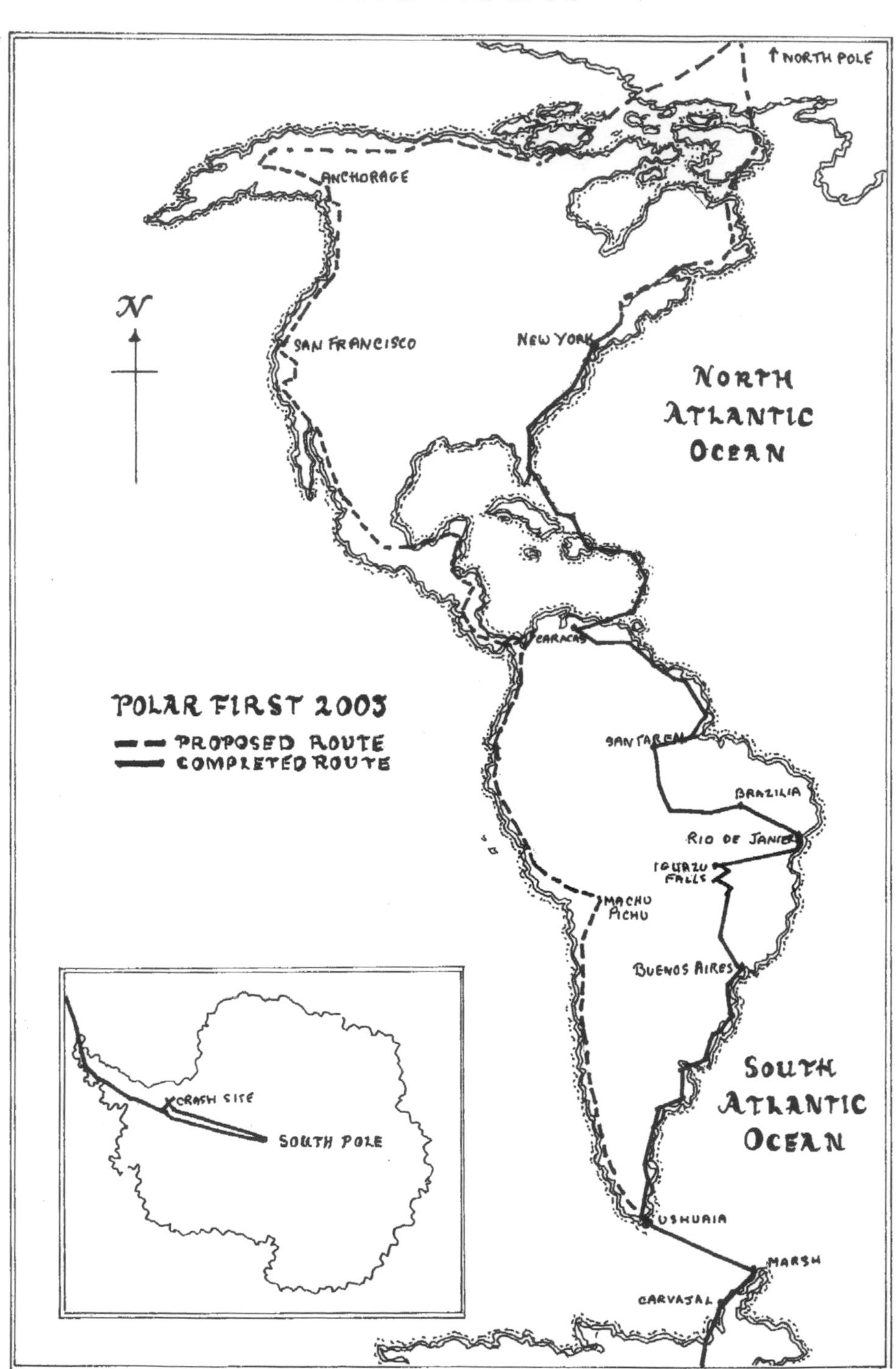
NORTH POLE
ANCHORAGE
N
SAN FRANCISCO
NEW YORK
NORTH ATLANTIC OCEAN
CARACAS
POLAR FIRST 2003
PROPOSED ROUTE
COMPLETED ROUTE
SANTAREM
BRAZILIA
RIO DE JANIE
IGUAZU FALLS
MACHU PICHU
BUENOS AIRES
SOUTH ATLANTIC OCEAN
CRASH SITE
SOUTH POLE
USHUAIA
MARSH
CARVAJAL

'Always in the big woods when you leave familiar ground and step off alone into a new place there will be, along with the feelings of curiosity and excitement, a little nagging dread. It is the ancient fear of the unknown, and it is your first bond with the wilderness you are going into. What you are doing is exploring. You are undertaking the first experience, not of the place, but of yourself in that place. It is an experience or our essential loneliness; for nobody can discover the world for anybody else. It is only after we have discovered it for ourselves that it becomes a common ground and a common bond, and we cease to be alone'.

W. Berry

N44FA

PROLOGUE

'You see things and say, "why?"
But I dream things and say "why not?"'

George Bernard Shaw

Left: N44EA

The approach of two small Twin Otter planes broke the months of winter silence at Patriot Hills. For four months of the year night prevails in this remote mountain range deep in Antarctica. There is no living soul. Temperatures plummet and the only sound is of the harsh winds that flow unobstructed for hundreds of miles off the polar ice cap, picking up speed as they go to form hurricane-force winds, which can blow for days on end.

The two planes landed softly, and the occupants climbed stiffly out of the closed confines of the cramped interior. Karl Z'Berg, captain of one of the Twin Otters and veteran of more than 30 polar summers, braced himself against the force of the wind and the freezing temperatures, quickly donning his habitual blue knitted hat, outer garments and goggles. He was happy to be back in the harsh and hazardous environment that he loved, drawn back to it almost spiritually year after year by the utter isolation and unforgiving beauty of Antarctica.

It was the end of a long journey from the high Arctic for the crews of the two Twin Otters. Also on board were Mike Sharp, the base manager, and Boris Mihovilovic of Antarctic Logistics and Expeditions (ALE) who had joined the Twin Otter crews in Punta Arenas. They had arrived to 'open up' the expedition base camp for the new season.

The only sign of the previous year's camp was the shrouded snowmobiles, parked close to where the two planes had landed, and numerous flags fluttering on the end of bamboo poles in the distance. The flags marked the position of the now buried and dismantled tents from the year before, the entrance to an underground food cavern and a buried hangar containing a yellow single engine Cessna airplane. Ten years previously the hangar was on the surface – it had been slowly buried each year and the roof now lay some three feet below the surface.

Under Mike Sharp's directions everyone went efficiently about their allotted tasks and within a couple of days the base camp was operable. The snowmobiles and snowplough were in action and the blue ice runway was clear and level in preparation for the arrival of the large four-engine Russian Ilyushin 76 transport plane, which would fly in from Punta Arenas, over 2,000 miles away on the southern tip of Chile.

The Ilyushin 76, would bring the remainder of the ALE team members, seasoned polar men and women from all over the world, all with a common passion – Antarctica. The Twin Otters were there to provide local transport and 'Search and Rescue' for explorers trekking to the South Pole and mountaineers climbing the 5,000-metre peak of Mount Vinson, the highest mountain in Antarctica.

Patriot Hills forms part of the Ellsworth Mountain Range, which lies 600 miles to the north of the South Pole on the Antarctic continent. Here the katabatic winds power off the ridges and down onto the flat plateau, forming great sheets of blue ice and a natural runway where large transport planes can land on wheels – if they can tackle the force of the crosswinds. The Twin Otters are ski equipped and capable of landing almost anywhere on the high plateau of Antarctica, providing the winds will allow it.

Summer temperatures at Patriot Hills hover around -20°C with winds seldom less than 25 knots. In winter the temperatures drop as low as -70°C, but no one has ever spent a winter there, so no one truly knows. With the wind chill factor it would be too much for any life form to survive. Patriot Hills also enjoys the dubious reputation of being one of the windiest place in all Antarctica; with the cold and the wind, suitable flying days are few and far between.

At the South Pole there is only one sunrise and one sunset each year. At Patriot Hills the first slither of sunlight pierces the polar twilight on 20 August and finally clears the horizon on 16 October. For four months there is 24 hours of daylight, then on 24 February the sun starts to disappear and is finally gone on 20 April. Today was the fourth day of full summer light. A lot of people had a lot of things to do in the following four months before Antarctica shut down again into the long dark winter.

RAF Kinloss, Scotland 00.55 GMT 20 DECEMBER 2003

Around the world, 24 hours a day, seven days a week, the banks of computers of aeronautical rescue coordination centres (ARCCs) monitor orbiting satellites picking up distress signals from emergency locator transmitters (ELTs) activated by people in trouble.

At RAF Kinloss in the far north of Scotland, Corporal Craig O'Reilly closed the front door of his barracks, braced himself against the cold and set out briskly for the short walk to the ARCC. It was 9.55pm; his duty watch was from 10pm to 7.30am.

The base lay wrapped in darkness. Only the light from the ARCC, the low building on the southwest perimeter of the airfield, cast a blue–white glow, fracturing off the icy gravelled path outside.

Squadron Leader Nick Phillips and Sergeant Gavin Thornton had been on duty for the last three hours and were able to report that it had been a quiet night, there had been no activations.

Corporal O'Reilly settled down to a routine watch, finalising paperwork and secondary duties, closing the log at midnight and opening the new one for the following day. By 1am there was little to do other than keep an eye on the screen and check the satellite information (SATS), which beamed earthward every half-hour.

England 01.00 GMT 20 DECEMBER 2003

In the county of Cheshire in northwest England my mother had a full house. Many of the family were gathered there; they would all be travelling south to Bedfordshire the following day for my niece's wedding.

All were sleeping soundly.

A hundred miles away to the east, across the Pennine Hills in Nottingham, Colin's partner Michelle and their two children were also sleeping. Michelle had just slipped back into sleep having checked their son Peter's blood sugar count, a thrice-nightly occurrence. Peter, aged 11, has Grade One diabetes and brain damage.

Further south in London, Tamara Hall, my personal assistant, in charge of Polar First 'Ground Support' was still up. She and her fiancé Ed Risso-Gill had just been to the cinema to see *Lord of the Rings*; they were on their way to Ed's apartment for some late scrambled eggs. Earlier that evening they had had a small celebratory Christmas party with our PR person, Sara Tye, and my husband's support team. Everyone was in high spirits, there was much to celebrate, and all was going well. Colin and I had achieved two of our targeted 'firsts': we had crossed the Drake Passage and reached the South Pole. Simon and Pen were still making steady progress.

As Sara was leaving she turned to Tamara and said: 'You know, we should have some sort of battle plan in case the unthinkable should happen. We should all know how to contact each other in case of an emergency over the Christmas break.' They exchanged contact details and wished each other a happy Christmas.

Patriot Hills, Antarctica 22.00 LOCAL TIME 19 DECEMBER 2003; 01.00 UTC 20 DECEMBER 2003

ALE had been operative for nearly two months and the season had gone well despite the usual weather delays. The ALE team was stretched to capacity with 68 explorers and mountaineers 'on the ice'. The walls of the radio tent shuddered under the familiar hammering as wind and airborne ice crystals battered the sides.

Inside, weatherman Jaco Wium adjusted his multi-striped woollen hat; everyone was beginning to don their more festive clothing as Christmas approached. He checked the latest weather satellite imaging on his computer screen. A few feet away on the other side of the tent, fellow South African, Jason Whiting, the communications operator, was waiting for the afternoon update from the ALE headquarters back in Punta Arenas. Both men were in their early 30s and spoke with an Afrikaans accent. Jaco was slightly taller and thinner, with a long, sensitive face, while Jason, with his fair colouring, had something of the Boer in his appearance, in spite of the fact he is half-English.

Jaco commented that the new images were showing widespread cloud cover to the north in the area where Colin Bodill and I were flying in our Bell 407 helicopter, 'November Four Four Echo Alpha' (N44EA), with Karl Z'Berg ahead in his Twin Otter plane carrying fuel for us. We had all set off an hour earlier under clear skies on the 300-mile journey north towards the Fowler Peninsula where we would meet Karl in his Twin Otter. He would then return to Patriot Hills and we would continue north to our next fuel cache at Camp Bravo on Alexander Island, another 370 miles to the north of Fowler, where ALE's second Twin Otter was positioned to provide our Search and Rescue cover.

The Twin Otters are fitted with autopilots allowing safe, straight and level flight in cloud. Colin and I were comparative newcomers to polar flight and the helicopter had no autopilot.

No one liked having both Twin Otters away from camp for too long, with so many expeditions on the ice dependent on them. There were three groups of mountaineers on the slopes of Mount Vinson and six foot expeditions, one of which was being made by my husband Simon and veteran polar explorer Pen Hadow. Simon and Pen were attempting to walk unsupported for 750 miles, from the coast of the Antarctic continent to the South Pole. If successful, Simon would be the oldest person by some 10 years and Pen would be the first Brit to go unsupported to both North and South Poles.

Jason laid down his headsets and went to peer over Jaco's shoulder at the weather picture.

'Not so good,' Jaco said, 'let's hope the helicopter makes it through to Camp Bravo otherwise everyone could be socked in for days and our crews won't be back for Christmas.'

The tent flap opened letting in a blast of cold air and Mike Sharp came in sporting his festive effort: a two-shades-of-blue fleece court-jester-style hat. He removed his snow goggles and outer gloves.

'Any updates?' he asked, brushing away ice crystals from his week-old beard and clapping his hands together to restore circulation. Outside it was -20°C with winds of 25 knots, bringing the wind chill factor down to -

35°C. Even in camp you had to be constantly on guard against the stunning cold and possible frostbite.

Jason moved over to make room for Mike to take a look and said, 'Just had Jennifer's half-hour report. Flight normal, they are north of the 79th parallel – clouds extensive there.'

The satellite phone buzzed. It was Karl in the Twin Otter; he reported solid cloud cover below for as far as the eye could see…

RAF Kinloss, Scotland 01.35 GMT 20 DECEMBER

At RAF Kinloss the peace was shattered by the claxon warning of an activated beacon. The three men quickly turned to their screens. A message was coming through from Chile. A British registered beacon had gone off in Antarctica. Corporal O'Reilly quietly picked up the phone and dialled his counterpart in the Falklands.

La Jolla, California 17.38 LOCAL TIME 19 DECEMBER; 01.38 GMT 20 DECEMBER

Eight hours behind London, the local time was coming up for 5.30pm on 19 December. It was a typical southern Californian winter's afternoon, the temperature 22°C (72°F), with blue skies. At the offices of Blue Sky Network, Jon Gilbert stood for a few moments looking out over the rooftops to the Pacific Ocean, enjoying the spectacular view from the window of their modern block. The office was quiet; only fellow worker Jonas Olsen and he were left. The rest of the staff had already departed for the long Christmas break and Jon and Jonas were sorting through a few last details before heading off themselves. Jonas had a flight to catch at 8pm to Palo Alto to the north of San Francisco, where he would be joining his wife and 6-month-old son. Jon and his wife Bobbie were going to have a quiet Christmas at home, right there in La Jolla.

As Jon turned away from the window his cellular phone beeped – an alert message had come through. Seconds later Jonas's phone also beeped.

CHAPTER ONE
Preparation

'Patience and perseverance have a magical effect before which difficulties disappear and obstacles vanish.'

John Quincy Adams

Left: CB & JM, survival training, Alaska

'We did it – now what about the big one?' Those were Colin Bodill's words to me within days of completing our record-breaking solo flights around the world in 2000.

Colin became the first person to fly a flexi-wing microlight solo around the world, while I, piloting my Robinson 44 helicopter, became the first woman to pilot a helicopter solo around the world, and the first person to do so without autopilot and in a piston engine helicopter. We had flown east–west, a journey that took us 99 days.

'The Big One' – to do what no helicopter pilot had ever done before, to fly around the world the other way, to fly via the South and North Poles. As with the east–west flights, you have to complete the journey in the same machine with the same crew, circle all the meridians and fly a minimum of 24,901 miles (40,075km) – the circumference of the equator.

We knew the risks if the engine were to quit. Three-quarters of the journey would be over hostile terrain, mountain ranges, equatorial rain forests, ocean crossings and the polar regions. The chances of survival are slim.

I had already put family and friends through anxious times with my previous flights around the world. Now the unanimous wish was that I should go back to painting pictures, planting my roses, doing nice, comfortable, grandmotherly activities and be happy to be given a new wheelbarrow, rather than a fuel bowser, which had been my 1999 Christmas present from my husband Simon.

Once again I reasoned with myself that there was still plenty of time for all that and my children were all grown up and very busy with their own lives, while Simon was running his own company and on an airplane much of the time. The argument was, of course, that they wanted me 'there' and they wanted me alive and not dead. I, for my part felt very much alive, I felt wonderful. Ever since I took up flying helicopters at the grand old age of 54, my life took on a whole new dimension and my love of adventure and challenge has had a field day ever since.

I had discovered the pure joy and freedom of flying, to soar like an eagle and hover like a humming bird where the beauty and splendour of the universe is all around you. Where you can travel the same route a million times and it's never the same. The light, the weather, the sunsets and sunrises all bring you untold worlds. You can dance the clouds, climb to the sunlit heavens or skim the forests – each flight a new adventure, a new challenge, your senses alert. You're truly living up there in the great blue where you follow no highway.

I have always loved a challenge, to test myself, to set goals, to go that one step further and ever since I made those first nerve-wracking solo cross-country flights after getting my pilots licence I have wanted to explore just that little bit further, to explore the skies and the world below.

In 1997, three years and 300 flying hours after getting my pilot's licence, I became the first woman to pilot a helicopter around the world with fellow pilot Quentin Smith. The aviation world thought we were mad and the helicopter manufacturer gave us a one in five chance of making it and said we wouldn't get as far as Pakistan. We flew east through Europe to Saudi Arabia, across the Indian Ocean, over the jungles of Borneo. We were fired on by pirates in the South China Seas; we witnessed the 'Hand Over' in Hong Kong; we made the 500-mile crossing of the Sea of Okhotsk from Japan to Eastern Russia and crossed the Bering Strait to Nome in Alaska; and from there journeyed southwards over the great glaciers and the Rockies to a surprised and happy Frank Robinson – the doubting helicopter manufacturer – in California. Finally we went onwards across the United States for what was potentially the most dangerous leg of the entire journey, the cold water crossings of the North Atlantic ocean, from Canada to Greenland, on to Iceland, the Faeroe Islands and finally back to Scotland…but we made it!

It had been tough: thousands of miles over water, the extremes of temperature, from the searing heat of the deserts to the Arctic cold of the far north. The elements dished up everything from sandstorms to blizzards. We had times of utter exhaustion, of disagreements, of frustration and moments of pure adrenalin-pumping fear. But then there was the flip side – the constant thrill of the challenge, of doing what no one had ever done before, the pure adventure, the beauty of our universe seen from the small bubble of a helicopter. To be able to soar and turn, to hover, to land almost anywhere, be it an iceberg or a sand dune. And we had the reward of raising funds for charity, to inspire others, to promote aviation and to share the great adventure through all the modern media channels. At last we arrived safely home, 87 days and 24,000 miles later, triumphant and saying 'never again'…

A few short weeks later I found myself once more looking to the skies and dreaming of far-off places. Once you have left the trodden path, have blazed your own trail, have known the freedom of the skies and felt the lure of the far horizon, it is difficult ever to let go.

And then I met Colin at an air show for record breakers at Woodford Airfield in the north of England. Colin, a quietly spoken north country man of medium height and stocky build, was already deep into planning a solo flight around the world in his microlight – with some help from various friends and his feisty and long suffering partner Michelle.

He said, 'Why don't you come too?'

I smiled saying, 'You've got to be kidding, and I'm way faster than you.'

'Want to bet?' was his quick reply.

Laughingly we shook hands. I was tempted. I had made my first flight with an infinitely more experienced pilot than myself and I had always had the secure feeling that Quentin would get us out of any serious problem. I needed to prove to myself that I could do it on my own.

Ten days later the bet was on.

Two years of preparation later and we were on our way.

It was tough; you have no one to turn to. The workload is huge, every day you must have everything in place for the day's flight. Clearances, flight plans, weather briefings, charts folded, all airfield frequencies sorted, route checked a hundred times, cameras and film at the ready and a drink somewhere you can reach with one hand. You have no copilot to do that along the way and no autopilot. When things turn nasty there's only you.

Only four days into my solo venture in 1997 I had a mechanical problem over the Mediterranean and I thought I would have to ditch in the sea. I was completely terrified and although I finally made it to Jordan, my confidence in myself was shattered. For the first time I began to wonder if I had taken on more than I could handle. Was I up to a solo flight in a small piston engine helicopter over thousands of miles of hostile terrain? No pilot, man or woman, had ever flown a helicopter solo around the world without an autopilot, or in a small piston engine helicopter, and I was after all just a bog-standard pilot while Colin, although in a flimsier, more vulnerable machine, was two-times World Microlight champion. But despite the doubts I was too committed and I didn't want to let Colin down, so I pulled myself together and on we went.

Colin nearly died on several occasions thanks to engine failure, severe turbulence in tropical storms, being forced down by fighter jets in China and having to make an emergency landing in a prawn breeding field miles from anywhere, where the military held him for three days before finally allowing him to continue to Hong Kong. But champions don't go easily and he always came through and never lost his cool. And we both made it around the world. Me in my helicopter. He in his microlight.

Colin dreamed of flying from earliest childhood, but it seemed like an impossible dream. He didn't have a privileged life. He grew up in a small mining community, his father, like his grandfather, had been a miner. When Colin was still a very small boy his mother was diagnosed with multiple sclerosis and his father had to quit going down the pits to look after her. The pension they lived on was negligible and to help ends meet Colin's father would sell their small coal allowance to put food on the table. Their only heating was a small coal fire, so Colin and his younger brother would go out after dark in the bitter winter cold to try and find lumps of coal on the slag heaps behind their house.

Searching the slag heaps continued until Colin was 12 years old; he then devised a better night-time sortie! His bedroom window was right beside the small railway that took the coal from the mines to the terminal. There was a bend some 100 yards before his house where the train had to slow down. He reckoned he could jump onto the moving train, then chuck a few lumps of coal off as he passed his house, ride the carriage to the terminal and then get in the empty train going back. It worked well, but the round trip took a long time. If he could just nerve himself to jump from the full train to the empty one going in the opposite direction, he could be home in half the time. Taking that first jump from the top of a fully loaded car into the bottom of an empty one was the greatest hurdle. It took him a little while to summon up the courage. But, he assures me, once he got the hang of it, it worked well!

Colin's first airborne efforts saw him running full tilt down grassy slopes. He was one of the early pioneers of hang-gliding in the UK; he built his own glider from pictures he saw in an American magazine and then, with no one to instruct him, managed slowly to increase the length of his airborne moments. A friend joined him and together they improved their technique to the point where they decided it was time to leap off a cliff in the Pennine Hills. They drew straws. Colin's friend got the short one but couldn't bring himself to go for it. The minutes passed, a small crowd gathered – alarmingly small dots far below. Colin turned to his mate with a grin and giving the thumbs up and saying 'I guess I gotta go' took a running leap – and made it safely to the ground! He said it was one of the most terrifying experiences of his life.

A few years later Colin built his own microlight, once more working from pictures in a magazine. He had a job as a welder in a factory at the time and spent his lunch and tea breaks cutting and welding bits together, much to the entertainment of his fellow workers. I believe his was the first ever microlight in Britain. The great day arrived for the launching. He trucked his machine to a flat field some 10 miles from the factory and, with only his hang-gliding experience and a rudimentary understanding of aerodynamics, he hurtled down the field and into the air. The only problem was that the winds were ferocious and he'd set the wing slightly out of kilter, so it would only fly around in circles. None the less, he somehow made it back to the factory to a hero's welcome from his fellow workers and the local press.

Colin later told me that the winds were so strong that day that he should never have been flying. 'If you paid me £10,000 today I wouldn't do that again!' he said.

Colin has twice won the World Microlight Championships and in 1998 he beat the world record for an open cockpit aircraft flight from London to Sydney in his little flexi-wing microlight.

When not in the air Colin likes nothing better than to be building or repairing machines, mostly microlights, but he's a dab hand at all mechanical and electrical gadgets – very handy if you're miles from anywhere.

So this was the man I met at the Woodford Air Show.

After our solo flights Colin got his helicopter licence and in 2001 was available to join me in my R44 helicopter for the London to Sydney Air Race. The only helicopter among 35 fixed-wing aircraft, we came third. Once again we had our share of good and bad times. We worked well as a team, not too many arguments, although I found that underneath that quiet, gentle exterior was a stubborn, wildly competitive person. A mutual friend of ours calls him 'Chief Jutting Jaw!' I have to admit that when it comes to stubbornness and competitiveness, I'm just as bad as Colin, but somehow we worked well enough together for both of us to feel confident about sharing a cockpit once more for our attempt on the poles, although I do remember Colin suggesting at one point that two helicopters might be better than one. After the London to Sydney Race we spent two months in Morocco on a filmset flying separate R44 helicopters. We ferried film crews and actors from one site to another, with frequent crossings of the Atlas Mountains – and continued to discuss going for the 'Big One'.

I wrote two books, one of which was published, and I made a five-part documentary series on flying solo. I gave talks and wrote articles for magazines. There are never enough hours in the day, which is the way I like it. There is no question of that nasty feeling that 'my life no longer has a meaning or purpose now the children have left home'.

On all our world flights we worked to raise funds and awareness for charities. My 1997 journey was for Save the Children and Colin's Australian flight was for the the Princess Diana Memorial Fund. And our solo flights were for Operation Smile, a small and very active charity that sends surgeons and nurses all around the world, operating on children and young adults with facial deformities.

Colin and I both felt a little guilty that we would once more be submitting family and friends to times of worry, but I did say that it would be the last expedition and what better year than 2003, the year of the 100th anniversary of flight.

On 17 December 1903 two brothers, Wilbur and Orville Wright, changed the world as we knew it forever when they made their first momentous powered flights at Kitty Hawke on the east coast of the United States. The entire aviation world would be commemorating the date. What a personal celebration it would be if we could reach the South Pole on that very day.

The most daunting and thankless task of all in putting together an expedition like this is always trying to find sponsors, not only for the flight but also for the helicopter. We wanted a larger helicopter than my small piston engine Robinson 44, in which I had flown on the previous flights around the world. We needed the added safety factor of a more powerful machine and one that had enough room to carry World Wildlife Fund (WWF) scientists and biologists from time to time and have room for all the necessary polar survival kit. And anyway, my original R44 helicopter was no longer available; it was residing in glory in the new Smithsonian Air and Space Museum at Dulles Airport, Washington DC. On top of that there was the actual expedition to organise: route planning, fuel, permits, clearances, working with the charity, filming...the list went on and on.

We needed information on the polar regions – the big unknown. I talked to Sarah Wheeler, the author of *Terra Incognita*, the story of her six months in Antarctica. Sarah told me much about the coastal areas and her experiences but suggested I should talk to polar explorer Pen Hadow to obtain information on the poles.

That introduction to Pen changed much in the lives of the Murray family. Pen proved charming, enthusiastic and helpful, just into his 40s and looking astonishingly like a younger version of Tony Blair. When I asked him what he actually did for a living the wider ramifications of his work became apparent: 'Well, I formed this little company called Polar Travel. I can arrange for you to go to the polar regions on board an icebreaker in five-star comfort, or you can pull a sledge!'

The sledge idea appealed, but I said, 'Sadly I'm too old to pull a sledge.'

'Not at all', he said. 'It's just a question of commitment.'

I thought long and hard about that one, not for me but for my husband Simon. Perhaps he would be interested? What fun it would be if we embarked together on a simultaneous adventure.

At breakfast the next morning I put it to Simon. His immediate reaction was, 'Walk to the South Pole? You've got to be kidding. I've got a company to run.'

I pointed out that he really didn't have to be away for too long. That he could be flown in and just do the last degree, the last 60 miles to the South Pole. It would only take 10 days.

'Anyway', I said, 'Pen is coming here tomorrow, why don't you talk to him?'

Pen arrived, the two of them hit it off immediately and after a fairly alcoholic lunch the deal was done. Simon and Pen had firmly decided to go and not just the last 60 miles, but the whole thing, the full 750 statute miles from the coast of Antarctica to the South Pole. They would do it unsupported and it would take at least two months.

From then on our house was flooded with every possible book on polar exploration, with us happily throwing awesome statistics and facts backwards and forwards to each other. I told Simon that Antarctica is larger that China and India put together, 'And did you know the continent holds 70 per cent of the world's fresh water and 90 per cent of the world's ice, and that it's the highest, coldest, driest and windiest continent on earth?'

'I know, I know,' he said. 'And, did you know that Antarctica is an ice desert? The annual precipitation is only 20cm, that's only fractionally more than the Sahara Desert.'

'And', he added, 'it also has the lowest temperatures ever recorded on earth. A staggering -129°F at Vostok, the Russian scientific research station near the South Pole. The average summer temperatures in the interior hover around -20°C to -40°C and then you have to add in the wind chill factor – and there's seldom a day without wind.'

'What about the winds?' I said, 'Antarctica has the most powerful winds on earth; I believe 200 knots have been recorded.'

'And', he replied, 'in the Antarctic Treaty that was signed on 1 December 1959 by 12 nations in Washington DC and came into force on 23 June 1961, it was agreed that Antarctica would belong to no one country and that it would be used for peaceful and scientific purposes only.'

'But Chile and Argentina still contest the issue between each other,' I said. 'Did you know that in 1978 the Argentine government, in an effort to strengthen its claim, went to the lengths of sending one of their pregnant citizens to Antarctica to give birth? On 7 January that year, Emilio Marcos de Palma was born in Hope Bay on the Antarctic Peninsular – the first and only child to be born on that frozen continent…' And so it went on as we discovered more and more about this frozen wasteland.

Preparations were seriously under way. Simon was to be seen dragging car tyres around the countryside, hoping to get his 63-year-old muscles fit for pulling a 150-kilo (300lb) sledge.

Our children despaired: not just one parent, but now both were heading for the bottom of the world. 'What about Christmas?' they said 'This will be the first time we haven't all been together.'

It was true; and the mere thought of being away from them all for so long was a real wrench as we had always managed to have the family together, despite everyone living in different corners of the globe. In 2003 our son Justin, his wife Pinyi and their two daughters Nicola (nine) and Joanna (seven) would leave Amsterdam and head off to Seoul in Korea where Justin would be the country manager for Cathay Pacific. Our daughter Christy with her husband Nick Powell and brand new baby son Domingo were threatening to leave London and go to Hong Kong for at least 5 years, where Christy and Suze, our elder daughter, were born and where Simon and I spent the first 30 years of our married life. Nick works with Simon in his asset management company, GEMS. Suze was living in London running her successful antique shop specialising in Chinese furniture and porcelain, but she too was constantly on the move, spending much of her time in China sourcing goods for the business. The family were all happy and active – including my 86-year-old mother Eleanor, living in the northwest of England, frequently exhibiting her oil and water-colour paintings, tending her beloved and rather large garden and playing 18 holes of golf most weeks. They all did their best to dissuade us. They were naturally concerned, but as always the support was there.

Preparation was the usual 'cart and horse' situation, the horse frequently getting muddled up with the cart. You have to raise the funds, but you must start putting everything else in place too, and hope that it will all work out on the day. A helicopter, avionics, insurance, route planning, clearances, permits, a charity, a documentary and of course, sponsors...

Yet again I had hoped it might all be a little easier this time – but it wasn't. It was much the toughest trip I had prepared for, despite the fact that Colin and I had successful track records and that we both had gained a certain level of notoriety. Getting sponsors proved immensely difficult thanks to a depressed market, the war in Iraq and SARS. For months SARS had virtually closed down Hong Kong, where I had most of my contacts.

I spent months trying to talk to someone serious in Eurocopter; many friends in France tried to help me, including Lionel Poilane, Chairman of the Helicopter Club of France; and, in the USA, Al Trenk of Liberty helicopters introduced me to Eurocopter USA. My hope was that they would supply us with a machine. My argument was that all previous east–west circumnavigations had been in American helicopters and I felt it was time Europe got in on the act...And so I kept trying.

We needed publicity to woo our sponsors. I was introduced to a dynamic young blonde who knew everyone in television, which led to many meetings in London and Washington DC with National Geographic magazine. It appeared that they wanted to make a documentary series with us and the World Wildlife Fund. I was told Eurocopter might be interested if National Geographic came on board.

In June I went to America, to Atchison, Ohio, Amelia Erhardt's birthplace, to receive the International Harmon Trophy for my solo flight around the world in 2000. I had been rated as having achieved the single greatest female aviation feat of the year. The honour was huge – previous recipients included Amelia Erhardt herself and Amy Johnson. I hoped the publicity would help our ratings with potential sponsors.

Our optimism took a sharp plunge in July 2002. Colin and I were at the British Helicopter Championships when word came through that Steve Brooks and Quentin Smith, my erstwhile copilot from my trip in 1997, had successfully reached the North Pole by helicopter. They had stolen the march on us. Were they attempting both poles? Were they out to beat us? Would they be the first? I felt kicked in the stomach. I had seen Quentin just a couple of short weeks before when he told me he was thinking of giving up flying! I had always been open about my plans – too open it seems!

The next news was that Quentin's engineer was in Anchorage and before I knew it they were in Mexico. It looked certain that they would be attempting the ultimate goal – the South Pole and to complete the full circle around the world via the poles. Could we even justify continuing? The name of our challenge – 'Polar First' – now had a mocking, hollow ring. To be second took away much of the impetus, the driving incentive, even though the whole venture had become so much more than just going for a 'first', it was the 'first' element that everything else was built around and it was how we were presenting our challenge. We knew only too well how Robert Falcon Scott must have felt to see Roald Amundsen's flag fluttering at the South Pole. Amundsen had beaten him to it by one short month. The parallels were there. Amundsen had told Scott he was going to the North Pole when all along his goal was Antarctica. Quentin had told me he was thinking of giving up flying...

The purpose of Scott and Amundsen's explorations were much, much more than just reaching the bottom of the world. They both spent over a year in Antarctica before their 'push to the Pole'. They built their base huts for 'over wintering'; they charted, mapped, studied the wildlife and collected rock samples, amassing a wealth of scientific information.

What we were attempting could hardly begin to compare with those heroic expeditions. We did however have goals apart from going for 'firsts'. We would be working with WWF and planned to devote a great deal of time recording, taking photos and sending back information to our website so that we could ultimately share our adventure and the work being done by WWF with a wide audience, particularly schools.

We simply had to put the thought of the possibility of being second behind us and get on with our own preparation – and there was always the chance that they might not make it. Several weeks later I heard that Steve Brooks had contacted various people about charts for Antarctica; there was now no longer any doubt of their intentions.

Time was evaporating. There were just 14 months to takeoff and we still had no word from Eurocopter. We had no helicopter and we were into August when everyone was on holiday. We had all the family together in France. Simon and I were deep in planning and get-fit programmes. Simon got plenty of Gallic comments like 'Monsieur, 'ave you lost your car?' when found dragging his tyres along the rural byways of the Dordogne.

I kept delaying phoning Lionel Poilane to enquire about Eurocopter, nervous of bad news. I felt I couldn't cope with another 'non'. Eventually I summoned up my courage. He was gloriously enthusiastic; he said he had already discussed the idea of a Cousteau-style documentary with Jean Francois Bigay, the CEO of Eurocopter. He said he expected good news daily. Three weeks went by and finally Lionel phoned, still enthusiastic: 'Jennifer darling, I am seeing the Vice President on Tuesday. I am rooting for you – I think you are just the right person and it will cost them nothing – just one or two helicopters around the world…'

Lionel's enthusiasm was infectious, but events around the world were bad. It was only a year since 9/11. War with Iraq was on the agenda, Saddam Hussein was refusing to allow in more weapons inspectors, Bush was having none of it and Germany was accusing Bush of behaving like Hitler. Stock markets were down, it was a lousy time for raising sponsorship and sometimes I felt I should be putting all my efforts into something weightier rather than attempting a world record first in a helicopter. It was always the thought that we would be working with WWF that kept me going forward – in some small way we would be doing our bit for the environment and aviation.

I also thought about what a friend of mine at the Royal Geographical Society had said to me: 'I like the fact that you have never pretended to be doing anything other than what you are – going for a first. That you don't claim to be an explorer, or attempting to give your challenge a scientific justification.'

At the time I nodded in agreement, although inwardly shaking my head and thinking 'She's got that wrong.' I am an explorer, we all are;

some just go a little further than others. We all have something in our hearts that drives us. Past explorers and adventurers discovered continents, islands, mountains, rivers, the creatures of the earth, weather patterns and ocean currents, and still exploration continues. We still don't know how much we don't know.

I contacted Dick Smith, the first person to pilot a helicopter solo around the world, and one of the world's great helicopter and fixed-wing pilot explorers. Dick was, I believe, the first pilot to fly a helicopter to the North Pole. He had given me many useful tips over the years and his books have always been a great source of reference and inspiration. I wanted his views on a north–south flight right around the world routing through New Zealand. His reply was direct and to the point:

> *Thanks for your note. I believe a Pole-to-Pole flight will be hard enough, receive just as much publicity and make just as good a film. I was originally planning a Pole-to-Pole flight when I headed my Jet ranger to the North Pole, but found it so hard and after seeing Twin Otters operating there I changed my mind about doing it in a helicopter and purchased a Twin Otter which allowed me to go right around the world via the Poles.*
>
> *Everything is possible, but if you decide to go right around the world via the Poles I believe there will be horrendous difficulties in getting approval to fly via Macquarie Island – they are absolutely paranoid about helicopters worrying penguins!*

We decided against New Zealand.

October 2002 was a bad month for the world and for us. Chechen terrorists laid siege to a theatre in Moscow and then killed many hostages; Washington was terrorised by snipers; and we got a final but polite 'non' from Eurocopter. And then at the beginning of November, en route to Hong Kong in search of sponsors, I received the shocking and desperately sad news that my dear friend and great supporter Lionel Poilane had died. He had been flying his Agusta 109 helicopter to his country home on the north coast of France, when sea fog had closed in as he was approaching his landing site. He apparently tried to land once and failed. He then circled out to sea for a further attempt but never made it. His wife and dog died with him. They left behind two young teenage daughters.

Now, as I write this, I know, but for the grace of God, my own and Colin's scenario could so easily have had the same ending. The last time I spoke to Lionel, his closing words to me were 'Courage Jennifer'.

I was going home to the UK from Hong Kong via California. I planned to visit several potential sponsors and tie in a book club lunch for 400 people in Los Angeles. My book *Now Solo* was one of five chosen for the event. But I still had to find a helicopter. I arranged a visit to Bell Helicopters in Dallas, Texas. Perhaps they might be interested in providing the helicopter.

Bell has a worldwide helicopter maintenance infrastructure and a reputation for global travel. Both Ross Perot Jr and Dick Smith had made their epic world flights in a Bell and, more recently, Ron Bower and John Williams had set a world speed record in a Bell 430.

I received an immediate and warm response to my letter from John Murphey, the CEO of Bell Helicopters. He wrote:

> *Regrettably I will miss your visit because of a scheduled business trip to Asia during that time. I will ask our President and COO, Glenn Hess, to host your visit. We would like the opportunity to give you an overview of Bell, visit our flight test facility to see our 609 Tilt rotor, and if you have the time we could try to schedule some time for you in our V-22 simulator. We will be happy to make any arrangements you may need for travel and accommodation whilst you are in Fort Worth.*

Did they think I was about to buy a helicopter when I was looking for the loan of one? No doubt they were going to be hugely surprised when I told them what I really wanted!

I was given hospitality Texan style – huge, generous and spontaneous. Everything went well and Bell gave me a heroine's welcome. I cautiously mentioned that perhaps they might loan us a helicopter with the possibility of our buying it at the end of the journey, though I wasn't at all sure that Simon would go along with that. Bell told me they would 'be in touch'.

Time was now disappearing at an alarming rate. I had gone down so many blind alleys. It was November already and there were just 11 months to go until we were due to take off.

Were Steve and Quentin already at the South Pole? They weren't the only ones with their sights set on the poles – I heard that Polly Vacher, a friend and fixed-wing pilot, was also set on attempting a flight around the world via the poles. Polly had secured her sponsors and was being supported by the British Antarctic Survey (BAS) in Antarctica. The BAS had given her special dispensation to cache her fuel at its Rothera base on Adelaide Island and the Americans had given her permission to place her other fuel cache on the other side of the continent at the New Zealand Scott base. I had also been in touch with BAS but received rather different results.

Pen Hadow had stressed to me that it was important to have BAS on side and that without their sanction, permits and clearances could be

The history of the bottom of the world

The history of the bottom of the world is all comparatively recent. It wasn't until Ross's expedition in 1839 that we knew for sure that there was even land there, indeed a whole continent south of the Antarctic Circle. Amundsen was the first to reach the South Pole in 1912, followed by Scott a month later.

Aviation is even more recent. The Wright brothers made that first ever motorised flight in 1903. In 1923 Allcock and Brown made the first non-stop flight across the Atlantic in a fixed-wing plane and the first plane to land at the South Pole was in 1957. It was only in 1981 that Ross Perot Jr became the first person to fly a helicopter around the world piloting a Bell Jet Ranger. So I say, set your own challenges, go out there, climb your mountains, reach for the sky, seek the far horizons – it's never too late!

National Geographic and some potential sponsors had wanted us to go via New Zealand as that was, in every sense, 'around the world'. We too liked the idea, especially as it would make ours a different challenge from that of Steve Brooks. The difficulty with the New Zealand route was the ocean distances – they were extreme. The longest leg was 700 nautical miles from the small island of Macquarie to Young Island, a barren, uninhabited hunk of ice and snow-covered rock lying some 500 miles from McMurdo, the American base on Antarctica. No helicopter has that sort of endurance, so unless there was a friendly cruise ship to land and refuel on, there was little hope. I checked out cruise ships and there appeared to be only one sailing per year!

difficult. So I emailed the Director, telling him briefly of our plans and asking if we might come and visit them at their headquarters in Cambridge. I received a reply from his Head of Administration and Logistics, and arranged a meeting in January. Shortly afterwards I received another e-mail that was obviously sent to me in error saying… 'Done, alas. She is coming to see me in the New Year!'

Simon in the meantime was going from strength to strength. He had persuaded Tetley's Tea to sponsor him; he planned to raise funds for the Royal Geographical Society; and already had an additional flow of funds from donors. He spent a night on Dartmoor climbing cliffs, falling in rivers and crawling in bogs in near freezing conditions with Pen and a former SAS man putting him through his paces, checking that his heart, soul and body were really up to the challenge. Unsurprisingly he came through with flying colours. He spent five tough years, between 1959 and 1963, in the French Foreign Legion during the Algerian War and has kept fairly fit ever since.

In December I finally managed to secure our first major sponsor. HSBC was in; we only needed five more!

Tamara Hall, the cousin of a friend from my childhood, came to work for me. An Oxford University graduate, young, bright and enthusiastic, Tamara was a godsend and the London headquarters was now a team of two. Colin was 200 miles north of London in Nottingham and was unable to play a very active role in preparations because he was busy supporting his young family as a microlight instructor.

The New Year of 2003 was upon us and the day of our scheduled meeting with BAS had arrived. Colin and I went to Cambridge determined to be as charming as possible despite the negative email.

We were ushered in to the Head of Administration's office, who acknowledged us with a nod and with a brief handshake waved us into a couple of chairs on the other side of his desk.

Once again we recounted our tale of upholding British traditions for adventure and exploration, we told him of our plans and how we were inspired by the scientific work that BAS were doing. His response was terse and to the point.

The gist of it was to the effect that Antarctica belongs to nobody, so they couldn't stop us going there, but we weren't welcome.

We were, needless to say, stunned. I tried to reassure him of our good intentions, but there was little more to say and I could see Colin was about to explode, so we hurriedly took our leave with Colin muttering something about, 'That miserable little man...and who's paying his bills I'd like to know? It's us, the taxpayer!'

That evening I went to the Royal Geographical Society with Pen to hear Caroline Hamilton give an inspiring talk about her trek to the North Pole. Faith was restored, a meeting of like minds – reaching for the peaks, going for the challenge. A far cry from the grey corridors of BAS. Simon summed it up nicely: 'The predatory animals of the Civil Service are more frightening than any Arctic polar bear!' and like Colin took the taxpayers' view. We were the ones paying for them in their endless examination of snowflakes.

As events were to turn out, we bypassed BAS in Antarctica. However, we were given helpful and friendly receptions both before and in Antarctica by the USA, Argentina and Chile who all operate scientific research stations in Antarctica. It was sad that our one contact in BAS was so unsupportive, especially knowing the immense contribution members of BAS have made and continue to make and the many people I count as my friends who have worked in the organisation.

I have tried to look at adventurers and explorers from the scientists' point of view and I suppose I would find people like us a nuisance, a possible hindrance to their work. They are busy and our contribution to Antarctica perhaps has little meaning to the scientific mind. On the other hand, they wouldn't be there either if they didn't have the spirit of adventure. But I think that the scientists who are actually out there in the field are a rather different breed from those who never venture forth. I like to think that ours was a one-off encounter and does not reflect BAS and its people at all.

I had to get my annual helicopter proficiency renewal. This offered a great chance to learn more about Steve and Quentin, as I would be doing the renewal with Quentin's father, Mike Smith. The Smiths ran and owned the helicopter facility where we kept our R44 helicopter. We are also somewhat related by marriage as Quentin's sister Sasha is married to my nephew John.

While making a 'confined landing' on top of a small concrete shed, I casually asked Mike how Quentin was getting on. Had he and Steve reached the South Pole? I was stunned and delighted to hear that they were still in South America. I knew that ANI's season would be over at the end of January and it was already the 21st. The short Antarctic summer closes in fast at the end of January, with temperatures dropping dramatically as the sun sinks rapidly ever lower each day on the horizon until it's gone and stays gone throughout the polar winter.

'They've left it a bit late.' I said.

Mike laughed, 'Well, you know Quentin!'

I asked what the delay was, was it the weather?

Mike was a little vague: 'Uh, well I think they are still working on their clearances and trying to get the army to cache fuel.'

It all sounded very encouraging from our point of view.

The news two days later I wouldn't have wished on my worst enemy. At 7am I turned on my radio to the breaking news: 'Two helicopter pilots have ditched off the coast of Antarctica, satellite phone call received from life raft.' I prayed they had both made it into the life raft and felt dreadful about my earlier hopes that they wouldn't complete their journey, when I had simply hoped they would be stuck in South America.

I phoned my sister Gillian (John's mother). She'd heard the news too but had been unable to reach Sasha. Then the next news on the radio was that they had both made it into the life raft. What a miracle. To get out of a ditched helicopter is tough and the chances are you will be well below the water's surface before you can get out. Helicopters sink like a stone, usually upside down as they are top heavy. If you manage to get out you still have to get into the life raft. In the freezing waters of Antarctica I would have thought it was nearly impossible. Even in a full survival suit you only have a few minutes before your hands would be too cold for you to be able to pull yourself into the raft.

I phoned Quentin's mother Mary. She told me that Steve had indeed jumped first but had few other details other than that they had said they had suffered complete loss of oil pressure and that Chilean and British ships were on the way. The following day we heard that after nine very cold hours Quentin and Steve were picked up by a Chilean ship and would probably be transferred to HMS *Endurance* and taken to the Falklands. It was good to hear they were both safe and well.

At breakfast the following day I was less than enchanted to open my *Daily Mail* and find that with clever graphics the newspaper had used a photo of my very distinctive red R44 helicopter, covered in its sponsor logos, ditching in the Antarctic!

A few days later I got an e mail from Nick Lewis who was helping us with our initial environmental evaluation:

> *As you can imagine, the events earlier this week may well have made things more difficult in many ways for private aircraft expeditions such as your own. Even though you are aware of some of the issues and problems of working in the Antarctic, it seems that the two chaps who ditched this week weren't. I don't have full details but it appears the expedition was not permitted through the normal channels, and the use of a single-engine helicopter in a Drake Passage crossing has raised many eyebrows. The Antarctic is after all a very different place from the Arctic where I believe these two other guys had gained much of their cold-weather experience. It was in many ways what all the National Operators fear: a private trip, with inadequate contingency, which then needs bailing out by the Government (in this case a foreign one). This obviously results in people asking the usual questions about use of government resources and taxpayers money etc. As a result I would imagine that from now on small private aircraft expeditions will face increased scrutiny from the permitting authorities.*

It was difficult to stay positive when negatives kept piling up. But then my confidence would rise again with positive news – more sponsorship came in, this time from YTL Corporation in Kuala Lumpur and '3', the mobile phone network in Hong Kong. We were nevertheless still desperately short, and only had a few months to go.

We went to the Helicopter Association International (HAI), the big helicopter expo in Los Angeles. There was news from Bell, which had agreed to sponsor us in kind: they would provide us with logistical support and spare parts, but no helicopter. We met many of our previous avionics sponsors who all agreed to supply us again, if we had a heli to put the goods in.

At the HAI we also saw Frank Robinson, the manufacturer of the R44 helicopter that Steve and Quentin had been flying. He told us that he'd been getting mixed reports on the ditching, but that it was generally believed they had run out of fuel.

As neither Eurocopter or Bell were prepared to supply us with a helicopter, Simon reluctantly agreed to make the down payment on a Bell 407 helicopter on a 10-year payback scheme on the understanding that the monthly payments would be covered by sponsorship and that at the end of the expedition the machine would be sold.

I agreed with him that we would sell our beautiful home in Somerset if I failed to get the necessary funding, never really believing it would come to that. Someone somewhere would surely come through.

Preparations for Antarctica continued to occupy much of our time. Pen gave me an introduction to Anne Kershaw who ran Adventure Network International (ANI). ANI was the only commercial organisation catering for expeditions in the interior of Antarctica at that time. We arranged to meet. Anne agreed that ANI would be able to cache fuel and provide Search and Rescue south of Adelaide Island, contingent on all the necessary permits and clearances and a very hefty deposit.

The Antarctic 'desk' of the British Foreign Office told us that as far as Antarctica was concerned, we were considered to be an American expedition as our helicopter was made and registered in the USA and we would be starting and finishing in New York. All our paperwork would be with the Environmental Protection Agency (EPA). Definitive documentation – an initial environmental evaluation (IEE) was required on every detail of our expedition once we left the shores of South America. The document ended up running to 50 pages and covered everything from Search and Rescue and disposal of solid waste, to listing the wildlife colonies that we would be flying over and their breeding seasons. We had to enlist professional help from two ex-BAS men – Nick Lewis and Dave Rootes. The IEE had to be submitted at least 90 days before departure.

Colin and I visited the EPA headquarters USA, in a vast structure occupying several blocks of downtown Washington DC, a necessary visit. The small print stated that without our environmental report we could be looking at a US prison sentence if we attempted to gain entry without the all-important documentation! We met professional courtesy and encouragement from representatives of the EPA and the National Science Foundation – the American counterpart to BAS, whose headquarters were across the road from the EPA. We advised them of our plans and of our hopes of visiting the South Pole and they were all friendly and appreciative that we had taken the trouble to visit them. They didn't foresee any problems, so we didn't have to worry too much about BAS!

From there we crossed a few blocks for an appointment with David

Hamlin at National Geographic. I had already visited him several months before. This time we were giving the National Geographic a presentation of our planned documentary, which we had prepared with the help of David and WWF. All departments were present and at the end they said they would 'be in touch'.

Next stop was Alaska. We spent a week there doing 'survival training'. Pen had put us in touch with Art and Damaris (Dee) Mortvedt, both in their early 50s. Art was a quietly spoken giant of a man with greying hair, penetrating blue eyes, moustache and beard. Dee barely reaches Art's shoulder, has dark wavy hair, a ready smile and is a wonderful cook. The two of them have survived just about everything the frozen wilderness of Alaska's far north can throw at you. Art has also spent many summers in the polar regions flying small aircraft.

They have lived in Alaska for the last 25 years, much of the time in a hut made out of sods of earth, far from another living soul and with their only mode of transport being a dog sled. They have now upgraded somewhat and live in a small community of 12 families, in Manley Hot Springs, 220 miles northwest of Fairbanks, Alaska. Snowmobiles and a small four-seater Cessna airplane have replaced the dog teams.

Fairbanks in early March was extremely cold. Our Alaskan Air 737 landed at around 8pm local time in near whiteout conditions with blowing snow and the temperature hovering around -30°C. After a good night's sleep in a comfortable log-cabin-style hotel, Art bundled us off to the nearest clothing store and got us kitted out in Fairbanks' warmest, though not the most glamorous-looking gear. We looked like Teletubbies, but we were warm and were to be very grateful for this in the coming days.

We visited a supplies depot to buy a small and compact kerosene cooker-cum aircraft engine-heater. It had a standpipe attachment to which you fixed a flexi hose when warming the engine. Art told us that when the temperature got below -35°C this would be able to de-frost the engine in about two hours!

Art and Dee had a charming little log cabin with hot and cold running water and electricity. Survival training was looking good. Then Art showed us our quarters 50 yards away – a small log cabin, no electricity, no water, one room with loft and the loo in a privy some 25 yards away down a small forest track disappearing into the wild.

Privies are a source of pride in Manley Hot Springs and the surrounding area. Art told us that it's a place where you can relax with the door open and commune with nature, and then, with a twinkle in his eye said, 'If the freezing air is altogether too much for you, or a bear happens along, you can shut the door and enjoy the interiors or yell for help!'

Everyone pasted their privy walls with pictures, mostly tropical paradise scenes. Odour is not a problem, solids freeze in an ever-rising pyramid.

The log cabin turned out to be luxury compared to the training he had in store for us.

The following day found us camped on the edge of a frozen lake having had a great couple of hours on snowmobiles along ice- and snow-covered forest tracks, lakes and rivers. We stopped at a cabin where an old man, Harold Smith, lived all on his own. Art thought he would invite us in for a cup of tea, that he would like the company, but he was happy just standing out in the cold and chatting for a few minutes. A fir tree next to his house was decorated with hundreds of little pieces of coloured cloth. At my questioning look, Harold gave a small rasping laugh saying, 'Oh those are the dawgs bootees, I just pick them up here and there, them dawgs are always losing them.'

Art explained they were for the husky dogs: 'Stops their feet getting sore. The snow balls up between their toes, so if they are going any distance, we put these little boots on them. As you can see they are just made of cloth with a Velcro strap, but they do tend to come off every so often, so Harold here, gets to decorate his Christmas tree.'

Shortly after meeting Harold we came across a father and son fishing for their supper through a small hole in the ice. So far they'd caught nothing. They seemed happy enough though, sitting on camping stools, giving the slushy, icy hole a stir or two every so often to stop it freezing over.

Scenically our campsite was beautiful, the sunset perfection, but as the evening got colder and colder, Art left us to put up the tents while he went off with his chainsaw on a snowmobile in search of firewood. He returned with an immense pile, but we were only allowed to build a small fire, which Art said was adequate. Every time he turned his back, Colin whipped on a couple more logs, saying, 'It's diabolical, he's sawn up enough for a month, this jolly is costing us more per night than staying at a Hilton Hotel and we've got a log restriction!'

I laughed and said, 'You're nuts, this is all about survival.'

'Why the log fire then? There won't be any log fires in Antarctica, or the Arctic, there aren't any trees.'

'Well,' I said rather lamely, 'I guess it's all about having it tough.'

We shovelled up buckets full of snow to melt over the fire. We boiled a kettle and had our mug of tea, the teabags froze solid the moment you lifted them out of the insulated mugs and when you tossed away the last few drops, they froze in mid air. We put up the tents and laid reindeer skins on the floor. We learnt about holding on tight until all tent pegs were secure. Polar winds, we were warned, can whip your tent away in a flash – gone forever.

The manufacturer stated that our enormous sleeping bags were good down to -60°C. Our night time temperature plummeted to -45°C. Art was in the big tent with the stove, he said he didn't trust us not to bump into it in the night. We were in a tiny tent where ice crystals were hanging inches deep from the roof before we had even got into our sleeping bags.

Colin is at heart a city boy and for him camping was a necessary evil. I had to laugh looking at him as I clambered into the tent. He was already deep in his sleeping bag, tugging the zip as high as possible and in a voice of deep resignation said, 'This is going to be a long, long night.'

Although he might complain when it came to sleeping out at -45°C, he is, of course, a man of great courage and stamina and remains icy calm in a crisis, especially when the chips are truly down, as I was to find out later.

The sleeping bag manufacturers' claim that the bags were good down to -60°C turned out to be overly optimistic. I woke in the small hours of the morning, practically frozen solid. Colin was actually climbing out of his sleeping bag for a pee, I longed for a pee too but when I tentatively reached a hand up into the small opening I'd left for air above my face, thousands of ice crystals showered down on me. I decided to cross my legs and wait for daylight.

Colin had a lot to say about frozen extremities when we finally dared surface a couple of hours later with the first light of dawn. To move an inch was to be showered by frost. We clambered clumsily out into a silent, frozen world where the first rays of light gave the cloudless skies a wash of the palest aquamarine. The full moon was still high and bright in the sky.

As Colin emerged out of the tent to face the day he firmly announced, 'Right, that's it then, we've done that, no point in camping a second night!'

'But that's why we're here.' I said.

'So? As I said, we've done that, so let's not waste time packing and unpacking frozen reindeer skins and camping gear on sleds, let's do new things, like seeing new places on snowmobiles.'

Thinking I'd never win this argument I just said, 'Let's see what Art says.'

Art's tent was toasty warm. He was happily heating the frozen remains of our night-before moose stew. He then half-wiped out the pan, poured in water and added the crushed oats for our morning porridge. It tasted delicious.

We were able to test out our new cooker–heater sooner than anticipated on one of the snowmobiles that stubbornly refused to start. The engine finally burst into life after an hour of hooded heat, although

I wondered how we would manage with the jet turbine engine of a Bell 407 helicopter, mounted on the top of the helicopter some eight feet off the ground. The snowmobile's engine is only a foot off the ground and Art's little Cessna plane engine is also moderately close to the ground. I hoped the overnight temperatures in Antarctica would never get below -35°C, the threshold where the heater would have to come into action.

Art covered every aspect of survival he could think of, from frozen engines to stopping a polar bear in his tracks. He told us we should have strap attachments on our gloves, and to wear three pairs on each hand, that the wind would pick them up, grab them and they'd be gone before you could say knife – 'And that goes for pretty much anything,' he said.

He showed us how to insert snow plates and pickets to anchor the heli to the snow and ice screws for the ice, how to build an igloo and dig snow holes. We would need a shovel and an ice saw and for the Arctic a rifle in case of polar bears. He impressed on us the need to check each other for frostbite and to keep our clothes and sleeping bags as free from condensation as possible; and he reminded us to take emergency kit like locator beacons and enough freeze dried food for three weeks in case we got stuck.

By the end of the week we even knew how to set a snare and were getting fairly confident at recognising the tracks of the abundant wildlife such as wolf, moose, snow leopard and arctic hare, tips to be saved for the Arctic. In contrast, the largest creature in Antarctica, other than the maritime creatures, is an insect – a half-inch long midge! Happily the bears of Alaska were all in deep hibernation. We drove dog sled teams, and made many snowmobile sorties.

I was also able to purchase wolf skin ruffs trimmed with beaver from Pam Reddington, the wife of a trapper living in Manley Hot Springs. These were for the hoods of our new polar jackets and Dee showed me the best way to sew them on. We had a great time and it was welcome relief from all the stress and worries back home. And happily for Colin, we only did spend one night in the tents.

While Colin and I were surviving in Alaska, Simon and Pen had set off for Resolute Bay in the far north of Canada, over 500 miles inside the Arctic Circle. Pen was going to spend a week with Simon, testing and introducing him to actual sled pulling. He would then set out on his attempt to be the first person to walk solo and unsupported to the North Pole from Canada.

The two of them nearly perished in attempting to get back to Resolute before a blizzard came in. They should have put up their tent and weathered the storm, but Simon had a plane to catch. There must be a moral in there somewhere! However, they survived. Simon caught the once-a-week plane back to civilisation and Pen set off on his lonely and dangerous voyage to the North Pole.

Things were beginning to fall into place for our trip. We secured two more major sponsors, Tommy Hilfiger and Holcim, the latter a cement company with head offices in Switzerland. Route planning was more or less completed, and all was agreed with WWF. Our clearances, a critical issue, were all being handled by Overflight, a small company in the south of England, although Tamara and I had to handle Antarctica.

We took on a young and enthusiastic PR company, who organised our website, on which we were running a 'flag' campaign – you could have your name on the WWF flag that we would fly at the poles. Tamara was trying to finalise the IEE, keep sponsors updated and generally coordinate with me on all aspects. The office, our erstwhile guest room, was filling up with expedition gear – charts, tents, survival rations and a life raft in case we ditched in the sea.

The WWF was putting together a programme of activities throughout South America. We would have one of their people on board for much of the journey and would be monitoring wildlife, doing aerial survey work and taking scientists and biologists into remote areas. As it ultimately turned out we were able to generate massive national TV coverage in Brazil and Argentina, promoting all the work organised by the world-wide infrastructure of WWF and put into practice by their dedicated field workers.

We still had no confirmation regarding a documentary from National Geographic.

The war in Iraq was in full swing; American troops were in Baghdad, SARS was still rampant in Hong Kong and markets were flat. Given the world situation it was amazing that we had secured any sponsors; we had approached many companies and had many doors politely closed.

We printed our own brochures on our large laser colour printer and Tamara spent hours putting them together. Each one personalised for each prospective sponsor. We made phone calls, appointments, sent emails. We made some progress but we were still behind and very under-funded.

Colin and I went to Polly Vacher's take off at Birmingham airfield in the UK with Art, who had come over from Alaska especially for the occasion. Coincidently, Polly had also done her survival training with Art and Dee. It was a grand take-off with Prince Charles in attendance; we all felt proud and happy for Polly heading off all by herself in her small plane. I felt not a little envious that all the preparation was behind her – the adventure had begun.

On 19 May 2003 Pen reached the North Pole at 10.11 GMT! Fantastic. The first man to do so unsupported, solo, from the Canadian side. He had an enforced camp at the Pole for several days, as the weather was too bad for the Twin Otter plane to come in and collect him. The papers made out that he was stranded and Search and Rescue was needed, but that was not the case. He had arrived two days ahead of schedule and had arranged and paid in advance for a Twin Otter to pick him up. He was hungry and surviving on half-rations as his food was running low, but he was in no danger and he had plenty of water.

A few days later, back in London, Simon and I were celebrating with Pen and his wife Mary his historic achievement.

We had happy family news. Our daughter Christy told us we could look forward to another grandchild in November, but by then of course, Simon and I would both be far away and we wouldn't see the baby until it was at least four months old. For the umpteenth time I wondered why I was putting myself through all this stress and potential danger when I could be enjoying our lovely family. Well, it was too late to back out and I would always regret not having a go at 'the big one'. It had been beckoning for so long. The ultimate goal, to do what no other helicopter pilots had ever done and the great polar regions beckoned.

Then a lovely letter from Charles Swithinbank, an eminent glaciologist who has written four excellent books on his experiences, boosted my flagging morale. Charles first went in to the Antarctic in 1949 and has spent three winters and many summers there. We had yet to meet but he had already given me advice and I had sent him a copy of my book, the account of my solo flight around the world in 2000. He wrote:

> *I have just finished reading* Now Solo. *I think it is the most gripping adventure story that I have read since childhood. I agree with the Robinson man who commented that 'you must be mad!' but it is an inspiring sort of madness. Thank God you survived that lot.*

He went on to talk about Cape Horn and Diego Ramirrez, off the tip of South America:

> *Those tiny islands might welcome an unofficial visit because they seldom see anyone (you seem to have a fondness for unofficial visits). Three Chilean navy lads live a couple of miles east of Cape Horn in a small wooden hut. A few yards away they have built a tiny chapel, one of the most inspiring places I know anywhere. Five minutes walk away is a magnificent monument to all those who have perished rounding the Horn. I think there is a helipad near the hut, but don't go zooming around more than you need to because of the wildlife (Magellanic penguins in burrows nor far away). A couple of chaps live on Diego Ramirez and there*

> *is a flat bit of grass near their house. But again, don't buzz more than necessary because of the wildlife (wandering albatross).*
>
> *Having met Colin, who struck me as very sane, I can only say that your descriptions of his landings, engine problems, alarms and excursions in a Chinese paddy field made him sound almost crazier than you in G-MURY (My R44 helicopter). It would be fun to discuss Antarctic terrain with you, and anyway I want to meet you to be able to judge whether, in spite of what you enjoy doing (and I secretly envy) you are really as sane as your copilot seems to be.*

I had the pleasure of meeting Charles shortly after that and was able to gain a little insight into his remarkable pioneering years in Antarctica, he gave me much helpful advice. Charles said such nice things about my book, but I felt like the Johnny-come-lately adventurer compared with him and all those who went there in those early days of man's infancy in Antarctica.

National Geographic pulled out. Their producer–director David Hamlin was nearly as disappointed as WWF, Colin and myself. We had all put so much time and money and effort into the preparation. WWF had lined up all their high profile scientists and locations had been chosen. We were bitterly disappointed. We were told their target audience is the 18–35-year-old bracket. David said, 'I want to see you go out and make the best f…g documentary ever!' At least he believed in us. Could there be any other setbacks? Could things get any worse? They did.

In August I got a phone call from Pen. 'I guess you know why I am calling?'

'No,' I said, 'but it's good to hear from you.'

'Then you haven't heard?'

It was the news that ANI, the company that had agreed to supply us with fuel and Search and Rescue in the interior of Antarctica, had announced they would not be operating that season. Utterly devastating. What could we do? Were there any alternatives? Could we go it alone? I was full of a million questions and Pen had no immediate answers, but he knew people and said he would call around.

The moment Simon made that down payment on the helicopter, we were committed to Bell. Without ANI or a similar company there would be no polar expeditions that year, there would be no one to cache our fuel or provide Search and Rescue cover. It meant our whole venture was off, or would have to be postponed for another year – and our monthly payments on a $1.6 million helicopter were due to start in October.

I told Pen that just two short weeks previously we had made the deposit on the helicopter and that Colin was already in Dallas at Bell

Helicopters doing their engineering and field maintenance course on the Bell 407 helicopter. How could I possibly finance payments if we were delayed a year? Everything was spiralling out of control, not least the finances.

This news from ANI meant that Simon's expedition was also in the balance. Could it all have been for naught? He said there was no way he could keep up the level of training for another year, plus there was the small issue that he had a business to run.

A couple of days later Pen gave me the names and contact details of two separate groups that might possibly take over the ANI set-up at Patriot Hills. 'They both need confirmation of funds, so what we need is to get as many expeditions as possible to back them and collectively we might induce them to do it,' he said.

One of the groups was a Russian company called Cerpolex operating out of Paris. They had a damaged Antonov 3 plane at the South Pole that had made a heavy landing there two years previously. The plane was sitting at the end of the runway at the Pole and the Americans were equally keen to have it removed.

The other group with a vested interest in going to Antarctica were two brothers, Mike and Peter McDowell. They too had a valuable damaged aircraft stuck in Antarctica, a DC3 that had blown over in a blizzard the year before at Patriot Hills. Pen thought we should contact both groups, but reckoned the McDowells might be the better option as Mike McDowell had been a founding partner in ANI with Giles and Anne Kershaw back in the early 1990s. Giles, a highly skilled and experienced pilot had spent many seasons in Antarctica working with BAS before setting up ANI. Tragically he was killed in an air crash there in 1991. Anne gamely and efficiently carried on the business until she sold out in 2000 to a group of accountants on the proviso that she would stay and continue to run the company for a year. The accountants were the ones who had cancelled the season and we found out later they had given Anne an hour to clear her desk and leave. She was devastated. We were all devastated.

We contacted both groups. The McDowell's would provide local transport and Search and Rescue by Twin Otter planes, while the Russians were considering ground transport. Both were working against time. The season was only two months away.

The Russians wrote back to Pen, they said:

> *We have plan to go this year to bring the AN-3 that is at the South Pole.*
> *We will bring 2 to 3 russian-vehicules (not the same kind that had been to SP few years ago or the ones that broke last year in Novolazarevskaya).*
> *We are still in contact with the Chilean army. Our vehicles can go in 4*

days between Patriot Hills and Pole (14 hours/day driving, 10h/day resting), carrying 6 pax and 1.5 ton.

Both groups planned to base themselves at Patriot Hills.

Cerpolex would attempt to make numerous journeys between Patriot Hills and the South Pole in their heavy track vehicles – a round trip of 1,200 miles. Which meant that any expeditions attempting to walk to the South Pole would have to make the return trip overland in one of the track vehicles, fitting themselves in among the parts of the dismantled aircraft for the four day journey back to Patriot Hills – it all sounded complicated, uncomfortable and a big anticlimax. However, Cerpolex introduced me to Gonzalo Campos, a Chilean man from Santiago who did freelance work for them and knew everyone. They told me Gonzalo would be able to arrange fuel and Search and Rescue for the northern sector of our route. I immediately got in touch with him; he sounded confident and efficient.

Emails and phone calls followed. The stress of the ANI situation was getting me down, what if neither of them came through? What if we had to wait for another year? How could I possibly handle the monthly payments for the helicopter that Simon had been reluctant to finance? The possibility of having to sell our home was fast becoming a reality. Failure was unacceptable, all we could do was continue as though we were going forward, yet time was so short and the situation seemed hopeless.

Our insurance broker was frantically trying to find companies to underwrite the helicopter and there were difficulties in getting the helicopter's auxiliary fuel tank made and certified. (It was a 280 litre auxiliary fuel tank, replacing the three forward-facing rear seats of the helicopter.) All this time Bell Helicopter's subsidiary, Edwards & Associates, were racing against time to get our Bell 407 completed – time that now had a hollow ring if we failed to get the Antarctic support.

Finally, a small ray of hope. On 12 August I got a phone call from Nick Lewis, the McDowell's man: 'I don't want to get your hopes up too much but it looks as though there's an 80 per cent chance that the McDowell's will take over the ANI tented base at Patriot Hills.' Nick said they needed firm confirmation in the form of deposits on our expeditions. They too had commitments to make. A Russian Ilyushin 76 with a seven-man crew from Azerbaijan had to be chartered for the three-and-a-half-month Austral summer as well as the two Twin Otter airplanes and pilots from Canada. Then there were all the Patriot Hills base personnel, cook, radio and weather operators, doctor, mountain rescue team and engineers, plus their 'home base' staff in Punta Arenas to be taken on. Profit margins, if any, were narrow, so much was weather-dependent.

And then five days later I got the following email:

ANTARCTIC LOGISTIC SUPPORT FOR THE 2003–2004 SEASON

We want to advise you that a group of us, including Mike Sharp, David Rootes, Nick Lewis, Peter McDowell and Mike McDowell, have joined together to offer Antarctic logistic support for expeditions. We will operate from Patriot Hills, Antarctica, for the 2003-2004 season. The operating company will be named Antarctic Logistics & Expeditions Ltd, [ALE]. Each person in this group has extensive Antarctic experience and in the cases of Mike Sharp and Mike McDowell, extensive experience with Patriot Hills operations and logistics...

I sat there, staring at my computer screen, wave after wave of relief flowing over me. I read the email again – we were back in business, perhaps we would be able to meet the helicopter payments, perhaps we would be able to get the rest of the funding…

I remember scrambling down the stairs to give Simon the great news. He was relaxing happily soaking up the last rays of Dordogne's late afternoon sunshine with a discarded *Financial Times* newspaper lying on the ground beside him. His first reaction was a great big smile and the words – 'Thought Pen would pull it off.' The big smile was quickly replaced by a wry smile and – 'Shit, now I've got to get on with hauling those f…g tyres around.'

Colin and I only had five weeks to go before leaving England for Dallas to collect our helicopter. There we would spend two weeks flight training on the Bell 407, leaving us one further week before our official take-off on 22 October from West 30th Street heliport, New York City.

We chose New York as the Everest of cities. It represents the pioneer spirit of North America, is a centrally accessible location and, to clinch it, Al Trenk, who had tried to help me with Eurocopter, and his daughter Abigail of Liberty Helicopters who operate the heliport, offered to sponsor much of the take-off. We were still under-funded, optimistically praying that the publicity on reaching the South Pole would generate new and enthusiastic sponsors.

Despite the good news regarding ALE, there were still more major hurdles to overcome, but somehow everything started to fall more or less into place. We got the insurance, at a hefty premium and the helicopter was delivered from the Edwards facility in Tennessee to Dallas, covered in sponsor logos, complete with certified auxiliary tank. We did our training on the Bell 407 and in between time rushed around Dallas sourcing various items like a 24-volt battery charger, remote generator and fuel pump. Colin reckoned we would be better off with the charger and generator than a spare battery. 'We'll look pretty old fashioned if both batteries go flat and we can't start the helicopter,' he quipped.

The generator was also to prove invaluable for pumping fuel from drums and recharging all our other devices – satellite telephone, cameras and computer. Bell Helicopters kindly offered to ship everything south to Punta Arenas in Chile for us, along with other Antarctic items for the helicopter such as cases of thin oil and snow baffles, the latter being protective shields to stop driving snow blocking the engine air intake.

On 16 October we lifted off from Bell Helicopters in Dallas for New York, but were back 10 minutes later. Colin still had the keys to our hire car in his pocket.

Raising further sponsorship wasn't over – St Louis, home to Anheuser Busch, was more or less on our route to New York and we had an appointment with August Busch and his son Steven – both of whom are helicopter pilots. We were met with enthusiasm and support, and in New York we happily added their beer logo – Michelob Ultra – to our helicopter.

Our preparation troubles weren't over – our young and enthusiastic PR company, who should have organised press conferences and our send-off, had done nothing other than bring themselves to New York at our expense.

However in the three short days before departure, we somehow managed to get things reasonably organised – we printed press packs and had a press conference with WWF, sponsored by Reuters, and held at Reuters' headquarters in downtown New York, and Art and Abigail Trenk, the owners of Liberty helicopters at the West 30th street heliport, gave us unstinting support.

And so, after all the months of preparations and anguish, on 22 October 2003 we took off from Liberty Helicopters West 30th Street helipad, waved off by our patron, the Duchess of York, WWF representatives, my darling husband, a bunch of stalwart friends and a smattering of journalists. The wind was icy cold and it snowed the following day.

schoolmaster.net
the meeting of minds

CHAPTER TWO
Ushuaia

'Only as far as we seek, can we go. Only as much as we dream, can we be. What you are is what you have been; what you will be is what you do now.'
Bhudist

Left: Alejandro, JM, CB

My journal entry on 5 December 2003:

> *We've made it here to Ushuaia – the southernmost town in Argentina – such a feeling of history – so many great seafaring explorers – the names are all around – we've crossed the Magellan Straits, we'll be flying down the Beagle Channel to Cape Horn and then onwards across the Drake Passage – can't quite believe we are here – all the months of planning, dreaming, thinking about 'worst case scenarios' – all the focus has been on reaching this point and the great Antarctic Continent – this is where the 'extreme' element comes in – extremes of weather – the cold, the winds, the altitude and the isolation.*

We had by then been 48 days into our journey, flying south down the Eastern Seaboard of the Americas. We flew over the translucent turquoise waters of the Caribbean, past the lava dust clouds and eerie desolation of the deserted volcanic island of Montserrat and onwards to Venezuela where we visited the world's highest waterfall – the spectacular Angel Falls that feed the mighty Orinoco River – and onwards over the jungle to Surinam. There we took WWF scientists deep into the rain forests to monitor the mercury levels in the water caused by the illegal gold mining and had tea with the outlaws.

The next stop was Brazil and the seemingly endless rain forests of the Amazon basin where we had a series of WWF field workers join us for different legs as we travelled up the mighty Amazon River. We visited fishery projects, monitored deforestation and the swaths of forest lost to the new 500-mile long highway joining Santarem on the Amazon with Vilhena, 500 miles to the south. We trudged through the forests to see the Golden Lion Tamarind monkeys who now, thanks to WWF, are no longer threatened with extinction – for the time being. In the case of the Tamarind monkeys, much of their natural habitat has been either destroyed or broken up into small areas separated by farmland and for these small, engaging monkeys to thrive and breed they need, like most creatures, quiet sanctuaries. Tamarinds also need corridors. As tree travellers, it only requires one line of trees to link to the next forest area for them to be able to move. WWF has done much in educating the locals about the sanctuaries of these lovely little orange monkeys needs to survive, helping them to understand that they can still have their fields while leaving some trees in place.

We crossed into the far north of Argentina at the Iguazu Falls where Anibal Parrera of the Fundación Vida Sylvestre, an affiliate organisation to WWF, joined us on our journey south to Punta Arenas. Colin had been happily looking forward to the company of a lovely Argentine woman, but Anibal turned out to be a very nice, good looking young man in his early 40s. Anibal has a vast knowledge and passionate interest in wild life and conservation and as we zigzagged our way south, we, or rather he, was monitoring wild life and performing aerial survey work. We learned much from Anibal about the land over which we were flying. On our previous flights we had endlessly speculated on much of what was below us – rock formations, creatures, vegetation, crops and marine life. Animals like polar bears were a cinch but others, like the weird prehistoric looking creature I saw when taking off from the Sondrestrom Fjord runway in Greenland, were completely unknown to us. I had radioed the air traffic controller, who had laughed and said, 'That's a musk ox!' It looked a bit like a buffalo with a long silky coat almost reaching to the ground. But Anibal knew it all and gave us a wonderful running commentary from his backseat in the helicopter.

However, it wasn't all one way. We were able to teach Anibal a thing or two as well – as our part-time radio operator. None of the people in control towers in Argentina's domestic airports spoke English and I regret that Colin's and my Spanish is virtually non-existent. Anibal did a great job and even learned some of the abbreviations that radio talk is riddled with. It was pretty chaotic but we somehow muddled through.

We flew over great cities: New York and its fabled skyline; Rio de Janeiro with its Sugar Loaf Mountain and the famous Jesus statue poised on the highest peak with arms outstretched; the vast sprawl of Sao Paolo with helipads on the top of every other skyscraper; and Buenos Aires where we felt we could have been somewhere in Europe with its beautiful old buildings and wide avenues. Further south we crossed the sweeping plains of Patagonia with the distant peaks of the snow-capped Andes, then onwards to Punta Arenas and finally Ushuaia.

The last 48 days had been hard work, but it was a treat and privilege to work with WWF and the Fundacion, to go off the beaten track and to learn about the flora and fauna and to see the birds, the beasts and the fishes in their own habitat, knowing that, even if it is was only in the smallest of ways, we were playing a part in trying to preserve our planet for future generations.

I enjoyed the WWF side of things more than Colin. In theory, Colin was all for helping WWF and their affiliates, but in the context of prolonging our attempt to get to the South Pole with the work we did for the WWF along the way, he was less enthusiastic. Although he was good natured about the delays, his heart lay in getting to the South Pole by mid-December. Colin also had a problem with bugs, especially the mosquitoes, who loved him. After one particularly long day monitoring wildlife and visiting projects, he sighed and said, 'I didn't plan to fly around the world as Richard Attenborough's assistant!'

On arrival in Punta Arenas, Gonzalo Campos was there to meet us. Finally I was able to put a face to the voice and the many emails that had passed over the months. Charming, urbane and with a ready smile, he was a family man in his mid-40s, had wavy dark hair with a touch of grey and a military, upright bearing. Gonzalo got us installed in our hotel and then, wasting no time, wheeled us off to the nearest notary where we had to sign a document exempting the Chilean government of any responsibility for us once we left the shores of South America, although they would be providing a 'flight following' service for the 450 miles Drake Passage crossing. We would be phoning in on our satellite phone every half-hour to report flight normal and give our coordinates.

Thankfully the final acceptance by the US government of our 50-page-long initial environmental evaluation had come through three days earlier. This was the all important document listing every detail about ourselves, our helicopter, our route and our activities while in Antarctica. We had been told firmly that the Chilean authorities would be giving no clearances or permits without the IEE and the notary document, so we were extremely relieved.

Permits had not been easy after the ditching of Steve and Quentin's helicopter earlier that year. I asked Gonzalo how the two pilots had managed to go without the normal permits.

'Well you know, they were here and they were so persuasive,' he said with a shrug and a smile.

I don't know how we would have managed without Gonzalo. He knew all the Chilean authorities, and had arranged our fuel and Search and Rescue for the entire northern sector as far as Carvajal Island at the southern end of the Antarctic Peninsula. From Carvajal to the South Pole and back we would be in the hands of ALE.

The fuel cache that Gonzalo had organised at Carvajal lay in the snows of the abandoned Chilean research station on Adelaide Island. No one had been in there for three years, but he was fairly confident that the fuel would be there and in good order. He said it would be up the hill beside the one-time skiway and that it might be buried so we should take a good shovel, but he had the coordinates and would give them to us later. It was not very reassuring, but there was no alternative. Needless to say Colin saw the half-empty glass and I saw the half-full one.

We could have tried to arrange for a ship to leave drums of fuel on Adelaide Island, but pack ice is fickle. One year the coastal area can be free of ice, the next year not. Ernest Shackleton found this out to his cost all those years ago in 1914 when his ship *Endurance* was trapped and crushed by the ice before he ever landed on the Antarctic continent. It was a miracle that all the expedition members survived. They made an epic journey by sledge and open lifeboat over pack ice to Elephant Island. Then Shackleton and five others crossed the Southern Ocean, in one of the open boats, James Caird, to South Georgia, a mere pinprick of an island in a vast and empty sea. It was one of the world's greatest feats of navigation. Then, undernourished, exhausted and with totally inadequate footwear and clothing, Shackleton, accompanied by two of his men, somehow clambered, stumbled and slid up and over the uncharted snowy mountain range on South Georgia to raise the alarm at the whaling station Grytviken. You don't want to trust to the vagaries of pack ice if you can help it – we settled for the three-year-old fuel supposedly sitting in the snow at Carvajal.

Our next stop in Punta Arenas was with ALE, where we were able to put more faces to names. We met Peter McDowell, the head of ALE operations, and Rachel Shepherd, his assistant in charge of communications. The ALE headquarters were situated in a small, rather dilapidated house, up a dusty road looking out over brightly painted corrugated iron roofs of the town. It was a cheerful touch in bleak and windy surroundings – pink, purple, green, yellow, every colour of the rainbow. Beyond lay the cold waters of the Beagle Channel, the Drake Passage – and Antarctica.

Peter McDowell greeted us in a room surrounded by charts and stacks of polar gear in every corner. A tall, lean man in his late 40s with several days' growth of beard, he was looking slightly harassed. They had seven mountaineers waiting to go to Patriot Hills who had already been waiting for 10 days for a weather window and the forecast wasn't good. Peter told us that the start of the season had been fraught with delays.

I was anxious for news of Simon and Pen who were already in Antarctica. I had managed to speak to Simon two weeks before while he was waiting for a weather window to fly in to Antarctica in the Ilyushin but had heard nothing since. I had tried many times to get through to his satellite phone with no success and was getting worried. To my relief Peter reassured me that all was well with Simon and Pen. They had also had to wait a week before finally getting a suitable weather window for the Ilyushin to make the 1,500-mile journey to Patriot Hills. The reason I hadn't been able to get through to them was because they only turned on their phone once a day to make and receive calls. He explained that calls had to be brief as they were relying on solar energy for charging the battery, 'Phone them at 11am, you might get through.'

According to Peter, Pen and Simon had spent several days at Patriot sorting their gear, before being taken by Twin Otter to the coast. They had now been on the march for several days and all appeared to be going well, though progress was slow. I was relieved to hear they were actually moving. Simon had been worried that the sledges were so heavy he might find he was going nowhere. He told me later that they had to unload half the sled's load for the first steep glacier gradients, haul the first lot to the top, then go back for the other half.

It was hard to believe he was out there, that their big adventure had begun and that, weather permitting, we would shortly be reunited for a tantalising couple of hours with them on the ice.

Peter asked a lot of searching questions to reassure himself that ours was no half-thought-through adventure. He wanted to know exactly what polar gear we had and our provisions for refuelling. We appeared to have everything other than a fuel filter – we had both forgotten that rather essential item. Peter was able to lend us one; unfortunately we were to find out later that the 'thread' on Peter's filter didn't fit with the thread on our fuel pump.

Peter was also able to supply us with several bottles of Prist, a substance that stops any water that might have got into the fuel from freezing and blocking the fuel flow, which saved us precious time hunting some down in Punta Arenas or Ushuaia. We had tried to get some in Dallas, but there's not much call for de-icing equipment there.

Peter drove us over to his warehouse where he had stored all our gear, which had arrived safe and sound from Dallas and London. As we bumped our way up the dirt track, Peter elaborated on the Antarctic weather. So far that season it had been appalling, even by Antarctic standards: 'We haven't been able to get the Twin Otters off the ground for 10 days now. It's blowing a hoolie out there, but at least we managed to get the South Pole expeditions to their start points. They're having a hell of a time though – complete whiteout. Still, they are on the ground and, as I told you, Simon and Pen sound to be in good shape – lots of jokes from your husband, he's really something!' We hadn't had too many smiles up to that point, so it was a relief to see a big grin spread across his face, and see his less serious side.

We hoped the weather would improve. We had studied weather charts and read many books written by or about the great explorers in Antarctica. All told the same tale of extreme weather and harsh conditions. We knew what we were heading towards, but now it was the real thing, the full reality was beginning to sink in and we were only days away from the big crossing.

And the delays, we wondered how long we would have to wait in Ushuaia in the southern tip of Argentina, our take-off point for our crossing the Drake Passage. Polly Vacher in her small single-engine Piper Dakota had been delayed a record five weeks – did the same fate await us? Polly finally got away at the same time as Simon and Pen, but not before kindly giving us an introduction to Jonathon and Roxanna Selby in Ushuaia who had befriended her on her arrival there. Polly also gave us the address of some self-catering, inexpensive chalets where we could stay in Ushuaia.

We now had a mass of extra kit – all essential for Antarctica – which we had to somehow fit into the helicopter for the short journey to Ushuaia, back in Argentina. Nonessential gear for Antarctica would be left in Ushuaia, but we had to get it down there. We had the boxes of oil for the oil change, the remote generator, fuel pump, battery charger, three weeks of food rations, cooker, survival suits and more.

We ended up having to feed the contents of my polar gear bag through the sliding back window where there was another six inches of space once the door was shut. We had crammed everything in so tight that the 'activation' switch on our Blue Sky Network tracker box got switched off when squeezing in the last items and we didn't realise until we got to Ushuaia. As a result, that was the only section of our journey that was never recorded.

We had hoped to take off for Ushuaia at 2pm local time; we finally got away at 6pm. We had been all set to go only to be told that the Argentine authorities at Commodoro Rivadavia Control had refused us permission to re-enter Argentine air space. Gonzalo had lengthy discussions accompanied by many gesticulations with the Chilean authorities while I phoned Jonathon Selby, who was meeting us at the airport in Ushuaia. He said he would phone the Argentine authorities and try and find out what was going on. Several hours and many phone calls later Jonathon called me and said, 'Commodoro know nothing of this, as far as they are concerned you are free to come!' And finally Gonzalo managed to persuade the Chilean authorities to let us go. He said with a laugh, 'You know we in Chile have many disagreements with Argentina, we have much competition and you know we both think Antarctica belongs to our own countries.'

There was no room for Anibal on our onward journey to Ushuaia. His journey and mission with us was over and he had to return to Buenos Aires and his family. It was time to say a sad goodbye. He had become so much a part of our team and done a great job as our auxiliary radio operator, although tending to get distracted on occasion by vegetation and wild life. We'd remember fondly our approach to Punta Arenas when there had been an Airbus coming in at the same time as us, air traffic control was telling us to 'orbit', to go into a holding, circling pattern, and Anibal was busy saying, 'Oh look, this is very interesting, this is natural virgin woodland!' We gave Anibal big hugs and some beautiful kites for his two young sons. The kites were in the shape of various birds that one of our sponsors had asked us to fly at various points – which we had done – but now there was no room for them.

It was also temporarily goodbye to Gonzalo. How different our circumstances were to be on our return and how grateful we were going to be to have Gonzalo's anxious, friendly face and endless help.

We made good time for the first leg of the journey to Ushuaia. We had met two pilots at the airport who had advised us to make a dogleg to the east to avoid the highest area of the mountain range between Ushuaia and Punta Arenas: 'In these winds the turbulence will be extreme, we've lost a few planes through the pass, go via Rio Grande,' they said.

Patagonia is renowned for strong winds that sweep the vast plains, and we had them in full measure as we headed southeast with 50 knots of tail wind to Rio Grande under stormy skies, shafts of golden evening light piercing the gloom. Conditions changed dramatically once we turned southwest at Rio Grande. The last of the sunlight was gone, the friendly plains were far behind us and we were into the foothills of the Darwin Cordillera, with powerful head winds and cloud obscuring many of the snow-capped peaks ahead.

These were the first serious mountains of our entire journey, and our first in a Bell 407. We braced ourselves for turbulence, for the wind sheer, the updrafts and the downdrafts of the mountains. We knew what to expect as we had been there so many times before in the smaller Robinson 44 helicopter. We need not have worried. In the Bell 407 we barely felt a thing as we slowly made our way up the deep valleys and over the snow-capped peaks to Ushuaia, tucked between the mountains and the waters of the southern oceans.

As we crested the highest peak we could see the airfield and the black strip of the runway on a small offshore island that was linked to the mainland and the town by a causeway. Everything was cold and grey in the fast fading light of evening. As we drew closer we could see the dark, low sprawl of the two and three storey wood and brick buildings of the town. Like Punta Arenas, many of the roofs were of corrugated iron, but there in Ushuaia, for the most part, they lacked the brightly coloured paint.

We hover-taxied down the runway where fine flurries of snow swirled over the black, wet surface. The air traffic controller told us to park beside a large hangar with a blue roof to the north of the runway.

Finally we had arrived in Ushuaia, the most southerly town in the entire world. The end of civilisation. We had crossed over into an unforgiving land, cut off by the black snow-capped mountains to the north, while off to the south lay the dark waters of the Beagle Channel and the last splintered fragments of the Americas before the southern oceans and Terra Incognita – Antarctica.

Our journey south from New York had all been through warm, tropical and semi-tropical climes. Even southern Argentina with its windswept plains had been warm and we'd enjoyed unseasonably good weather in Punta Arenas. Now we were surrounded by a harsher beauty. Ushuaia, the capital of Tierra del Fuego, the land of fires, was named it was said after the inhabitants of 10,000 years ago who had to light campfires to keep themselves warm. Today the population stands at a little over 38,000.

Jonathon and Roxanna were there at the airport to meet us, along with their lovely eight-year-old daughter Gabriella who reminded me poignantly of my two grand daughters, Nicola and Joanna, who were much the same age; they all had long, dark hair. Gabriella had inherited her mother's Latin good looks. Jonathon looked like the Englishman that he is with his fair, freckled skin, rather abstracted air, warm, half-apologetic smile and scruffy clothes. Besides being a thoroughly nice family, Jonathon and Roxanna were heaven sent – via Polly. Jonathon is an IT whiz and meteorologist and has developed and patented 'Sky Eye', an Iridium satellite weather aerial linked to a bank of computer monitors that give the latest satellite weather images. Roxanna is bilingual in Spanish and English and knows everyone and everywhere in town.

As we drove into town Jonathon asked us if we had heard the news on Polly? We shook our heads. Jonathon explained that Polly had had to turn back! She had made it to Rothera, the BAS research station, the one where we had been told we were not welcome. At Rothera she had to wait a further week for a weather window for her onward flight to McMurdo, the American Antarctic base, 2,140 miles away. Finally there was a weather window and she had set off on her long journey, but weather changes very fast over there and there is no full satellite coverage. The head winds had picked up and as Polly approached her 'point of no return', her fuel tanks were half empty and the wind strength was steadily increasing. She had to make the agonising decision to return to Rothera – her fuel margins were unacceptable.

Colin and I were stunned and asked Jonathon what she planned to do. He said, 'Well, the problem is, she doesn't have enough fuel at Rothera to get to McMurdo and Rothera don't have or won't give her any. She's stuck. She's got her fuel cached and waiting in McMurdo but of course she can't get there. We're looking into the possibility of getting some fuel from the Argentineans at their Marambio base, but that would mean that Polly would have to backtrack 300 miles in the wrong direction. Marambio is to the east of Marsh on the northeastern tip of the Antarctic Peninsular; Polly hasn't got the fuel capacity to get to McMurdo from Marambio, which means she'll probably have to come back here.'

Bad as her news was, we were to fare worse.

Colin made some pithy comments about BAS and the reception we had been given all those months ago when we had visited their headquarters in far away Cambridge. 'Those wankers at Rothera,' he said, 'I bet they've got fuel. The Argentines will help!'

Jonathon told us that the situation at Rothera was delicate and Polly's husband, Peter, had appealed to him to tread softly, not to do anything to aggravate the situation. What a desperate time for Polly. She must have been feeling so low and her husband Peter was already in New Zealand waiting to greet her in triumph. What was she going to do? I wondered if she would still be at Rothera if and when we flew south down the Peninsular. Our route would take us close by as our fuel cache at Carvajal lay only 60 miles further along the coast of Adelaide Island.

We told Jonathon and Roxanna how we had become especially pro the people of Argentina since our stay in Buenos Aires. We had been given a surprise reception on arrival at Aeroparke airfield by Colonel Jorge Reta. He had laid on a military brass band, a guard of honour and had even found the oldest living aviatrix (the rather daunting title given to a female pilot) to present me with a bunch of flowers – I'm still not quite sure whether I should be flattered by the latter gesture or not! Colonel Reta had invited us to spend Christmas at their Marambio base and had given us an Argentine flag to fly at the South Pole. Little did we know how precious that flag would be to us in the days ahead.

Helicenter, the Bell Helicopter agents in Buenos Aires, had also given us immense and friendly help. They had given the helicopter a thorough servicing at their own expense and had looked after us very well. One of their team, Rodolfo Lagos Marmol, had taken us to a polo match where we had seen some of the best polo players in the world and the Helicenter boss, Alejandro Servidio, had entertained us lavishly at his home, serving up a full barbeque. He had also arranged to have his chief engineer, Lucio Garcia, come to Ushuaia to give the helicopter a final service before our departure to the frozen south. All very generous and spontaneous. They were hospitable, lovely people.

It was still twilight at 11pm as Jonathon drove us up the twisty, dusty road and turned in the gates to the Aldea Nevada self-catering cabins that Polly had recommended. Colin thought it all a bit primitive and far too rural. We dropped off our bags and headed back into town to Ushuaia's still busy main thoroughfare, San Martin Street, for a late supper with the Selbys in a warm and welcoming little restaurant called La Rueda. We managed to get the one remaining free table. Ushuaia was enjoying 'peak tourist time'. For the next couple of months there would be cruise ships plying the route to and from the Antarctic Peninsular as adventure tourists enjoyed the wonders of the frozen continent in five-star luxury. And then there were the others like us, who were going it alone. Ushuaia attracts pioneers and adventurers from all over the world.

The Selbys were no exception. They had met in Punta del Este Harbour, Uruguay, in the winter of 1990. Roxanna had been crewing on board a 42-foot fibre-glass Argentine boat while Jonathon had his own small, rusty 29-foot Becket. It was love at first sight. Roxanna had abandoned the comfort of her 42 footer and sailed away with Jonathon into the sunset – to New Zealand and the harbour at West Auckland. There they got married and started their own company, Xaxero Marine Software Engineering, while still living and working on board the 29 footer. In 1995 their daughter Gabriella was born. They needed more room and with business doing well were able to purchase their current boat *Anahera*, a ferro-cement 40 footer Donovan. A few years later they had set sail once more for South America, first to Tahiti then onwards to Chile and the Patagonian Channels, finally arriving in Ushuaia in December 2002, where for the first time in their married life they lived in a house – 'for weather reasons', Roxanna said.

Roxanna and Jonathon were running their IT business from their rented two-bedroom wooden house, located up one of the many steep and dusty, unpaved roads perched high above the town. Their yacht lay at anchor in the harbour along with an assortment of other small craft.

I don't remember what we ate that night in Ushuaia, but I do remember that it was delicious. I think we finally got to bed around 2am. I went to sleep thinking how nice that for once we would be staying in the same place for at least three whole days.

That was on Friday. Jonathon had told us that weather-wise the earliest possible date for our crossing would be Monday when the winds were forecast to be light, but the satellite images were showing extensive cloud cover for the Antarctic Peninsular. Tuesday looked better and we needed at least two days of preparation before we would be ready to go.

I suppose we might have managed somehow without Jonathon and Roxanna, but I know we would never have been ready and able to make a 4am departure three days later. Roxanna knew where to go and who to see, she spoke the language and Jonathon was able to give us the latest satellite weather imaging with pinpoint accuracy. Without Jonathon we would have had to rely on a standard email meteorological forecast printout that Commodoro Rivadavia, 300 miles to the north, sent out each day. They could never have given us such precise times and on the evening of our intended departure the promised weather email failed to come through at all.

The next morning I finally managed to talk to Simon on his satellite phone. I had also asked the base at Patriot to tell Simon his wife wanted to hear from him! It was so wonderful to hear his cheerful voice. All was going well, spirits were high, but he had shin splints, which didn't sound too good considering he and Pen had only completed 40 miles with 700 miles still to go. However it was obvious that they were optimistic, committed and focused on the Pole when Simon said, 'Darling can you get us some bacon and eggs and leave them at the South Pole…and anything else solid you can think of…and we'll need a frying pan and some butter! See you in a few days…I'll be the guy in blue!' he added before wishing us a safe journey over the Drake Passage. Simon was dressed for the expedition in blue and white and Pen in red and white.

Back at the Selbys we found Jonathon seated at his computer. His opening words were, 'Tuesday is still looking good.' Colin and I went over and stood behind his seated figure as he flicked through the satellite images on his various screens. 'But you will need to make an early start, around 3am, any later than that and you'll be stuck for days.' He went on to explain that an extensive area of low pressure would be moving in fast on Tuesday morning which would replace Monday's stationary high. 'When those winds come in from the northeast,' he cautioned us, 'they hurtle down these mountains with hurricane force, so once airborne there will be no turning back, but the low will give you tail winds for the first leg of the journey.' Jonathon finished his weather briefing quietly nodding his head and smiling as if in agreement with himself and said, 'I'll be putting my boat out on its storm anchorage.'

The realities of what we were about to do were hitting home. I felt the familiar knots of anxiety in my stomach that I always get before a big water crossing, conjuring up thoughts of catastrophic turbulence, head winds, zero visibility and low fuel warning lights far from land. This was the biggest and potentially most hazardous water crossing either of us had ever attempted. This was the tumultuous southern ocean with all its potential dangers. It was the thought of this crossing that had kept me awake at nights with all those worst case scenarios and we were approaching D-Day. We were checking the images, talking through the final details and now we had the added knowledge that our point of no return would be within minutes of take-off instead of halfway across the Drake, thanks to the hurricane force winds up our backside.

I glanced over at Colin who was looking thoroughly relaxed and in answer to my questioning eyebrow said, 'Right, looks good to me. I'm starving, let's all go and get something to eat.' Roxanna scooped up Gabriella and we all piled into the car and headed into town for some breakfast. We discussed Polly's long wait and the wait of the mountain climbers stuck in Punta Arenas, who as far as we knew were still waiting for a weather window for the Ilyushin to transport them to Patriot Hills. For us the odds were getting better that we would reach the Pole on the 100th anniversary of flight, although Colin was far from optimistic and constantly told me I had not allowed enough time. But getting the timing right in a place like Antarctica is fiendish. If you go too early in the Austral summer, then you risk a long wait like Polly's. If you wait till January, which is high summer in Antarctica, the month with statistically the highest temperatures and least precipitation, you might get unlucky. Blizzards are still frequent. You can find yourself grounded for days on end and sometimes treks and flights are abandoned for the entire season.

We discussed all we had to do in the next couple of days before heading south. The helicopter had to be prepared, provisions purchased, a flight plan filed and forward coordination with Gonzalo and ALE sorted.

Lucio Garcia, the engineer, was arriving later that day from Buenos Aires to service the helicopter, draining off all the oil and replacing it with the special thin oil that should not coagulate in the extreme cold. We would be there to help. The snow baffles needed to be fitted and the fuel filter connected to our handheld electric fuel pump and all our kit had to be sorted. I got out our shopping list and a rather crumpled copy of the email I had been carrying around from a New Zealand helicopter pilot called Jim Wilson.

Some months previously I had been put in touch with Jim, who for many years had been operating out of various coastal Antarctic scientific research stations. I had sent him a list of questions. His quick and detailed response had been immensely helpful and confirmed how tough the elements could and probably would be. Colin and I checked the list of things he recommended we take.

We don't use engine heaters down to about minus 25/30 deg c, but do fit double ni-cad batteries for as much electrical power as you can get for starting. Ni-cads work well in the cold, but lack of power will cause you major hassles on cold start-ups. We use a 'red box' portable battery and NATO plug that can be carried and recharged on 110 volts or 225 volts at a Base. A 'red box' runs 28 volts DC.

We do not anti-freeze. However, we do use FSII Fuel Shell Anti-Icing Inhibitor in Jet Fuel. Jet A1 plus FSII = JP8 or Jet A1 with anti-icing additive. Check your Flight Manual – you may be able to get around this with an airframe fuel filter. (I am not checked out on the Bell 407). EPIRBs are 406 SAR-SAT with an interface with the GPS for rapid position update on the satellite. Interface only compatible with some types of GPS. Speaking of GPS, we navigate in True, just set your GPS to TRUE or set the variation to ZERO. The variation runs 120 deg plus and is confusing when using topo charts for navigation. The Americans at the Pole use grid for runway and winds etcetera, just subtract 180 deg for TRUE. Rule of thumb – near enough.

Tie-downs on the snow/ice use ice screws or 'Deadman Flat Plates' with tie-down rings attached, buried in snow. Use maximum tie-down strength ratchet straps for very high winds. Count on decent blizzards – prepare for the worst that is. The wind is the bit that will hurt you, damage from flying objects, blade flap, and helicopter blown over etcetera. Use generous blade bags and climbing ropes for blade tie-downs. Have holes in them so snow does not melt then refreeze. Fit big tie-down rings on airframe, so you can use them with ratchet straps with thick gloves on. Get a good set of bungs made up for exhaust, air intake etcetera. It is better to push bung in with gloves on than to try and fit covers. Take snowbrush and shovels etcetera to dig out after a blizzard.

CLOTHING – Use high quality sunglasses suitable for flight over flat light areas that will give surface definition. Bausch and Laumb have some good ones. Try and avoid too much tint if you can. Dress for the cold as required, do not use the heater too much, it will tire you out at high altitudes. Salopette bib type overall wind proofs are very good, as you can put on/off jackets easily. The key to it is good polar fleece undergarments, i.e. t-shirts, longjohns etc and good 'wind proofs.' Plenty of gloves for dirty work i.e. refuelling then lighter pair for flying etc.

Plenty of sun cream on your face, hands, sunburn from glare and wind burn etc. Do not let Jet A1 get on your hands, use rubber refuel gloves. Earth fuel pumps, static electricity very bad.

> *Check your fuel burns carefully for higher power settings with strong head winds. High altitudes on plateau will reduce fuel consumption. Think about portable oxygen. Antarctic pressure altitudes are 2000 feet above normal for indicated altitudes due to low air pressure. Often at sea-level, standard day is 970 mbs, and lapse rates are higher than 30 feet min.*
>
> *Kind regards Jim Wilson.*

We had most of the items or the equivalent but we still needed two of the most essential – the 'dead man flat plates' and ice screws for securing the helicopter to the snow and ice. Roxanna could not think of anywhere we might be likely to get them. This was a real blow. There were no hotels or shops where we were going. We needed the precaution of sufficient supplies for three weeks of self-sufficiency in case of blizzards. We already had our dehydrated, freeze-dried packets of food, our cooker and the tent and sleeping bags that Tamara had sent over from England. We had debated what provisions to buy in the UK and ship out and had opted to get as much as possible in Punta Arenas and Ushuaia as shipping costs were exorbitant. We had been told we would be able to get basic expedition gear locally, but even those, according to Roxanna, were in short supply. Little was available, which was surprising considering the healthy flow of sailors and expeditions. We had counted on being able to purchase items like the 'dead man flat plates' and ice screws, either in Punta Arenas or Ushuaia. We drew a blank with both.

Colin argued that we wouldn't need them, that the helicopter weighed one and a half tons: 'Our helicopter is going nowhere, small planes are so much lighter and their wings act like sails, it's essential for them to be secured, we should be OK,' he reasoned. On this occasion, I was the pessimist, I remembered the not so small DC3 lying broken at Patriot Hills, which despite being secured had torn free in a blizzard and blown belly-up suffering serious damage. There had also been that blizzard that nearly cost Simon and Pen their lives in the Arctic, when Pen was giving Simon his 'sledging training'. They had lost their way. Pen's sledge, which was being towed behind his snowmobile, had turned over, and the contents were strewn for miles across the ice.

I was only partially reassured and pointed to the line in Jim's email where he had emphasised how wind would be our biggest enemy. We checked our shopping list – matches, lighter, fuel for cooker, billycan, teabags, rubber gloves and much more. So we shopped, worked on the helicopter, tested equipment, visited Flight Services at the airfield and generally ran round in ever decreasing circles.

Jonathon checked to see if we had the best programme for sending emails via our Iridium phone from Antarctica. He took one look and said, 'I can tell you right now, that won't work, I can set you up with the programme I gave Polly, hers is working fine.' And ours did too. Every time I was to log on in the days to come I silently blessed Jonathon. To have no website updates from Antarctica would have been sad and disappointed our sponsors. What a day and age we live in – mobile and satellite phones, emails, tracker systems, emergency locator trackers, GPSs – and how quickly we take it all for granted. There I was worrying about being able to send out emails, while less than a hundred years ago explorers disappeared for years with no knowledge of what was going on in the big world, or the world of them. News of Scott's death in Antarctica was not known to the world until a year after he had perished.

Modern technology is obviously a big safety factor but the drawbacks are there too. Many were the times when, tired at the end of a long day, it would have been nice to forget about the outside world, to write up one's daily journal or record the scene with a paint brush quietly. Now it's all satellite phones, downloads and digital cameras.

On one of our shopping trips we got a good old-fashioned billycan with a wide top, which we would be able to shovel snow into. The can would be big enough to hold plenty of snow so that, when melted, we would have water to pour into our foil containers of dehydrated food and still have some over for much needed mugs of tea.

Ushuaia had no bacon for Simon and Pen, so we had to make do with smoked Parma ham, but we got everything else we needed and more. Colin persuaded me that we too should have fresh eggs, butter and a couple of loaves of bread, despite my insistence that we had more than enough dehydrated food and pleading lack of space in the helicopter. He likes his creature comforts.

Lucio the engineer arrived from Buenos Aires and we found him working away in the cold outside the hangar. He had planned to bring attachable wheels so that we could roll the helicopter into the hangar, but they were too heavy and he was managing without them. He had already started draining all the oil, cheerfully resilient to the constantly changing weather. One moment the skies were heavy and lowering with an icy wind and hail, then the winds would drop, the sun would come out and it was almost warm. But most of the time we were freezing, getting conditioned for the days ahead.

We dumped all our kit in the hangar along with most of our gear from the helicopter so that we could sort and pack. Colin tested the generator with the electric fuel pump. It worked like a dream, but it was only then that we discovered the screw thread on the filter didn't fit with the one on the pump. Lucio and Colin both thought that our chamois leather filter cloth would be adequate. I prayed they were right.

We went to the harbour to check the sailing schedules and get the contact phone numbers of the various cruise ships that would be crossing the Drake Passage the coming week. It was reassuring to know that two ships were scheduled to cross on the Tuesday, one coming and one going. We wanted to give their captains a call and ask them to keep a listening watch for us in case of emergency.

At the airport Colin once more put in a bid for a Monday departure, suggesting we should file a flight plan and if it was 'no go' then re-file for Tuesday. I was pushing for Tuesday, I didn't like the idea of cloud cover at the end of the journey. Tuesday was much more appealing, with the prospect of strong tail winds to begin with, even though we would be running before the storm. I also didn't see how we could possibly be ready by Monday when everything would be shut on Sunday. Colin reluctantly agreed, with his standard comment, 'You're the boss.'

The next issue was our departure time. The lady handling our flight plan told us that we would have to wait until 6am when the airport opened as we had to go through the correct immigration channels. Trying to convince her of the urgency, we explained that it was essential to leave earlier before the storm hit. She nodded her head slowly in understanding and picked up the phone to see if anything could be done. Lengthy discussions followed. Finally there was vigorous nodding and smiles. She hung up the phone and turned to us with a grin, saying, 'Alora, it is all arranged, it ees a domestic flight, immigration will not be necessary!' And then added that the airport authorities had given permission for the airport to be opened two hours early, free of charge, at 4am as we were working with WWF. We were given instructions to go into the airport by the back entry. What a result. Happily the authorities chose to ignore the fact that we would be flying to a Chilean base on King George Island.

With smiles all round we departed for our evening rendez-vous at the Rivadavia Grill, where we were told, 'All you can eat for $5 dollars.' Several large Fueguian lambs were sizzling over open coals, occupying a large part of one side of the restaurant. As everything was closed on Sunday, we accepted the local Aero Club invitation to a 'fly-in' – and more barbecued lamb.

I woke early on the Monday morning, to the distant call of seagulls and the smell of the pine trees. The sunlight was flickering through the thin flowered curtains that fluttered in the breeze from the half-open window. The sky was blue with puffy white cumulus clouds. I lay there watching the early light patterning the simple wooden walls adorned with a small print of Van Gogh's *Sunflowers*, slightly repetitious of the privy in Alaska! I savoured the moment, the quiet, the peace, the comfort and the warmth under my cosy duvet. In those waking moments the world felt friendly and secure. Even the wind had softened. I thought of home, of my family, of my daughter Christy and her husband Nick so far away in Hong Kong with Talitha, their three-week-old baby daughter, and how Christy had called me the night before her birth. She'd been a little nervous and said, 'Oh Mum, I wish you were here', and how helpless I'd felt and how much I had wanted to be with her as I had been for the birth of their son Domingo. Instead I was far from home and in a rather ungrandmotherly fashion I was in the process of trying to fly a helicopter to one of the remotest parts of the world. I had so many mixed emotions. This was for me, it was my moment, I felt an overwhelming sense of happiness, but also loneliness with home and family so very far away.

In all my world travels, and I have been to many far-flung places, I had never felt so remote, or felt the foreign-ness so strongly. Everything felt foreign and England so distant. Perhaps it was that I had never been to South America before, or didn't speak the languages, or maybe it was that I was just getting older. I was overwhelmed by a longing to be with my own in my own land in my own comfortable bed, where I could wake up without an alarm clock, enjoying a slightly slower pace instead of the long gruelling hours we had ahead. And then there was Simon out there somewhere on the ice. I thought of the past journeys and the one to come and the challenges we had set ourselves. There had been little time to think of the dangers ahead, of the big sea crossing and beyond, but now the realities were piling in. My appetite was suddenly gone and the adrenalin high setting in.

The tiredness was par for the course, yet the 'foreignness' was unusual. It was strange, for everywhere we had met with overwhelming friendliness, especially in Ushuaia, where the Selbys, complete strangers, welcomed us like old friends. They couldn't have done more to help us in every possible way, from ferrying us around town to making final purchases and providing us with the crucial weather information, giving us virtually all of their time. On the couple of occasions when they had to attend to some activity of their own, they had been immensely apologetic. And yet the huge feeling of being out of one's environment was there – perhaps it wasn't so strange given the circumstances.

Our passage south had involved few major water crossings, only island-hopping through the warm Caribbean. On our previous world flights there had been major water crossings all the way, first the warm water crossings: Mikonos to Jordan, Kuwait to Dubai, Muscat to Pakistan, Danang in southern Vietnam to Hong Kong, to Taiwan on to Japan. And then the cold waters: northern Sakhalin Island to Magadan in southeastern Russia, across the northern Pacific Ocean by the Bering Straits to Nome in Alaska and finally, the toughest and longest of all, the North Atlantic crossings, Newfoundland to Greenland, Iceland, the Faeroes and ultimately Scotland. It all added up to more than 7,000 miles over water. Water is a killer if you have mechanical problems, and all helicopter pilots fear it. This time we had seldom been out of sight of land but all that was to change the next day. We were preparing to fly over 527 nautical miles of the most hostile water on earth. No single engine helicopter had ever made it across. I thought of Steve and Quentin's 'ditching' earlier that year. They nearly made it. They were only 30-odd miles off the tortuous coast of Smith Island when they went down. However, Smith Island has little to offer as a safe haven or indeed anywhere for even a helicopter to land, it consists of one towering 6,900-foot-high frozen mountain rising steeply from the water's edge.

Freezing fog, low fuel, whiteouts, hurricane-force winds, the perils of Antarctica saturated my thoughts; and then I thought of my meeting with Charles Swithinbank back in Cambridge all those months ago when we were pouring over charts. He'd pointed out the little British Antarctic Survey hut at Fossil Bluff on the Antarctic Peninsula and said, 'Now that's a beautiful place, that's the sort of place for a honeymoon.' I pulled myself together; it wasn't all bad, Charles helped me to see Antarctica through a different perspective.

I was brought back to reality with a loud knocking on my door. It was Colin saying 'I think we should go today!' 'Fair weather, must fly' was always Colin's motto. But he knew we wouldn't be ready for hours. I made some remark about not wanting to arrive in the dark and then laughed at myself. Dark? We were heading where there would be no sunrises or sunsets. The sun would not dip below the horizon for another three months. Even at our touch-down point on the northern tip of the Peninsular we would be enjoying 24 hours of daylight.

I got dressed quickly. Once out from under that comforting duvet it was freezing and I wanted to telephone all the family before leaving the next morning. I borrowed Colin's mobile phone as for some reason I had been unable to get any reception on mine since arriving in Ushuaia. Reception was poor under the pine trees, so I climbed a little way up the hill behind the cabins, slipping my way up over the pine needles and into an open field of long green grass. The scene reminded me of the northwest coast of Scotland where my sister

Gillian lives – mountains, wild flowers, pine and birch trees and, in the distance, the sea and scattered islands.

I managed to get Suze on the line, I hadn't spoken to her for weeks and although there was so much to catch up on, neither of us had much time to talk. As usual Suze was rushing. One of her 40-foot containers had arrived from China that morning full of furniture for her shop and the traffic wardens were giving her grief: 'Mum I've got to go – I love you, stay safe!'

In Korea it was 6pm local time. Justin was still in his office at the airport and happy to hear that all was going well and wanted to know if I had managed to talk to Dad. I briefly gave him our news and he told me that all the family were settling in well in Korea and looking forward to joining Suze and Christy in Thailand for Christmas. He too wished us a safe crossing, said he'd be following our crossing of the Drake Passage on our website and what a relief it would be to see us safely across.

Then I managed to get through to Christy. Baby Talitha was of course heavenly and she was in the middle of feeding her. Domingo, aged 18 months, insisted on talking to me too. They were all concerned for our safety. 'Mum we can't wait for you to get back home safe,' Christy said and then it was time to say goodbye to her. I stood there for a few moments, still in their worlds, being able to imagine what they were all doing – how much I loved them all.

The rest of the day was something of a blur of activity. The wind was already picking up as we headed down the hill in the direction of the Selby's house. It was further than we thought, not helped by the fact that we couldn't find their house. Tempers were frayed and we ended up going off in different directions, each convinced the other had got it wrong. More by luck than remembered landmarks I found the house, but then had to go and find Colin – a bright blob in his yellow jacket among the grey and weather-worn buildings.

Roxanna had bought a small synthetic Christmas tree and some coloured lights. Gabriella was thrilled and Jonathon was grumbling over the cost: 'And where are you going to put it?' he asked. 'We'll be on the boat for Christmas.' Then he turned his attention back to the computer screens and the satellite weather images. He said we still had a window, but it had narrowed – it was even more essential that we got away by 4am: 'That will be your last chance for the foreseeable future,' he said, looking up from his computer screen with his lop-sided grin.

I told Jonathon that we had been unable to find ice screws or snow plates. He suggested we went down to the port to pay a call on his friend Darrel Day on his Australian yacht, *The Spirit of Sydney*. Darrel had recently purchased the yacht and was busy refurbishing it in preparation for a journey to the Antarctic with a team of mountaineers. They planned to climb various challenging never-before-climbed peaks on the Antarctic Peninsula, including the mountain on Smith Island. Also on board would be Steve Irwin, of Aussie croc-hunter fame, and his National Geographic team.

The day had turned bitterly cold, the wind had got up and a squall of sleet hit us as we clambered over two moored boats to reach Darrell's yacht. All were battened down on their storm anchorages ready for the 'big blow'. Darrell's cabin was chaotic. Coils and coils of rubber hose lay in all directions, he was in the process of putting new insulation on all the hundreds of feet of electric cable that modern ocean sailing yachts now have. But among it all he managed to find one snow picket. He told us that it was sufficient to anchor a 2-tonne yacht in a force 10 gale. He had no ice screw but he did have a special little hook device he had fashioned for pulling the yacht's rope or the helicopter ratchet straps, through the V-shaped hole made by the ice screw – but we still had no ice screw.

'Let's hope there is more snow than ice where we're going,' Colin said.

We spent a happy hour with Darrel exchanging tales. On parting he gave us a rather dusty zip-lock bag filled with a congealed-looking brownish powder saying, 'It's an energy drink, an ovaltine/chocolate mix with glucose, left over from the Abo's sailing and climbing expedition. They sure had a taste for it and it'll give you some variety!' We all wished each other good luck and a happy Christmas as we climbed back out over the coils of cable, and out into the bitter cold where the sleet had turned to flurries of snow that swept across the grey water of the harbour.

The next hours were spent in the bitter cold with Lucio finalising everything with the helicopter. Test flying it, double checking everything and finding a home for all items. There was all the survival equipment for the 'over-water' stretch – life raft, life jackets, survival suits, 'three-minute' air supply cylinder and emergency locator transmitters (ELTs). Next there was everything necessary for Colin's and my survival in Antarctica – tent, sleeping bags, cooker, fuel for cooker, matches, food and lots of warm clothes. There were all the essential items for the helicopter's survival – remote generator, 24-volt battery charger, electric fuel pump, 'tie downs' for the blades to stop them slamming up and down, ratchet straps to secure the helicopter to the snow picket, all the fuel and spare cans of oil. Finally, all the other paraphernalia, like two video cameras, two still cameras, one digital, one normal, as well as all the attendant equipment – chargers, film, tripod and laptop computer. The final item to go in that night was Colin's box of one dozen fresh eggs, which fitted snugly into the small gap between the top of the 19-gallon auxiliary fuel tank and the ceiling of the small luggage compartment.

It had been getting colder and colder and once again everything took far longer than we had expected. Roxanna had gallantly filmed and taken pictures along with running various errands, but it was past 7pm by the time we got back to Jonathon, his computers, a welcome cup of tea and a digestive biscuit. That was the first food we had eaten all day and, as it turned out, the last. Food came a poor second to sleep and neither of us were particularly hungry.

We hung around with Jonathon and Roxanna waiting for the Commodoro Rivadavia weather centre to send through their final weather briefing – it never came, but that would have been more of a formality as we had Jonathon's briefing.

All that remained was for Roxanna to call Commodoro Rivadavia's air traffic control for the phone number for our 'flight following' for the following day. It was time to say goodbye. We called for a taxi, gave Jonathon, Roxanna and Gabriella all a big hug and thanked them profusely for all their endless help. They had put their own lives on hold for the three and a half days we had been there and Jonathon assured us that he would continue to monitor the weather until we reached Carvajal on Adelaide Island. They have our undying thanks. By the time we left we were too tired to even think of a hot meal, all we wanted was sleep.

It was gone 9pm by the time our taxi driver dropped us off at the cabins with promises that he would pick us up again at 3am the next morning – and a further five minutes after the taxi left when Colin realised he had left his mobile phone in the helicopter. It was our only communication with the outside world as there were no telephones in the cabins and my phone was still not working. Colin wanted to go and collect his phone. I told him not to bother. 'The taxi driver said he would be back at 3am. I'm sure he will be,' I said.

Colin was not so sure, 'What happens if he oversleeps and no one comes and all because of a failed taxi we miss our weather window?' It was as well he did go, as the taxi never appeared.

While Colin set off to retrieve his phone, I made my way wearily over to the cabin 'offices' to pay our bill. The proprietor, Raphael Fank, apologised that he didn't have the 'swipe' machine for credit cards in that office and asked me to go down to the other offices further down the hill. So down we went and at the same time he showed me the letterbox on the railings in which to drop off our cabin keys in the early hours of the morning. Raphael said we could leave any bags we didn't want to take with us in the cabin and he would collect them the next day – all very friendly and helpful.

Colin arrived back as I was finishing the major part of the sorting out of bags. We left behind all our exposed film and video footage, along with much of our clothing, charts, printer and so on – it added up to two full duffle bags.

It was 11.30pm when we finally stumbled into our beds. Butterflies and hunger were replaced with overwhelming tiredness and the concern that we would only be getting a few short hours of sleep. Our polar weather gear was laid out and waiting and our alarm clocks set for 2am. It was all about to begin.

Antarctica – the last great frontier on earth – and we were going there.

CHAPTER THREE
The Drake Passage

'Let us probe the silent places, let us seek what luck betide us;
Let us journey to a lonely land I know.
There's a whisper on the night-wind, there's a star agleam to guide us,
And the wild is calling, calling...let us go'
Robert Service

Left: Flynig over the Drake Passage

I woke from the deepest sleep to the sound of Colin knocking on my door and the alarm ringing all at the same time. D-Day had arrived. I clambered out of bed and took a quick look out the window to check the weather – inky black with the wind sighing through the pine trees, but no rain and no snow. It would do.

A large mug of tea would have been good, but we had no teabags and more importantly we didn't want to be caught short halfway across the Drake Passage. We had a long water crossing ahead of us and I had learned my lesson the hard way when we had made the eight-hour journey from northern Newfoundland to Greenland in 2000. On that occasion we were only two hours out when I knew I wasn't going to make it and had rashly announced the fact over my radio, much to Colin's delight. Colin has a camel-like capacity and could manage 12 hours at a stretch in his microlight. I never had to go through that sort of training – in a helicopter you can land virtually anywhere, except over water. So this time I wisely opted for no tea.

Outside there was total darkness – no moon, no stars and no gleaming taxi headlights. Colin was pacing up and down with intermittent checks outside. I was feeling groggy with lack of sleep and the early hour. I forced myself to get out the video camera to film the pending crisis. The interesting things to film are always when you least feel like filming or when you physically can't! This was one of those occasions and Colin was telling me to stop and help look for the taxi driver's card which he had given us the day before. After a frantic search, with both of us accusing the other of having it last, we found it in the sack of rubbish. Colin got through to the taxi company who thankfully operated a 24-hour service and were able to send a cab within minutes. Our erstwhile driver was no doubt comfortably tucked up in bed.

We remembered to drop off the keys to the cabin in the box on the railings and then followed an interesting conversation explaining to the taxi driver, who spoke no English, that we didn't want to go to the main airport entrance. But with plenty of hand flapping we managed to direct him along the now familiar dirt track leading to the hangars. All was shrouded in darkness, no lights anywhere, and when we reached the airport security barrier the black figure of the sentry on duty loomed out of the night. He had been warned of our coming. He checked our passports by the light of his torch, shone it briefly on us and with a smile said, 'Good luck' and 'Vaya con Dios' as he lifted the barrier. We continued on along the track that followed the airport perimeter fence, then curved inwards and circled around the dark shape of the hangar where, on the other side, our helicopter sat on the concrete apron, briefly illuminated by the arc of car headlights as our driver swung in and halted some 20 feet away.

Goodness knows what he thought, but the taxi driver too wished us well with a 'Vaya con Dios' as he climbed back into his cab and headed back to town, plunging us once more into total darkness.

We carried our various bags over to the already laden helicopter. Our sleeping bags and padded jackets alone took up a ridiculous amount of space and we would be twice our normal 'hot weather' size by the time we had put on our survival suits over our cold weather gear. The helicopter tanks were also full to the brim. We had five and a half hours of fuel for a four-hour journey in 'still' air – a fairly slim safety margin. We prayed that the predicted head winds for the last section of the journey did not intensify. For once past the point of no return – which, with the threatened storm on our heels was shortly after take-off – there was no turning back.

We got out our two small torches and while Colin stowed the last items on board and did the checks I set up the camera on the tripod ready to start filming. We were to find out later that virtually none of the footage came out. All there was to show of our final moments before departure was the indistinct sound of our subdued voices and the slight movement of black on black.

It was 10 minutes to 4am, the Bell 407 was packed and we were ready to go. The first hint of dawn illuminated the angry, threatening clouds building in the skies to the north, while beckoning us south was a golden strip of light on the far horizon.

Clad in our survival suits, we climbed awkwardly into the cockpit and secured our safety harnesses. We then attached our hand-held ELTs and three-minute air supply units to our suits. The air units consist of an eight-inch-long aluminium canister with rubber mouthpiece containing three precious minutes of extra life saving air in the event that you have to ditch at sea and are trapped in a fast sinking helicopter – usually upside down. If this happens, anything that is not attached to you is unlikely to make it out of the helicopter. So we were looking something like a couple of Christmas trees with all our attachments.

The waiting and the preparations were over and with it the worries and tensions. It was action time. I felt a little quickening of my heart as we carried out the pre-take-off checks. It was my day as captain – Colin was on the radio, we knew our routine. There was the lovely moment when you hear the high-pitched whine of one powerful Rolls-Royce jet turbine engine firing up – but this time was special, this was it, the long anticipated day. The dim light of dawn lent a dramatic quality to the moment.

We completed the final checks at exactly two minutes to 4am and were set to go as the light came on in the control tower. Unlike our taxi driver, the air traffic controller was there for us, and for no extra charge they had opened two hours early.

Colin pressed the intercom and radioed the tower. 'Ushuaia Buenos dias, November Four Four Echo Alpha requesting flight information for departure to Marsh Teniente Frei.'

'Good morning,' came the reply, 'QNH 960 (millibar pressure setting), runway 06 in use, climb to 8,000 feet on a heading of 140 degrees – clear to take off from present position.'

Never had the helicopter been so heavy as I slowly raised the collective lever and, once light on the skids, eased the helicopter forward into a sliding take-off with Colin cautioning me to watch the power gauge. Colin was always giving instructions and back-seat driving was normal. As an instructor it is second nature constantly to monitor your copilot. For the most part I would say nothing, though from time to time I'd remind him that I had matters in hand and that unless he thought I was actually about to kill us, then please shut up! He'd then laugh and apologise. On this occasion, he need not have worried and I need not have been so cautious, the Bell 407 had power to spare as we crossed the runway in the gathering light and headed out across the black and leaden waters of the Beagle Channel with the Ushuaia air traffic controller saying, 'N44 Echo Alpha, airborne at 04.03'.

We checked all systems. Everything looked good as we climbed quickly away to 5,000 feet, where we found we had a delightful 25 knots of tail wind. The land, still shrouded in darkness, slipped away below us.

We headed south. The last of the islands was the fabled Cape Horn. We talked of all the mariners, the great seafarers who had plied their way through that treacherous piece of water, of the ones who had died in the attempt and of the tiny chapel and monument to all those who had perished. I thought of the chapel. Charles Swithinbank had talked about it in the letter he wrote me after I visited him in Cambridge on that beautiful summer's day in far away England, when he had suggested landing and visiting it. But there was no question of our dropping in on our outward journey, and with the weather closing in behind us we had to conserve every ounce of fuel. The only direction we were going was forward, and as fast as possible. We hoped that on our return journey, with the prevailing southeasterlies, we would be able to drop in.

With a final backward look at the stormy skies, and the dark shapes below of the last of the Americas, we turned our sites south, to what appeared to be an altogether friendlier scene. The golden light on the far horizon remained, while the thin blue light of dawn streaked the skies with pink and gold. Far below, the grey seas were calm. I thought again of all the imagined dire scenarios, of what could happen flying across the Drake Passage in a single engine helicopter – and how 'the point of no return' had always been around the halfway point. We were already committed. 'Well at least it takes the decision factor out of the equation,' Colin said with a grin.

Ushuaia air traffic control handed us over to the headquarters at Commodoro Rivadavia. Colin would be talking to them every half-hour via our satellite phone, giving our coordinates and reporting 'flight normal'. We would stay in touch with them until we established a two-way frequency on the radio with Marsh base on the northern tip of the Antarctic Peninsula. It was comforting to know that the Argentineans knew what we were doing and approximately where we were. We never did contact any of the captains of the cruise ships. It was even more comforting to know that our Blue Sky Network tracker box, linked to our satellite phone, was giving out our exact location every 30 seconds, and incredible to think that anyone following us on our website could see exactly where we were, what height we were at and what speed we were going – thanks to the tracker box.

Our immediate problem was that we were cold. The outside air temperature at 5,000 feet was -9°C and we had no heating. We didn't dare risk turning on the heat. When storing the fuel for the generator and stove we hadn't thought about the hot air vents in the back of the helicopter. Had we put one of the cans up against one of the vents? The chances of any danger were slim but it was better to be cold than frazzled.

I had wisely put on my small 'tent boots' – canvas, down-filled bootees, over my survival suit, which had all-in-one feet. Colin had opted not to wear any boots. He only had a pair of thin socks under his survival suit and only two layers of fleece under garments to my three, but then again, I feel the cold a lot more than he does. Regardless, we were both freezing. I thought about the icy water far below and as always on long water crossings I mentally ran through

Helicopters seldom fall out of the sky

Contrary to what most people think, helicopters seldom fall out of the sky. If your engine fails you quickly lower the collective lever, which flattens the rotor blades. You then have no forward wind resistance and the air, instead of flowing over and down over the blades, pushes up from below and you float down like a sycamore leaf at approximately 1,500 feet per minute. The higher you are the better off you are as you have longer to prepare yourself. Even so, it all happens fast and over water it's incredibly difficult to judge your height, especially if there is a big swell.

At 40 feet you flare the helicopter into wind, just like a duck landing on water with its body tilted back and feet forward. Your copilot makes a leap for it, clutching the life raft, all at less than 20 feet – difficult to judge! Then the pilot ditches the helicopter with zero forward movement, tipping the blades into the water on the passenger side, in the hope that you won't make contact with the blades as you exit – and that the engine and transmission will hurl forward on the now empty side. The trick then is to get out of the machine before you are too deep in the water. The problem is that helicopters, unlike fixed-wing planes, sink like a stone and are top heavy so tend to turn over. You find yourself disorientated, sinking fast and unable to get out until the water equalises – that's when those precious three minutes of spare air can save your life.

ditching procedures. I checked once again that my emergency air supply and locator beacon were firmly attached to my life jacket. The life raft was on the ledge behind Colin's head.

We had done 'the dunker course', and got out of a sunken capsule at the RAF base at Yeovilton back in England. It was not even remotely fun and it all happened so very fast – and that was done with divers at hand to rescue us in a lukewarm pool. The water we were flying over was 2ºC.

We decided to descend to warmer climes and see if we still had a good tail wind. At 2,000 feet it was -3°C with 22 knots of tail wind. That was the best we could do as we now, rather worryingly, had patchy, low sea fog beneath us. An hour later, the fog was gone, only to be replaced by extensive areas of thin stratus cloud that forced us slowly up to 3,000 feet. We debated going below the cloud, but were anxious to keep our tail winds.

The cloud layer thickened below us and the gaps became fewer. We were 250 miles out and had solid cloud cover – and were still on top. Should we turn round and look for a gap? Or should we continue and hope for clearer skies? Below lay Eternity. We wished we had played safe earlier and sacrificed our tail winds. The further south we travelled, the colder it would get and the danger of icing in cloud would increase – and how high was the cloud base?

This was a situation we had both been in before. Colin reminded me of his dramatic flight to Crete at the start of his solo microlight flight to Australia. It was March and the weather was appalling. As always he was flying high, up at 14,000 feet to avoid turbulence, with solid cloud cover below. He was nearing Crete and had to get down through the clouds. The moment he entered cloud, the super-cooled frame of his microlight was coated in thick frost. He made a towering spiral descent at 2,000 feet per minute, breaking out of the cloud a couple of hundred feet over a storm-swept Mediterranean.

Jonathon's weather satellite images for the period had shown some areas of cloud for the middle section of the crossing: 'Difficult to tell the thickness of the cloud from the satellite images,' Jonathon had said, but he had reckoned it would probably not be too thick. The cloud area in those images had shown more extensive areas of cloud near the Antarctic Peninsular.

We opted to continue onwards and after the 6.30pm call to Commodoro Rivadavia we would call Jonathon for the latest weather, only to realise that Jonathon's phone number was stored in Colin's mobile, which was in the pocket of his jacket in the back of the helicopter. To climb through the small bulkhead aperture from the cockpit was possible for me, but only just. Colin is too big. I had tried it, back in Ushuaia, in case of an emergency, like a blockage in the auxiliary fuel pump over water. Clambering into the back had to be done with great care not to knock either the collective lever controlling the power or the cyclic stick controlling the direction. Both are infinitely sensitive and a good old knock could see you flipping over in a heart-beat. Then all the attachments, life jacket, air supply and ELT would have to be removed before attempting the twist and wriggle operation in my cumbersome survival suit through the narrow bulkhead opening behind my head.

We decided it was safer to leave the telephone where it was. There wasn't too much we could do about it other than be reassured that the skies were clear ahead, or panicked because they were not. To turn around and back-track, using up precious fuel to look for a hole in the clouds, seemed about as promising as finding one ahead. So we continued and tried not to have negative thoughts about wishing we had descended earlier. The positive side was that we still had 10 knots of tail wind with a fairly strong cross-wind component, which was exactly what Jonathon had predicted for the mid section of our crossing.

Time passed – it's strange looking back, we had planned to phone various people who we knew would be watching our crossing on our website, but we never did. We weren't fighting turbulence or poor visibility, but we were constantly monitoring everything: that the fuel from the auxiliary tanks was transferring to the main tanks, that all the temperatures and pressures were correct, making the half-hourly calls to Commodoro Rivadavia and of course looking for a glimpse of the ocean some 3,000 feet below us. We were totally focused on the flight with no room for outside thoughts.

Several times we thought the cloud looked thinner ahead, only to find little change, just a small drop in the height of the tops of the cloud. Finally we did get a momentary glimpse of the grey world below and were slightly reassured to see that the cloud was thin in places and the base looked to be a good 1,000 feet above the water. But we didn't want to risk descending through even 1,000 feet of cloud. The outside air temperature was now -7°C, and not much warmer inside. The danger of icing was there. Even the smallest film of ice can be catastrophic – ice can build up quickly on the rotor hub spreading outwards to the blade tips that spin at 400mph. The result would be blade stall and then you would fall out of the sky.

After what seemed forever, but was actually only half an hour since finding ourselves with total cloud cover below, we found a small gap and quickly dropped through, leaving behind the false security of the friendly sunshine and tail winds for a grey world and a slight head wind. It was a huge relief to be on the right side of the cloud. The waters of the Drake Passage were blessedly calm and the long, shallow swells unbroken by white caps.

Visibility was good and 10 minutes later we spotted a cruise ship on the far horizon, the only shipping we saw during the entire crossing. In a strange way the ship made us feel even more alone. It was only 7am and we could imagine all those people, wrapped in luxury, snug in their beds, with perhaps a few early risers enjoying coffee and bacon and eggs – it also brought home to us how hungry we were. We hoped we might be able to get some breakfast when we got to Marsh. 'It's the only place in Antarctica where there is hotel accommodation of sorts,' Gonzalo had told us. 'It's a Chilean and Russian base and DAP Airlines operates out of there – they used to bring DC3s in until one went off the end of the runway into the sea.'

We had been cautioned that the northern end of the Peninsular was renowned for bad weather, freezing rain and fog. If planes have the endurance, pilots heading to the interior avoid Marsh and head straight to Rothera, halfway down the Peninsula, where the weather tends to be fractionally better. We had neither the endurance nor a welcome at Rothera, the British Antarctic Survey base where Polly was stranded. We wondered whether she was still there.

When we were half an hour away from Marsh airfield on King George Island, Commodoro Rivadavia told us to report when we had made radio contact with the base. Then in the distance we spotted what we thought was another cruise ship but it turned out to be a great flat tabular iceberg, with sheer sides of deepening turquoise, large enough for half a dozen helicopters to land on. Soon everywhere we looked there were bergs of every shape and size, glorious solid shapes in our watery world, and then we saw the first sign of life, two small Antarctic terns.

There were breaks in the cloud; early morning sunlight sparkled off the ice and water and high above we could see thin wisps of cloud against the palest of blue skies. The far horizon looked more ominous: there appeared to be low cloud over where King George Island lay.

In hazy conditions, light over water can play a thousand tricks. Horizons are not where they seem and cloud is water and water is cloud, especially if the ground is snow covered, as was the case as we approached the coast of the Antarctic Peninsula. Clouds, snow, sea and icebergs were indistinguishable one from the other. We were both straining our eyes in an attempt to separate them. We were entering the spiritual, unforgiving world of the long awaited frozen south.

Our GPS was reading 30 miles to go when Colin managed to raise Marsh on the radio with air traffic control wishing us a cheery 'Good Morning'. Colin phoned Commodoro Rivadavia for the last time, telling the controller that we had 25 miles to run and we were two-way with Marsh. He thanked them for their service and they in turn wished us a safe flight.

Gonzalo had purchased 11 drums of fuel for us from the Chilean government for our outward and return journey – we prayed the drums would be there as promised. Our next fuel cache was altogether less certain. The Chilean government had happily sold us seven further drums of fuel at their abandoned research station at Carvajal, 340 nautical miles further south down the peninsula. The station where we were told no one had been for three years. 'Although', Gonzalo had said, 'possibly a ship could have gone in and helped themselves to a little fuel.' But he thought it unlikely as the cache was on the top of the hill and about half a mile from the sea.

With only 10 miles to go air traffic control asked if we had the runway in sight. We hadn't. Not only could we not see the runway, we still couldn't be sure of land. Our brief spell of sunshine was gone, the cloud base was down to 500 feet, with blowing snow. We made a note of suitable offshore alternate landing spots on tabular icebergs. At five miles we were finally able to spot the low ribbon of land rising from the grey and frozen sea, cluttered with pack ice. The cloud enveloped the land to the east of where the airfield appeared to be and to the west didn't look a great deal better, yet never did a destination look more beautiful. Antarctica, which had beckoned to us for so long, was in our sights.

We still could not see the runway until we were practically over it. Hardly surprising, as all was white. The runway was solid ice with drifting snow and virtually indistinguishable from the surrounding snow covered slopes. We could see the tower but no buildings. Colin's only comment was, 'There's got to be something wrong with you if you want to live here – are you sure we can get some breakfast?' He then reported: 'Airfield in sight.'

ATC Marsh came back: 'November Four Four Echo Alpha clear to land runway 11, wind 090 degrees, 20 knots, QNH 989 millibar.' He asked us if we were familiar with the helipad! We looked at each other and laughed – what a question! There we were, the first-ever single-engine helicopter to make it across the Drake, feeling like conquering heroes and he was asking us if we were familiar with the helipad. That certainly put us in our place.

There are a number of helicopters that operate around the coast of Antarctica, working with the various different countries scientific research stations, as well as the helicopter operated by DAP airlines based at Marsh, which provided local transport and Search and Rescue. Like all the other helicopters it had been brought over the Drake Passage by ship. Few have ventured to fly any distance into the interior. ATC told us to hover taxi down the runway and that at the far end we would see the Chilean station to our right and the Russian station to the left. We were to land at the Chilean one.

The slightly higher ground on either side of the runway had hidden the cheerful and welcome sight of the two stations – to our right, a cluster of red painted buildings, nestling in the lee of the hill that now came into view. On the left we could see the rather scruffier Russian base, which was in need of a fresh coat of paint. The helipad was a little to the right of the runway, some 50 yards from the sea. It was easy to understand why the DC3 airplane had ended up in the water, as the threshold of Runway 11 was just yards from the water's edge, while the far end is 1km from the sea, straddling the narrow neck of the island.

We were being waved in by a heavily wrapped up marshaller in polar gear wearing ski goggles and leaning into the wind. The ground was nearly obscured by the blowing snow. Beyond the helipad at the water's edge was the reassuring sight of some 50 blue plastic drums of Jet A1 fuel sitting in the snow. We touched down on the Antarctic Peninsular at 08.22 local time (11.22 GMT). The journey across the Drake Passage had taken 4 hours and 19 minutes.

CHAPTER FOUR
Marsh-Patriot Hills

'The last frontier,
A frozen world of infinite, unforgiving beauty.'

Left: Rothera, Adelaide Island

As we opened the doors of the helicopter, the full force of the elements hit our already chilled bodies. We both dived to retrieve our outer jackets, hats and gloves. It was desperately cold. The marshaller came over. He shouted a brief welcome, then pointing to the fuel drums and trying to make himself heard above the howling wind yelled something like, 'Your fuel is over there.'

The drums were 50 yards away, slightly downhill of our position and I wondered if we were expected to roll them up the slope. The marshaller obviously realised we could hear little of what he was saying, so he hurried over and shouted in Colin's ear, pointing to the huts, giving us the good news that breakfast was being served, that we should follow him and that after we had eaten he would take us up to the tower by snowmobile to file our onward flight plan to Carvajal. Then we could refuel and be on our way. The directive had obviously been: 'Be courteous but see them on their way as quickly as possible.'

The wind appeared to be strengthening. The huts that the marshaller had indicated were fast vanishing in the blowing snow as I hurried after Colin, who hadn't even bothered to take off his survival suit. He'd just flung his jacket on top, jumped into his big padded snow boots, grabbed his gloves and the moment the marshaller had finished speaking he did a runner, leaving his duffel bag sitting in the snow beside the helicopter in danger of being blown away. Life in Antarctica appeared to be every man for himself.

In the few moments it took to bundle the bags back in the helicopter and follow Colin to the huts I was frozen – such a joy to dive inside the building, shutting the door against the wind and perishing cold. It all felt rather like school. I looked around at the large canteen that we were being taken through, with its stainless-steel fittings, cream walls and concrete floor and the rows of empty trestle tables, alarmingly empty of any sign of breakfast. Happily we continued on and were ushered into a small room where a group of officers from the Chilean Navy were seated at a long table enjoying coffee, ham, cheese and pancakes with condensed milk. The room, like the canteen, was plain but warm and the windows covered in a rime of frost. The officers were dressed immaculately in uniform with plenty of gold braid.

A capsized Zodiac boat was the reason for the presence of these officers and the larger than usual number of craft anchored offshore. They told us that the day before a group of seven Koreans had been some distance from the base in the Zodiac when disaster struck – we never got all the details, but a big Search and Rescue had been mounted. I asked the officer if the Koreans were all OK. He nodded his head and said that the rescue operation had been successful, and then added rather casually that six had been rescued and one had died. The officers were friendly and between mouthfuls asked a few questions about our journey, but I think they were also on a tight schedule and perhaps saw us as another set of potentially foolhardy adventurers who might need rescuing.

We were famished. Even pancakes with sickly sweet condensed milk tasted delicious. We were just tucking into a second helping when the officers got to their feet and the marshaller hurried back into the room and, holding the door open, told us the snowmobile was waiting outside. We gulped down our coffee, took one last bite of pancake and hurried back out through the canteen. In the foyer we passed the six rescued Koreans. A forlorn little group, huddled together, anxiously looking up and listening to a rather tall Chilean officer, who I imagine was giving them instructions on what to do next. I felt very sorry for them. 'Poor sods' was all Colin muttered as we followed the marshaller out into the howling elements and the waiting vehicle.

We had a choice – one of us to ride pillion, the other to climb onto a sled that was attached behind the snowmobile, which looked like an overgrown battered shovel. I ended up on the shovel. I think I had more protection from the wind than Colin, but mine was certainly the bumpier ride. I saw very little but rather enjoyed the novel form of transport as we lurched and bounced several hundred yards up the slope through the blowing snow to the tower. I was hunched up in a tight ball, one hand holding on to the side of the contraption, the other holding the hood of my jacket tightly around my face. Neither of us had had time to locate our inner woollen hats or balaclavas and I'd given up on learning the drawstring technique on the hoods with their Alaskan wolf-skin ruffs.

Like the canteen, the control tower building was a uniform cream inside. We passed a young woman on the stairs, clutching a pile of documents. She gave us a disinterested glance as we passed; she looked as though she could be British. I'm afraid my rather jaundiced thought was that she was probably with the British Antarctic Survey and said as much to Colin.

'Don't be daft, but even if she is she's probably OK, she's come here, hasn't she?' he laughed.

All was quick efficiency in the tower. I filed the flight plan while Colin checked the latest satellite charts. The weather, just as Jonathon had forecast, was looking good for our 350-mile onward flight to

Carvajal. 'You'll never get a better day for flying down the peninsula,' he had predicted.

'Have you got the fuel coordinates?' the controller asked, glancing up from the flight plan I had just handed him. I assured him that I had, and double-checked them against the ones he had for the Carvajal base. They tallied.

'You know that no one has been in there for three years?' he asked.

We knew only too well. 'The drums will probably be buried in the snow. Have you got a shovel?' I replied 'yes' on all counts. He wished us a good journey and reminded us to call in and close our flight plan on arrival at Carvajal.

Once more outside we skidded and bounced our way back down the hill to the warm splash of our red helicopter sitting on the helipad, and were delighted to see that refuelling help was at hand. Two base personnel had already rolled six drums over to the helipad and offered to help fuel up. The marshaller told us to be sure to replace the empty drums with the others by the water when we were finished, then, turning his snowmobile around he gave us a wave and a shouted goodbye and was gone in a flurry of snow.

Colin and the two helpers did the heavy fuel work and got the generator and fuel pump out. I attempted to regain some semblance of order in the back of the helicopter. I found Jonathon's telephone number and also checked the position of the hot air vents – there were no tins of fuel up against them, but various bags were covering much of them, so I cleared a little space around them, then I took some photos and video footage. Colin was complaining as he worked as his hood wouldn't stay on: 'My ears are dropping off, wish I knew where my balaclava was.' He never did find it.

Shouting to be heard above the wind he said, 'Gonzalo Campos also said the drums of fuel at Carvajal will be well buried, we're going to have a job finding them.' I yelled back that I was more concerned about the state of the fuel after sitting there for three years, 'Remember Saglek?' He grimaced and nodded his head.

In 2000 we had used a drum of fuel at the disused airfield of Saglek in northern Labrador. On that occasion, because of the weather conditions we had opted to fly via Labrador to Greenland instead of taking the shorter over-water route from Iqaluit on Baffin Island. On arrival at Saglek we found out that the 'disused' airfield was anything but abandoned. It was a US–Canadian early warning radar station. However, after all our initial shocks, and the military checking us out through Goose Bay, we were made welcome. But they had no Avgas fuel for our piston engine machines. We had estimated before setting off from our last airfield that we would have just enough fuel to make the long 500 miles over water crossing going the Saglek route. The margins were narrow, but when an unopened drum of what smelt and looked like regular car fuel was found, we hungrily set about emptying the contents into our machines. It had looked clean enough and we reckoned it would be well diluted with the good fuel already in our tanks. It wasn't until halfway through transferring the fuel that we noticed large amounts of rust and water in the bottom of the bucket that we were using to transfer it. For the whole of that long flight our ears were attuned for the slightest hiccup, but other than a couple of heart-stopping coughs, the engines ran smooth and we made it across.

While we were talking and refuelling, we saw a man battling his way over from some distant buildings. He was sporting a long red beard dusted with snow and, like everyone else, heavily disguised in ski goggles.

'Hello, my name is Alejo Contreras. I am Chilean, I am with DAP airlines.' Alejo was interested to know who we were and what we were doing – he'd heard rumours he said. 'Picking up fuel in Carvajal? You know no one has been in there for three years?' he said. I told him that we knew that. 'The fuel will be buried. Have you got a good shovel?' This was getting to be a routine. I told him we did, but he wasn't convinced and wanted to look for himself. I couldn't see much of his expression due to goggles and hair, but his voice said it all when he saw our small but sturdy fold-up shovel that I pulled out from under the tent and sleeping bags piled high on top of the big auxiliary fuel tank. 'You need a real shovel, I will lend you one, you can give it back to me when you return. You will have some big digging, if you can find the drums, but you have I think got the coordinates, I hope they will be accurate.' He went off to get his superior shovel.

Our next visitors were two young Chinese students from Beijing University. They were spending two weeks at the station studying cold weather systems. They were charming and very curious as to what we were doing – I think they thought we were mad, though they understood the WWF side of our venture.

Alejo returned with a 'proper shovel', for which we were to be infinitely thankful. 'The drums, you know, will be up on the hill near the old ice skiway. You have to be careful too for crevasses. Some Chilean's were not careful and they fell down a crevasse on their snowmobile – they died.' Carvajal was getting more interesting by the minute. He continued, 'One of the reasons the station was abandoned was the problem with crevasses in the runway. But that is late in the summer, now you will, I think, be OK.'

Coping with crevasses on the ground was something we were new to. We had flown over them and studied plenty of photos, but understanding where we were likely to find them and recognising the snow-covered cracks was another thing. But I was reassured by the thought that we were unlikely to be wandering far from the helicopter.

Refuelling finished, Alejo quickly helped us roll the drums back from whence they had come. The wind and the cold kept conversation with Alejo brief. He gave us his satellite phone number and told us to please call him if we needed his help or advice. We thanked him and said we would keep in touch and would take good care of his shovel. His warmth, friendliness and concern were in sharp contrast to the helpful but brusque, military efficiency we received from the Chilean military. As we lifted off we could just make out Alejo's small figure over by the DAP hangar as he waved us farewell.

The journey south down the Peninsular went without a hitch. The weather improved almost immediately and we enjoyed blue skies nearly all the way. We phoned Jonathon back in Ushuaia, who told us there would be slight cloud cover in about 20 minutes, but that would quickly clear, and that is exactly what happened.

And the scenery – what a festival of glory! All the long months of preparation, all the stress, all the tiredness, everything was worth it for a day like that. The times I have lifted off into the great blue and felt a shiver of pure joy, the elation of flying, to be at one with the universe. Now in Antarctica, with no trace of man's imprint, we were surrounded by the might and majesty of God's creation in its harshest most beautiful form, yet calmed on that day by the blue skies and silent, ice-packed sea.

Colin was a little more pragmatic. 'Where are all these wildlife sanctuaries you had to list in that document for the American government? Hard to believe that an egg could survive around here.' It was hard to imagine, but we did see the occasional sea bird and later we flew over leopard seals lying on large hunks of pack ice and basking in the sun.

For 300 miles we travelled south between the peninsula and the chain of offshore islands. The names of those islands tell their own story of the men who'd first been there and of the heroes, many of them British, like King George Island, Livingston and Nelson. Some are descriptive like Snow Island, Low Island and, a short distance to the east, Lower Island. The Frenchman Jean-Baptiste Charcot was a little more imaginative; he called one 'Pourquoi Pas? Island' – the name of his ship.

The Carvajal base on the southern end of Adelaide Island was originally built by BAS, but was later abandoned in 1976 in favour of the site at Rothera some 60 miles to the northeast. There they are able to maintain a hard surface runway at sea level instead of the ice skiway high on the hill at Carvajal which, as Alejo had informed us, tended to develop crevasses. Also Rothera was less prone to the vagaries of the pack ice blocking access from the sea.

Around 15 miles out from Rothera I called the base on the radio requesting to pass overhead. We were hoping we might meet with a greater degree of friendliness than we had received at their headquarters in Cambridge back in the UK. Perhaps they would even invite us in for a cup of tea and we could visit Polly if she was still there? We were, after all, all Brits far from home. Under normal circumstances we might have actually asked for permission to land, but Polly's husband Peter had said, 'Please don't aggravate the situation' – Polly's two week overstay while trying to arrange fuel with the Argentine base was apparently a bit fraught, although she was doing her best to 'earn her keep' doing odd jobs, including cleaning the loos. It must have been a tough and lonely time for her, stuck there having had to abort her onward journey and feeling unwelcome to boot.

We could see the base clearly from 10 miles away, the huts and runway silhouetted against the sea, hugging the low mountainside on a small, flat promontory of land. A friendly, but incurious voice immediately answered my call and gave us permission to pass overhead – but there was no chat or offers of a cuppa. There was no sign of life as we passed overhead the runway. I asked the man on the radio to say hello to Polly for us. He replied with a cheery 'Will do!' and that was that.

We knew that all the scientists have an intensive working programme during the short Antarctic summer and don't want interruptions from expeditions. That is understandable, but Rothera gets none of the foot expeditions and those made by Polly, Colin and me were the only airborne ones to pass that way that year and we didn't even land. So, shunned by our fellow countrymen, we flew onwards to our abandoned Carvajal station, which was to prove one of the best of times.

Under a calm and cloudless sky we flew up and over the mountain range on Southern Adelaide Island and there, below us on the coast, we could see a cluster of huts, and like the ones back at Marsh, they were all painted red with black roofs. Beyond them floated icebergs of all shapes and sizes on a sparkling and frigid sea. We couldn't see the skiway or the fuel drums.

'Turn back up the hill, the skiway is up there somewhere,' I said and added confidently in response to Colin's pessimistic muttering, 'I'm sure these coordinates are a 100 per cent accurate,' fervently hoping they were.

We circled around and sure enough, beside what looked like a possible skiway, we could just make out a small cluster of blue drums that mercifully were not fully buried.

'Don't appear to be many there,' Colin said as he circled them, 'and it's going to be a hell of a job digging that lot out.'

We were anxious to park as close as possible to the drums, but equally anxious to check that the snow was firm enough to hold our weight. The surface had a honeycomb texture from the constant melting and freezing and it all looked rather dicey. We couldn't see any tell-tale cracks or sunken areas that might suggest a hidden crevasse but, as mentioned before, neither of us had any crevasse experience. We spent a fair amount of time gingerly setting the helicopter down then lifting off and resetting, with me holding my door open and checking the skid positions and how much they sank into the snow as Colin put more and more weight on them. Thank goodness for the lovely weather. It would have been a nightmare hanging out the door of the helicopter if conditions had been the same as they were at Marsh a few hours earlier. But it was high summer on Adelaide with the temperature a balmy +3°C. In the coastal areas of Antarctica when the sun is out and there's no wind you can be in shirtsleeves, and we had one of those days, well nearly, once we got digging.

Finally on the ground and satisfied that the helicopter wasn't about to disappear down a crevasse, we had a chance to survey the scene – our kingdom. It was breathtakingly beautiful. We stood under a cloudless sky in the great silence of that frozen wilderness so far from civilisation, enjoying our first landing in Antarctica outside an airfield. We were on a high plateau, about half a mile from the cluster of huts some 300 feet below us down a gentle, featureless slope. The huts lay close to the water's edge where the majestic icebergs drifted slowly by. Beyond them we could see for miles and miles across the pack ice to the distant peaks of the mountain range of Alexander Island, where, somewhere, on the far side of those mountains, was our next fuel cache – Camp Bravo.

Colin interrupted my musings on nature's wonder to point out that all was not perfect in our world: 'Will you look at all those rusty old fuel drums dumped over there?'

I looked to where he was pointing, and there in the middle distance was an enormous pile of drums, thousands and thousands of them.

'Just look at them all – and that environmental document thing that you had to do for the Americans telling us when we crap we must put it in a bag and bring it out of Antarctica in the helicopter, that's a laugh!'

The drums must have been there for years, rusting and leaking their last residues of fuel, an eyesore that the snows will never fully bury, unlike in the interior where temperatures never rise above freezing and the snows ultimately bury everything. Still, two wrongs don't make a right and huge efforts are being made to 'tidy up' Antarctica. In the early days stuff got dumped any old where. Now the more responsible countries demand

How to bury solid matter

Colin wasn't entirely correct as we were in fact allowed to bury solid matter. But to give you an idea of the detail required of US expeditions in the IEE document here's a small example.

> *Sewage consists of faeces and urine; toilet roll will be removed from Antarctica. On average, a human produces 135–270g (wet) of faeces per day (this equates to 35–70g of dry solids). The moisture content of faeces is 66–80%, and the remainder is nearly 100% organic matter (Mara, 1987). The amount of urine produced per person per day is 1.0–1.3kg. The proposed activity will therefore result in the production and burial of approximately 6–12kg of dry solid faecal matter and 42–55kg of urine.*
>
> *Inevitably, there will be some litter lost or be blown downwind at the camps or caches, including lightweight materials such as paper and plastics but also heavier items such as empty drums.*
>
> **Assessment**
>
> *All garbage and toilet paper and food waste, if any, will be stored in the helicopter for disposal outside the Antarctic treaty area. Human waste will be buried. The relatively small amounts of human waste generated by the expedition is considered to have a low impact at a local and regional scale.*

the toughest controls over any of their citizens going south, as we knew only too well.

Refuelling took every bit as long and was every bit as tough as Colin's gloomy predictions, but the good weather held and as it turned out we were in no hurry – much to my relief and Colin's frustration. We had been on the go for close to 12 hours and I was ready to call it a day. Colin wanted to continue while we had the weather window – given half a chance I think he would have ploughed right on to within a few miles of the South Pole and camped there until the 17th to ensure we got there on the all important day. However, the weather further south was the deciding factor.

Shortly after touching down at Carvajal I had phoned Antarctic Logistics and Expeditions (ALE). Mike Sharp answered, welcomed us to Antarctica and asked a few questions about the weather and our crossing of the Drake Passage. He then told me that the weather at Patriot Hills was appalling, that they had had no flying for three days and had been unable to cache our fuel at Fowler or further north at Camp Bravo on Alexander Island. It also meant that the Twin Otter plane was not in place to provide Search and Rescue so he said he would appreciate it if we remained at Carvajal. So we were, to my secret relief, stuck.

An hour after landing and deep into digging out barrels, Colin said, 'Do you know what? We haven't closed our flight plan.' Thank goodness

VFR flights

All flights are made either under visual flight rules (VFRs) or instrument flight rules (IFRs). For VFR flights you seldom file a flight plan unless you are crossing borders or sometimes when taking off or landing at large international airfields. We were flying VFR – so it was a rare occasion to make a landing outside an airfield that necessitated the closure of a flight plan. If you land at airfields your flight plan is automatically closed. It's the easiest thing in the world to forget when you are outside an airfield, and if you don't close your flight plan within half an hour of your specified time of arrival, Search and Rescue operations are usually launched.

he remembered. We could have had a full-scale, wildly expensive Search and Rescue launched on our behalf. Colin phoned Marsh. The staff were fairly relaxed, merely saying they were beginning to get worried.

When we took part in the London to Sydney Air Race, one of the contestants flying a Second World War Piper Cub monoplane ran out of daylight and had landed at a very comfortable and welcoming farmhouse in France. The pilot forgot to close his flight plan and a major Search and Rescue was instigated at vast cost and not a few red faces.

Alejo's shovel was a godsend. Ours probably would have done the job but would have taken about five times as long. Colin was doing all the hard work. My efforts were puny compared with what his muscle power could achieve, although I had the odd go at digging when he was having a pause and would then add my weight heaving and pulling drums into an upright position. The disheartening thing was finding that a drum was unusable after hours of digging – either the seal was broken or it was only half full, or both. The risk of there being water in the fuel was too great to use anything other than sealed drums.

As we were now in no hurry we decided for extra safety that we would let the drums stand upright beside the helicopter for a couple of hours to let any possible contaminants settle while we went off to explore the huts at the bottom of the slope. Remembering the fate of the Chileans on their snowmobile, who disappeared down the crevasse, I insisted that we roped ourselves together as we made our way down the hill to the base huts. Looking back, it was daft as the ground was as safe and smooth as our Somerset hills. We ended up sliding down fast on our backsides, much to the surprise of a group of Adelie penguins, which were sedately making their way on the lower slope past the huts.

The Adelies were to provide delightful company for the following days, along with a large group, or more correctly 'pod', of elephant seals, which we practically fell over on rounding one of the huts. They seemed to prefer basking on the stones and concrete that had been warmed by the sun to lying on the ice. There were also many nesting birds – skuas, fulmars, terns and petrels. We were not alone.

Elephant seal are enormous. The largest of all the seals, the males can grow up to 4.5 metres (15ft) long and weigh up to 4 tonnes (8,800lbs). Ours seemed to be all female as none of them had the distinctive snout of the male, which they inflate to impress the ladies. The females are a lot smaller but still weigh in at 900kg (2,000lbs) and looked huge to us. I thought they were wonderful and could have watched them for hours. There was something so comic in their movements. Much of the time they seemed to just lie around in a large heap, letting out all sorts of snuffs and grunts, idly scratching themselves with their prehensile flippers; then one would raise its head up and roar at its neighbour who in turn would rear up and roar back. But that appeared to be altogether too much effort and they would both collapse back down again, give a few final snuffles and go back to sleep. Every now and then one of the innermost seals would decide it wanted to go to the sea for a meal of squid, causing mayhem as she lumbered across her sleeping companions.

'Ugly great smelly brutes, good for nothing. They go for a dive in the morning, gulp down half a tonne of fish then spend the rest of the day lying around farting and belching!' was Colin's opinion of the seals. He said he liked the penguins, but when I mentioned that I hoped we would get the chance to see Emperor penguins at some point, he looked surprised. 'But we've got penguins here.'

'These are Adelie penguins,' I replied.

'Well they're all the same, just different heads!' Shaking his head and smiling, his final comment was, 'I just want to get to the South Pole and back to civilisation.'

Keeping a respectable distance from the seals, we set out to inspect the huts, hoping to find an open door. Charles Swithinbank had told me that the bases generally observed an open door policy. He had spent many months at Carvajal, which in its BAS days was known as Adelaide, where among other things he had plotted out the skiway.

If there was an unlocked door it was buried deep in the snow on the leeward side of one of the buildings. All doors and windows that we could access were firmly locked and barred, but a bolt appeared to be no obstacle at all for Colin. One moment the door of one of the more promising looking huts was impenetrable, the next it was swinging wide with no visible sign of forced entry – he is a man of many talents.

Peering gingerly into the frozen, silent depths we could just see what looked like gym apparatus and a snooker table. Beyond it was pitch black as all the windows were blocked by snow and ice. Our torches were in the helicopter so we groped our way along the table, bumped into a wall in the inky blackness, felt our way around a corner and saw a glimmer of light. It turned out to be a shower room complete with washbasin, washing machine, dryer and sauna. Further along the corridor was a row of pine bunk bedrooms, four beds per tiny room with towels and blankets folded neatly at the end of each bunk. Everything was spotless and fresh and icy cold. It was as though the occupants had left only a few days earlier instead of three years previously. The beds looked most welcoming but all our kit was up the hill in the helicopter and besides there was still all the refuelling to do and we wanted to be ready to leave at a moment's notice.

At around 8pm we trudged back up the hill, un-roped. The sun was only fractionally lower in the heavens than it had been at midday and the air was still calm as Colin got our little generator going and attached the electric fuel pump. I took some video footage and photos and set up the tripod so we could both feature in a couple of shots. The work division was going well!

Even with an electric pump and Colin's strength, it all took time and it was close to 10pm by the time we had repositioned the helicopter down by the huts and lugged an assortment of bags up to the dormitory hut, with Colin making his standard comment about how much luggage I had and how little he had. I made my standard reply that the extra weight was all the camera equipment and computer.

Carvajal was rather like one of those 'end of the world' movies where pockets of humans survived in places with all the mod cons but nothing works. It was all fairly basic but everything was there, just no electricity and no water. We had to melt snow for cooking, drinking and washing water, a slow process on our very small cooker. With the aid of a torch we found a large saucepan in the kitchen to supplement our billycan. The kitchen turned out to be the room beyond the games room, which we had groped our way through earlier.

The next day we tried to dig the snow away from one of the kitchen windows but soon gave up. The windows were buried deep under three years of accumulated drifts of ice; we would have had to saw it out, chunk by frozen chunk. The wind swirls around the huts, keeping some sides clear and others buried.

Inside the hut the temperature was even colder than outside, though the sun on the north side where the dormitories were raised the level by a couple of degrees. The only garments I took off indoors were my hat and gloves; everything else stayed on until I clambered into my sleeping bag, then the top outer layer came off. Colin followed the same routine except for the memorable and ambitious moment when he bravely took a shower.

The washroom, our new living quarters, also got a bit of sun but had nothing very cheerful about it. Unlike the bedrooms with their wooden beds and colourful curtains and blankets, the washroom was stark and bare with more of the dreary cream colour paint. The plastic tiles on the floor were old and worn and so were the shower, sink and assorted machines. But the main thing was that we were indoors and it was all spotlessly clean. There's no dust or bacteria in Antarctica.

We put the cooker with a heaped saucepan of snow on top of the washing machine, lit up, and waited for the snow to melt. 'How about a little drink to celebrate being in Antarctica?' Colin said. It seemed like an excellent idea to me – the temperature in the washroom must have been hovering somewhere around freezing as we sat there, huddled in all our layers of clothing. In Ushuaia we had purchased a half bottle of whisky and another half of bacardi rum – our emergency rations. Colin's favourite drink is bacardi and coke, but there was no coke. Then he remembered that somewhere along the line we had acquired a can of Red Bull. The combination wasn't great, but he drank it. My whisky was less of a success. I had opted for whisky remembering what a lifesaver it had been when some years previously I had gone trekking with a group of friends in Bhutan. One American companion had introduced us all to Jack Daniels in sweet tea – pure heaven at the end of a long day's hike. But it wasn't Jack Daniels and I had no hot tea as the kettle hadn't boiled. None the less, it did have an excellent effect and once the snow had melted and the kettle boiled, our freeze-dried 'expedition food' was delicious. We had a choice of cod and mashed potato, beef ragout or spaghetti bolognese. The meals come in foil packs into which you pour the boiling water, give it a stir, seal it shut for five minutes and it's ready to eat.

We also had the one dozen fresh eggs, the two loaves of bread and the two cartons of milk. We had big plans for breakfast the next morning, but decided to have a couple of hard boiled eggs with our cod and mashed potato. They tasted of kerosene. On take-off from Ushuaia we had filled every last square inch of all the fuel tanks to capacity, which caused the 19-gallon aux tank in the luggage compartment to vent a small amount of fuel out of the top seal, where the eggs were sitting. The result was that everything stored in the back compartment, bar the expedition food, which luckily was encased in kerosene-proof foil, smelt and tasted of fuel.

It had been a long day. When we finally got to bed it was nearly 20 hours and what seemed like a lifetime since our early morning start way back in Ushuaia. Colin chose what was obviously the boss's room on the dark south side of the building. It only had one bed, was fractionally bigger and definitely colder, and had the empty frame for a television fastened on the wall. I thought he was nuts when there were all the sunny rooms, but he said the sun, which of course we now had 24 hours a day, would keep him awake. I think he liked having the boss's room and dreaming of TV, and maybe the darkness did play a part. But it was a miserable room compared with the sunny one I chose, of which there were about eight.

I slept like a log, once more woken by Colin, this time saying it was nearly 8am and time to call ALE. I am a morning person, but when it comes to punctuality, Colin's in a league of his own. He offered to make the call, but I wasn't letting him anywhere near the phone – I wanted to keep on amicable terms with all the team at Patriot Hills and Colin's fuse was getting shorter by the minute and he only half believed that the weather was bad at Patriot Hills.

I couldn't get a good signal in my room, so I hastily clambered into my outer trousers, boots and jacket and hurried outside where blue skies and calm seas still prevailed. Mike had asked me to call in again at 8am; it was 8.05 when I got through to him. 'We were expecting your call five minutes ago,' he said in a no nonsense voice, then went on to say, 'I'm afraid conditions are still poor here. The Twin Otters can't get off the ground and we don't expect much improvement in the next 24 hours. We haven't been able to get through to Rothera but last reports said the weather was poor at Fossill.'

Colin, who had followed me out and was catching some of the conversation, muttered, 'That's utter crap – just look, we can practically see Fossill,' and tried to grab the phone – I held on.

I suggested to Mike that we might phone our friend Jonathon back in Ushuaia to see if he could give us a more accurate reading for Fossill. I also gave Mike Jonathon's phone number so he could check direct. Mike asked me to call back at noon, adding, 'and I'd appreciate it if you could be on time, we give all the expeditions set times to call in and we need to keep to the schedules.' Chastened, I assured him I would and said goodbye.

'How can he say the weather is poor at Fossill? Fossill's right over there and the sky is as clear as a bell,' Colin exclaimed, flinging his arm in a southerly direction. He was right, but it was in ALE's best interest to get us in and out of Antarctica as quickly as possible. 'That's just it, the trouble is they know we have a reasonably comfortable set-up here, they've had some weather delays and now they're giving precedence to the other expeditions. Next time he calls tell him we can't get in the huts and are sleeping in our tent!'

I told him to relax, we still had a week to get to the South Pole and the most important thing was to make it there safely and not to be too pressured about it all. Easily said, but of course we had been focused on

Top: Take off from New York CB & JM with our Patron, The Duchess of York
Bottom: N44EA near the Angel Falls, Venezuela

Top: JM crossing river Suriname
Bottom: JM & CB with WWF & goldminers in Suriname

Top: Colin flying kites, on shores of Amazon
Bottom: Patagonia, Argentine

Top: JM & CB holding the Argentine flag in Buenos Aires
Bottom: Jonathon, Roxanna and Gabriella Selby

Top: N44EA fully loaded for Antarctica
Bottom: 4am take off across the Drake Passage for Antarctica

Top: Marsh, Antarctica approach
Bottom: Adelaide Island

Top: Carvajal huts
Bottom: The ALE team at Camp Bravo

Top: Mike Sharp & Fran Orio at Patriot Hills
Left: Karl Z'Berg with the washing up team, Doc Martin and Martin Hartley

Securing N44EA with ice screws

Top: Jason at Patriot
Bottom: Jaco

Top: Jaco, Doc Martin, Colin and Martin
Bottom: Geoff Knight & his polar bike

Top: Simon & Pen heading south
Bottom: Thiel Mountains, waiting for fairer weather

Meeting up with Simon in Antarctica

Top: JM & CB at the South Pole
Bottom: Colin on snow sled being taken to Ilyushin

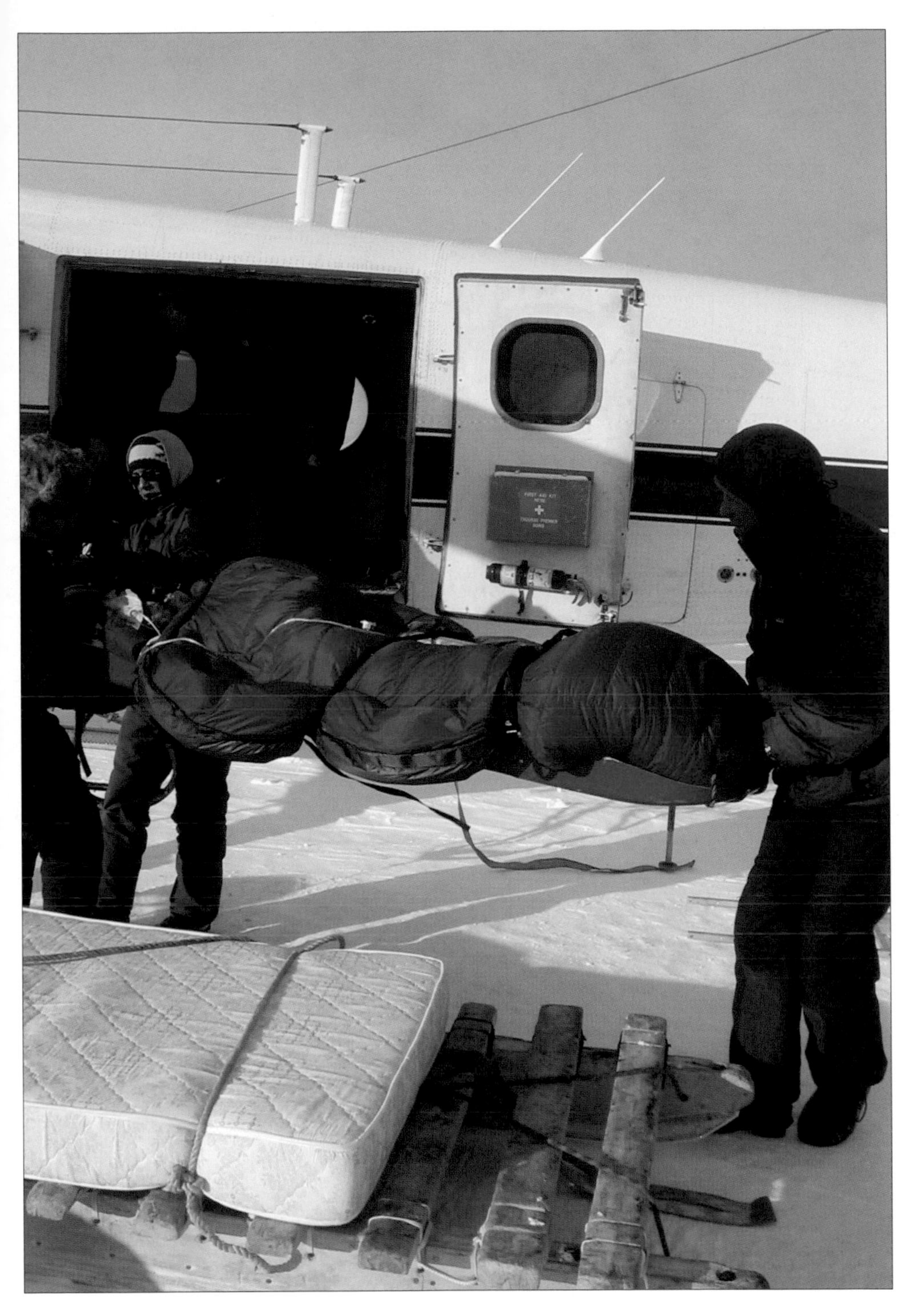

Colin being lifted out of the Twin Otter at Patriot Hills Rescue

Top: Colin being lifted into the Ilyushin
Bottom: The Ilyushin 76 at Patriot Hills

this deadline for a long, long time and it was frustrating being stuck when we had such good flying conditions.

Many months before I had received a form from the Federation Aviation International, in charge of everything to do with light aviation, asking members how they would be celebrating the one hundred years of flight, asking what airfield members would be flying from and to give the coordinates – and the pleasure it had given me to put, 'The Amundsen Scott Polar Base, South 90.00.00, West 00.00.00!'

Despite the frustration of the delay, Colin had a good time – he found a shed with three snowmobiles inside. Their engines had been dismantled and none of them had been used in the three years since the base was abandoned. He spent the morning happily reassembling one of them and by early afternoon had it working. With a grin he turned to me and said, 'You know if we're stuck here for a week, I reckon I could fix the generators and have this whole place up and running and we could have a sauna!' My immediate reaction was more prosaic – that we could find ourselves with a whopping bill for fuel if and when Chile was to reopen the base. At $2,000 a barrel, fuel didn't come cheap at Carvajal.

At 11am I tried phoning Simon and Pen and to my happy amazement I managed to get through. Pen answered with whoops of joy to hear that we had made it safely across the Drake Passage. He said they were fine, 'But here's Simon.'

Simon was reassuringly his old familiar self and his opening words were, 'Hi darling, where the hell are you – we're running out of vodka!'

I laughed and told him we were stuck on Carvajal. 'Patriot Hills say they've had a whiteout for days and haven't been able to cache our fuel.'

'Tell me about it, that sun has been damned illusive, can't see a thing and it's a hell of a lot steeper than I thought and the wind is a nightmare.'

'What about your shin splints?' I asked.

'Oh they're much better but frostbite is playing games with my fingers and toes,' Simon laughed.

'You mean you've already got frostbite?' I asked, alarmed.

In a very relaxed tone he said he'd got the upper hand for now. We talked and laughed some more and I told him we were fully intending to come and visit them on the way to the Pole, but if we were really pushed for time, we would have to wait for the return.

'Try and call me before you leave Carvajal, got to stop now, running short of juice, still have to make our daily call to Patriot, fly safe' – and he was gone. I realised how much I was missing him and how incredible it was that we might see each other in a few short days.

I took pictures of the seals and penguins and the ever-changing seascape. I sat there and watched the frozen world drifting by, the offshore icebergs – a great sculpture park on the move, some the size of three-storey buildings, the pack ice, the call of the sea birds and the oh-so-human penguins and their comic antics.

I charged up my computer and sent out updates and photos to our website. Sending out just one picture took around 15 minutes, with a little prayer that you wouldn't lose the signal halfway through and have to start all over again. How thankful we were to have Iridium as a sponsor. All expeditions try to get satellite phones sponsored – few do. The air time costs per minute are huge, but thanks to having the prototype Blue Sky Network tracker box on board the helicopter, which works in conjunction with the Iridium satellite phone, we were offered all the air time we could use for free.

In 1997, when I was flying around the world with Quentin, we had a problem in Eastern Russia when the helicopter wouldn't start. We tried to phone our engineer back in the UK on our satellite phone, which in those days was like a laptop computer with fold-out antennae panels and the air-time had cost a bomb. On that occasion the card ran out of credit before we could get an answer. Happily we managed to start the helicopter with a set of jump leads from a tractor. On this trip it was a joy. We had full communication all the time, unless we failed to plug the charger in properly in the helicopter – which on the final vital occasion would prove to be the case.

The only downside of the day was the continued bad weather news from ALE. By the second call Colin was beside himself: 'All those climbers, that's what they've been doing, I knew they would, I told you they would, the Ilyushin has been in and out and they've been taking those f…g climbers to that Saint Vincent mountain and they haven't brought our fuel.' With a grunt of disgust he stamped off into the snow adding, 'And you have been so nice to them!'

Colin on the warpath was almost comical – his normally quiet, even-tempered voice rose about half a decibel and you could almost see frustration puffing from his already puffed out, polar-clad figure as he disappeared up the hill. This was the sort of situation where being an optimist makes life so much more comfortable. I felt reasonably confident that we still had plenty of time to get to the South Pole, while Colin, a self-confessed pessimist, was in despair of us ever getting off Carvajal. I'm sure my relaxed attitude added to his frustration.

I felt slightly less relaxed when a few minutes later I glanced out to sea – where only moments before I could see to the limitless horizon. A great wall of sea fog had appeared from nowhere, rolling in across the sea, obliterating everything in its path with alarming speed. Now I was only too happy to be safe and secure with both feet on the ground, instead of out there in a helicopter over the water and pack ice. It was scary how fast the scene changed from one of calm and beautiful peace to one of awful beauty and infinite menace. I followed Colin's retreating figure, heading back to the safety and security of our icy quarters as the first tendrils of fog came sweeping remorselessly in.

Later, over spaghetti bolognese and a cup of tea, we tried to have a sensible conversation about our ongoing prospects. I said that the weather was obviously foul at Patriot and that Simon had confirmed the weather was ferocious with winds of 70 knots. The Ilyushin has been waiting for nearly three weeks for a weather window to bring the climbers in. They were the same climbers we had met in Punta Arenas and had already been waiting 10 days when we got there.

'That's just it,' Colin retorted, 'You and your optimism, and then you talk about people having to wait three weeks for a weather window, so I can't think why you are so confident of us getting halfway across Antarctica in a few days.' He certainly had reason on his side and after witnessing the fog I felt far less confident, only too aware of how fast the Antarctic weather could change. But ALE only had the two Twin Otters at Patriot and both were needed to cache our fuel. They had to position two drums on the Fowler Peninsular at 'F' Cache, 233 nautical miles north of Patriot, and then they had to position another four drums 350 miles beyond that at Camp Bravo on Alexander Island, a flat area some 30 miles east of the British Antarctic Survey base at Fossill Bluff. One Twin Otter would remain at Camp Bravo until our return from the South Pole. That team would be providing Search and Rescue for us as well as for all the other expeditions and would also be taking out empty fuel drums. ALE now had a lot of expeditions out there and any one of them could have an emergency at any time.

'And anyway,' I added, feeling tired and fed up, 'Those f…g mountaineers are climbing Mount Vinson, not Saint Vincent.'

'Mount Vinson, Saint Vincent, whatever, it's ridiculous, it's those guys at Patriot Hills…' Colin was off again.

'The weather's been perfect, you could see for miles and now that sea fog has rolled in. I bet we've lost our window, it's diabolical,' he moaned between mouthfuls of spaghetti.

The next day it was the same story – no flying at Patriot. However our sea fog had in fact disappeared and the weather was once more perfect and with it my optimsm. I spoke to Jason, the radio operator, who said it was -11°C at Patriot, with low cloud and whiteout conditions. He sounded rather cheerful about it all, but then we were to find out he was always cheerful.

Perhaps it was just as well that we were delayed. On checking out the helicopter Colin found that the rubber seals on our two extra fuel containers had shrunk due to the cold and our precious fuel was seeping out. Thankfully, only a small amount had escaped into the bottom of the helicopter and we were able to mop it up, but the smell was awful and we had to find some replacement rubber to seal the connection point. First all the fuel had to be drained off into another container – then we had to find some suitable rubber to replace the other. Happily Colin found what he was looking for in the snowmobile shed – two nice thick bungey circles of rubber, which he was able to fashion to fit the tank outlets. It all took time – but usefully filled Colin's morning.

To relieve his afternoon 'waiting frustration', Colin went off to explore the hut interiors while I decided to pay another visit to the penguins and seals. Mike Sharp had told me on the phone – when I was being so nice – that he had been in Carvajal back in 1976 with BAS when they were packing up the base for the move to Rothera and had driven out the last dog team. He had also mentioned that you could usually walk across the pack ice to a large colony of penguins on a small island slightly to the east of the huts. So I followed a group of six penguins that I had spotted on the hill behind the huts. They were making their way purposefully eastwards and looked incredibly comical, one behind the other, waddling along, intent on their destination.

The moment they reached a slight downward slope, they flopped down into 'sledge mode' one after the other and whooshed to level ground, then up they would get and continue on their way to the water's edge. The pack ice that Mike had referred to wasn't there. So I could only view them from afar as they swam across to their sanctuary on the island.

I plonked myself down in the snow, loving every moment of the aloneness and the frozen silence, only broken by the occasional distant call of a sea bird. I thought of the early explorers. One of the exciting things about Antarctica is that discovery and exploration is all so recent, so immediate. You can have the privilege of knowing people who were involved in serious early exploration, like Charles Swithinbank who was there in the comparatively early days, or know someone who knows someone like Fuchs and Hilary who made the first motorised trans-Antarctic expedition in 1957. I knew my grandfather who knew Ernest Shackleton and they were good friends!

I thought of how the first confirmed sighting of Antarctica was as late as 1820, how the first landing on the coast was in 1834 and how it wasn't until 1897 that a multinational expedition went in. The men on the expedition got stuck in the ice and remained so for a year. Several lost their sanity due to the Antarctic winter and hardship on board, aggravated by the language problem between all the many different nationalities. There were several Norwegians onboard including Roald

Amundsen, whose party in 1911 were the first to reach the South Pole, beating Scott's party by a month. Shackleton nearly got there in 1908 but, low on food and fuel and with the short summer months drawing swiftly to a close, he had to turn back just 96 miles from the Pole.

I half wished I could have been there, to be where no man had ever been before. Then I thought about the downside, the immense danger, zero communication with the outside world, the clothing, the equipment and the food. In a perverse sort of way I rather liked the idea of that side of it, too, but consoled myself with the fact that no woman was ever included in these expeditions so in those days I would in all likelihood have been the poor anxious wife left at home stitching my tapestry.

At least I was there, even if a little late, and could experience for myself, in a small way, the challenges that all those who went before encountered – and besides it was quite probable that we would touch down in places where no one had ever been before. When you think of the size of Antarctica, and how comparatively few people have ever been into the interior, it makes for a lot of untrodden ground. Imagine all of the USA and Mexico with just a few scattered camps along the coastal areas and no more than 400 people in the whole of the vast interior; 300 of those are in one spot – the South Pole – and you begin to get an idea of the scale of things down at the bottom of the world.

The stresses and strains of the 21st century seemed a lifetime away as I watched the penguins splashing into the icy water and popping their little heads up again as they clambered out onto their island. I thought of the weary commuters on underground trains and buses, of motorists stuck in traffic jams, and felt pretty good.

It was time to call ALE once more. I made my way slowly back towards the huts, retrieved the satellite phone, sat myself down on the skid of the helicopter and pressed the phone's recall button. I got the engaged signal. On the third try Jason came on the line. Nothing had changed – the whiteout prevailed. The only encouragement was that they were expecting better weather within the next 12 hours. 'Call again at 8am,' he said, and with a cheerful 'goodnight' was gone.

The sound of splashing water greeted me as, torch-less, I groped my way through the dark games room to our quarters. It was Colin's 'shower' moment. He had ambitiously melted a large amount of snow and boiled up saucepans full of water and was making full use of the shower stall facilities. He'd even managed to wash his hair. He poked a wet head around the shower curtain and with a happy smile said it was wonderful, adding that he'd melted enough snow for me to have a shower too. Then he asked what the latest from ALE was. On hearing that it was still 'no go' he disappeared once more with grunts of disgust and 'Didn't I tell you so.'

I opted for a mug of tea over a shower. It seemed a warmer option and meant we didn't have to melt any more snow that night, as long as we used it before it froze solid again. When I turned round to the stove to make my tea I found several bars of chocolate, a tin of mushrooms, a tin of tomatoes and a packet of linguini pasta. 'Where did all this come from?' I asked in amazement.

'I've been exploring,' Colin said. 'You can't imagine the provisions I found in this little attic. There's tons and tons of stuff, tons of sugar, tons of pasta, teabags, chocolate. It's unbelievable.' It all looked delicious but we had no tin opener and washing up would have been a nightmare, even with the extra melted water. We ended up having our own expedition food – beef goulash. The Carvajal stores were far too complicated, but the chocolate was good and it was reassuring to know that we could survive there indefinitely if we had to.

The next morning the skies were again blue to the far horizon, where the distant peaks of Alexander Island still remained tantalisingly clear and visible. But now the news from Patriot Hills was encouraging. Mike said they were hoping to cache the fuel at Fowler within the next few hours.

'But that's only Fowler,' said Colin after I rang off. 'We can't go until they get to Camp Bravo. If we have to stay another day we'll never get to the South Pole on the 17th, we've only got five days to go.'

It was true. We phoned Jonathon for his reading on the weather. He said that the satellite images had shown clear weather for the peninsula ever since we got there and that it looked good for the following day, and reminded us that he couldn't give accurate forecasts south of our present position. 'The more remote you are, the fewer the satellites.'

I asked for news of Polly. Jonathon told us that the Argentine base at Marambio was doing all they could to help and they had some Avgas fuel. Now Polly was waiting for a weather window. 'The weather's always bad at Marambio,' he said, 'But hopefully she will be there in the next couple of days, then she will fly back here to Ushuaia – and join us on our boat for Christmas. We're taking it down to Puerto Williams, the small Chilean port just to the south of here. Come and join us if you're back in time.' I laughed. It sounded like a great idea. 'We'll call you from the South Pole!' I said.

At midday Mike told us the crews were at Camp Bravo! He reported that visibility at Bravo was good, with high Cirrus clouds at 20,000 feet; the temperature was -6°C with winds from 100° at 42 knots.

We had not bothered to pack as we had been convinced that the Twin Otters would not reach Camp Bravo until late in the day at the earliest. Colin had got the pan on the boil for a shave, and despite my protestations and his desperation of the last three days to be on the move he insisted on going ahead with it. The result was, that with all the ensuing sorting, packing and shaving, donning of survival suits and giving orders, we succeeded in leaving two full bags of kit behind – one full of food, pots and pans, the other with Colin's personal kit. We left the bags sitting in the snow outside the hut and didn't register the fact until we unpacked at Patriot Hills. It was strange that neither of us saw the bags as we lifted off, especially mine which was bright yellow, but I guess our sights were set on the fogless far southern horizon, across a now familiar sea with its bergs and pack ice to the towering peaks of Alexander Island. Somewhere beyond lay Camp Bravo, 214 miles to the south. Thankfully, other than a large supply of Colin's underpants, there was nothing in the bags that we couldn't borrow from people at Patriot Hills

We were on the move again and we were on a high. The sun was shining and we were once more heading south, intoxicated by the challenge, by the extremes of that wild and wonderful place, of being there on our own, not part of some large group or organisation. To be free as a bird, yet always aware that we were living life on the cutting edge...I felt marvellous.

The 30-mile sea crossing was uneventful. It was our last water crossing before the South Pole. We only had a few knots of wind, the world was picture-postcard perfect and it was hard to believe that the whole scene could change as rapidly as it had done when the fog rolled in. I told Colin of my experience crossing the Davis Straits from Canada to Greenland back in 1997. The scene had been so similar, with calm and friendly seas, pack ice and bergs. It had been evening and everywhere was washed by the golden light of the setting sun. We'd landed on a large berg and taken pictures and the world was glorious and then the sun sank below the far hills, the skies turned grey and with it came the sea fog. The following hours had been tough, and we had been beyond the point of no return, but there was a happy ending. We had been able to weave our way under and around the fog and four hours later had made it to the haven of Sondrestromfjord on Greenland.

Colin then told me of his hairy crossing in his microlight over the shark-infested Timor sea from Indonesia to Darwin on the north coast of Australia and how all had gone well at first; then the storm clouds had got larger and larger. He'd had to make a 60-mile detour to avoid the worst of the storm, but the winds and turbulence were so severe he thought the fabric of his wing would be torn to pieces. He too had made it, thanks to sheer skill and a little luck. The detour and head winds had cost him dear though and he was flying on fumes as he staggered into Darwin – with a military escort. Colin had been spotted miles out to

Polar phenomena

In the days to come we were to learn more of the strange phenomena in polar regions of the illusions caused by the light, of the blowing ice crystals and featureless white, where the ground appears to slope up, when in fact it is entirely flat or even descending. Ridges appear where there are none and distances are hard to judge. Whether you are on the ground or in the air, the effects are the same. In the Arctic we were told we would encounter the 'black skies' or 'water sky' – the vertical black shadows that reflect stretches of open water. The disorientation is called 'Fata Morgana' or Arctic mirages, and they are caused by the reflections of water and ice that create illusions of solid, well-defined features where there are none.

Although we faced all these unique polar phenomena, navigation was no problem. We now live in the happy days of GPSs, which we appreciated greatly in the vastness of Antarctica, where there are so few visual landmarks, and most of all when the visibility is poor.

sea and escorted in – though there had been little the military could do for him other than give him the comfort of their presence. He made headlines in all the papers the following day and was given a hero's welcome on his arrival in Sydney Harbour.

Colin prevailed on me to swing slightly to the west of our course to avoid any possibility of icing over the mountain range between Fossill and Camp Bravo. I wanted to see the place that Charles Swithinbank had said was perfect for a honeymoon, but finally agreed it was a safe precaution. However much you study and are told about general conditions in foreign parts, it's not until you are actually there and experience it first hand that you can begin to have a full appreciation of them.

We had no visibility problems that day. We could see for miles and Jason had given me the coordinates of Camp Bravo. In the days before GPSs you had to be incredibly accurate if you were going to have any hope of finding a couple of drums of fuel in a featureless snow desert. We were flying at 1,000 feet above the ground, in the lee of the Colbert Mountains, with only 10 miles to run to Camp Bravo – we could see no sign of any tent or plane. At one point Colin thought he saw them. We were by then in two-way communication on the radio with the camp and he told them that we thought we had them in sight – it proved to be a rock! Despite the clear skies, we only spotted their bright red tent when we were a couple of miles away.

It was strange to see fellow humans, even though we had only been on our own for a few days. There were four of them there, two men and two women, all young and very fit looking, with big smiles of welcome. The captain of the Twin Otter was John Lekich and his copilot David Palfreeman. Di Gilbert and Heather Morning, both in their 20s, were from Scotland, seconded for the season from the Cairngorm Mountain Rescue team. Di was dark haired while Heather had white-blonde pigtails and looked as if she belonged in Heidi country. The girls' role was to trek in on foot to rescue us if we happened to crash where the Twin Otter couldn't land.

We parked beside the fuel drums, which were positioned close to the Twin Otter. All were located some distance from their tent – they obviously weren't risking any chance of our blowing their tents over with our downwash. The team invited us in for a cup of tea and a slice of banana bread made by Fran Orio the cook at Patriot Hills. The four of them were in high spirits. They were enjoying the best weather they had seen in days and were released from all the normal base camp chores. A few hours earlier on their arrival at the Fowler fuel cache they had spoken to Mike Sharp at Patriot Hills, who had told them they could expect temperatures around -11°C with winds gusting up to 30 knots. Instead it was a balmy -2°C with little wind. They told us that when they had left Patriot Hills earlier that morning the skies were clear, with 25 knots of wind. Colin then quizzed them about the weather over the past week and John Lekich confirmed Mike's reports that there had been blizzard conditions: 'That's Antarctica for you,' he said.

The team was on holiday and planned to have a good time skiing until our return. 'Don't be too long though,' John said, 'We're already missing Fran's cooking and we want to be back for Christmas.'

Christmas! We had almost forgotten about Christmas – it was 12 December. Strange to think it was just days away. I asked them if they had news of Simon and Pen, as I had failed to get through to them that morning. They said that the latest they had heard was that they were in good spirits and a day ahead of schedule. It was hard to believe that we might see them the next day. Everything was somehow difficult to take on board and I was still pinching myself that we were truly in Antarctica. To me it had become a mythical place that I had dreamed about, worried about and spent many weeks studying as I pored over charts, researched information for the IEE, drowned in correspondence with ALE, talked to pilots, got permits...Finally we were actually there, there in Antarctica and it was everything I could have hoped for and more.

Colin was on a roll, too – we were on the move. John phoned through to Patriot Hills to say we would be on our way in 15 minutes and confirmed that we would be checking in every half-hour on the hour.

The group walked back to the helicopter with us and offered a helping hand with refuelling, suitably impressed with our little generator and fuel pump, which made the transfer time so quick. 'You better get a move on now,' Heather said, 'if you want to make Patriot by supper time!'

We needed no second bidding and as soon as we'd refuelled we said 'See you in a few days,' as we climbed back on board, ready to head ever south to Fowler and our next two drums of fuel. John told us they were near some rocks, as whenever possible the policy was to cache fuel near a landmark.

The weather remained good and in the air we marvelled at the great emptiness, nothing upon nothing, the endless white with myriad light reflections, blue skies with swathes of ice crystals and us. We were the only living things for miles around. Colin wasn't impervious to our surroundings, either, and every so often he would surprise me with unsolicited comments about the beauty of it all.

With all the strange and new light effects and illusions we cautiously remained at 1,000 feet above the ground and were thankful that we had the added reassurance of a radar altimeter to give us our height above the ground. The regular altimeter, which is mandatory equipment for all aircraft, relies on accurate barometric pressure readings and gives you your height above sea level. With the vast distances we were covering in the Antarctic, you couldn't count on pressure readings remaining the same from one region to another, and the depth of ice was ever changing.

We headed south towards the two lonely green drums of fuel and a marker flag. Three hours later we found them positioned close to the low outcrop of snow-capped black volcanic rock, the only rock to break the surface in that frozen desert of ice for as far as the eye could see.

Our confidence in the accuracy of our radar altimeter was short-lived. On landing beside our fuel drums and while doing our 'shut-down' checks, we noticed, disturbingly, that it was telling us we were still 50 feet above the ground. It was obviously reading through the snow. 'That's not so good, we'll check it again at Patriot,' Colin said. The temperature had dropped to -12°C but the wind had also dropped since the Bravo party went through. So refuelling was easier than it had been at our first Antarctic stop at Marsh on the northern peninsula, where although the temperature had only been -7°C we had had 30 knots of wind, and the wind dramatically chills the human frame – if the outside air temperature is below freezing every 10 knots of wind nearly doubles the chill effect on the body. There had also been moisture in the air at Marsh, while the ice desert of Antarctica's interior is as dry as any desert of sand.

We flew onwards across the Ronne Ice Shelf and were soon able to see the distant pinnacle of Mount Vinson, Antarctica's highest peak, on the far southwest horizon. Then, slowly, the whole of the Ellsworth mountain range came into view and the evening sun reflected off the snowy peaks. Colin had been making the half-hourly calls to Jason at Patriot Hills giving our longitude and latitude and reporting 'flight normal'. On the next call, Mike was staffing the radio he reported, 'Visibility good, but it's blowing a hoolie here – winds gusting up to 55 knots.'

We knew the reason for the existence of Patriot Hills was thanks to the blue ice runway. Blue ice is where there are hurricane-force winds to break down the natural structure of the snowflake into unique microscopic balls that can fit through the eye of a needle. So, in the lee of the mountains and with the powerful winds hurtling off the upper ridges, Patriot is the perfect site for an ice airstrip. The location was first discovered by Charles Swithinbank and Giles Kershaw back in 1975, and has seen many a dicey crosswind landing in the intervening years.

The downside for the big Ilyushin transport plane was that all winds are crosswinds on the runway and there was always a wind, hence every landing required skill and nerve. The agreed maximum acceptable wind was 25 knots of cross wind on the runway. In our helicopter we had the advantage of being able to land into wind, but one of our big worries would be after landing and cutting the engine. The danger was that as the rotor blades slow down, they droop slightly and slap up and down – the greater the wind the greater the slap and the greater the danger of the blades hitting the tail boom.

The prospect of those katabatic winds, which can reach speeds of 200 mph, and the cold air pouring off the mountain range brought back all too vivid memories of the near catastrophic winds I had encountered coming off the Greenland ice cap in 1997. We had been told at Sondrestromfjord that we could expect severe turbulence on the east coast after the 400 mile crossing of the ice cap, which like the Antarctic plateau rises to over 9,000 feet. But nothing could have prepared us for the winds we encountered. We had been enjoying 55 knots of a constant northwesterly, giving us some 40 knots of tail wind. Then we had started our descent off the cap, marvelling at the turquoise depths of the crevasses. One moment all had been smooth, the next we were being tossed around like a rag doll. For 10 minutes – which felt like an eternity – we had battled to gain altitude, to get out of the grip of those fearsome winds tumbling off the cap. We could see the distant ocean, far below, churned into a maelstrom of foaming white by the force of the winds slamming into the water. I prayed now on our way to Patriot Hills that we were not going to find ourselves in a similar situation.

Soon we were able to identify the glacier field of Hercules inlet. The rising ground was the only indication that marked the point where two miles deep below the surface of the ice, water ends and land begins. The nearest open water lay 300 miles to the northeast across the vast Ronne Ice Shelf. And it was there, at Hercules inlet, that Simon and Pen had started their 700-mile trek from the coast to the South Pole. It was surreal to know that they had already been there and I remember Simon saying, so very long ago, way back in another world, back in England, how old-fashioned he would look, if he climbed into his harness only to haul for all he was worth and find he was going nowhere! They were pulling 300 lbs apiece.

During my first phone call with Simon on the ice he had told me that they had indeed stood there wondering just that, and had made a few more jokes about whether they were going to get any forward movement. He told me they had strapped on their harnesses and attempted to haul their 300-pound sledges up that first crevasse-ridden slope – they did have forward movement, but only just and had ended up having to take half the load off, then come back for the other half. After that the gradient had flattened out enough to be able to keep everything on the sledges.

From 1,000 feet up and a mile out, the splintered crevasses in the glacier merely looked like icing ripples on a Christmas cake. We descended to 300 feet and as we drew closer we could see the great fissures, the blue ice and blowing snow screaming across the surface of the ice. It all looked very unfriendly. It was good to know Simon and Pen were now clear of the coastal grounds and the glaciers ahead were, for the most part, well charted, although Simon had said the going continued to be steeper than he had imagined. The dangers were there, Antarctica with its great depths of snow can hide many a crevasse, the only reminder being the deep hollow boom of tons of snow on the move, echoing upward from the deep valleys now filled with the accumulation of 50 million years of snow – snow that has never melted.

At 10 miles out we turned and flew inwards towards the mountains and our ground speed dropped dramatically from 110 knots to 70 knots as we came up against the outer force of the katabatic winds coming off the Elsworth Mountains. I was nervously braced for the onslaught and for the full fury as we got ever closer. We were still unable to see the camp, but we could see the snow blowing off the mountain ridges that poured down onto the plain below, and then we saw the tiny specks of the little tented camp that looked so vulnerable, so insignificant in that infinite expanse. Man's brave and fragile toe-hold in a hostile world.

As we drew closer we spotted a small band of people through the wind-driven surface snow, legs braced, leaning at some 40 degrees into the wind, signalling where to put down. The strong winds were constant, no rolling, tumbling turbulence that day, just a powerful headwind – but nonetheless, I anticipated a tough landing. I need not have worried – once again our Bell 407 handled like a dream. We landed with the ice crystals screaming by the helicopter and our welcoming committee waving directions and greetings. They obviously knew about the problem of blade slap for someone quickly drove a large snowplough over and parked it a short way in front of the helicopter, to give it a modicum of protection and prevent us losing a rotor blade. We checked the radar altimeter. The reading was only 10 feet out but the ground at Patriot was near solid ice, with virtually no snow covering.

The moment the blades stopped turning someone else had a hefty great ice screw and drilled holes in the ice for our ratchet straps to secure the helicopter. I had difficulty forcing open the door of the helicopter against the power of the wind – it was a trial of strength just getting out and not being blown over. We were beginning to get an understanding of the polar winds.

All was quick efficiency. Mike Sharp came over and introduced himself, shouting against the noise of the wind: 'We've been waiting supper for you, let's get tied down here, we can sort you out later.' We were only too happy to agree.

But Colin had more than just supper on his mind, saying in a hasty aside to me, 'We're going to have a hell of a job getting our tent up in this wind – and we're not going to look very professional.' He was right, we had yet to unpack it and check it out. We had intended to have a trial 'tent-putting-up' exercise in Carvajal but somehow never got round to it. Then, as we hurried after Mike, he pointed to a couple of small yellow tents, and to our delight said, 'You two might as well use those. No point in putting anything up in this wind. They are Heidi and Liz's tents, you met them at Camp Bravo, so they are empty for now. By the way, you'll be glad to hear that Simon and Pen are going strong and Simon's shin splints seem to have cleared up. I'll brief you over supper.' All good news as we made our way through the camp, ably assisted by the gale at our backs.

The mess tent was the biggest structure at Patriot, a 40-foot long tubular affair with windows. We entered the vestibule area with a blast of wind and snow behind us. There was a series of wooden pigeon holes for depositing hats, gloves and goggles. Then, with the outer door closed, we were able to make our way into the main hut without lowering the temperature. Trestle tables were arranged down the room with a pot-bellied stove and kitchen at the far end where Fran Orio, the cook, held sway, dishing up endless delicious meals. Fran is Scottish, in her 40s, small, efficient and neat, with close-cropped grey hair and a smile for everyone. During the UK summer and early autumn she cooks for sporting parties on the Scottish islands of Islay and Jura, then in the Austral summer she heads for Antarctica to look after all the hungry souls at Patriot Hills. Her banana bread was superb and the shepherd's pie, salad and fresh baked bread that first evening were heaven sent. It was our first proper meal since the Aero Club barbeque back in Argentina.

It wasn't until we got into the canteen that we really got a chance to see the faces of all the eager hands that had helped us tie down and secure the helicopter. Thanks to all the outer layers of hats, goggles, furry hoods and blowing snow, everyone had been pretty much concealed. Shaving and hair washing were obviously not frequent occurences. Everyone looked rough and tough and cheerful – all gathered for dinner. Besides Mike there were the two young South Africans – Jason Whiting, whose principal job was to handle communications, and Jaco Wium, whose expertise was meteorology. There was also Martin Rhodes, the doctor who was known as Doc Martin, and the pilot of the other Twin Otter, Karl Z'berg, and his copilot Paul Rask. Also in the immediate gathering were Martin Hartley, a photographer who came out with Simon and Pen, and a tall thin Australian called Geoff Knight who was planning to ride a bicycle to the South Pole! There was a group of camp personnel responsible for maintenance of everything mechanical, along with driving the tracked vehicles, handling construction, refuelling, loading and unloading the Ilyushin, and a score of other camp activities. Finally there was Lawrence Burke, the Twin Otter engineer, sitting with the three engineers working on the DC3 airplane that had rolled over in high winds the year before. They were planning to fly it out when and if they had 'fixed' it.

Mike told us that all the expeditions and climbers had enjoyed the last 24 hours of clear skies after the previous days of white out. He said with a laugh, 'I think Simon and Pen are having far too good a time, and that husband of yours uses up all their precious satellite phone battery telling jokes!' It was good to hear. 'But', Mike reminded us, 'they still have a long way to go; they're only 80 miles into the 700, the elevation at present is only 2,000 feet and energy levels are still high.' Smiling he said that Simon and Pen were on red alert for our visit and planned to take a day of rest – it all sounded wonderful.

Britain was well represented that year in Antarctica, as besides Simon and Pen there were four other British expeditions. Two British girls, Rosie Stancer and Fiona Thornewill, were going solo and unsupported from the coast to the South Pole. The other two expeditions were supported, which meant their sledges were considerably lighter as the Twin Otter would fly in a couple of times along the route with re-supplies. One was a group of five heading south and the other group was heading north. The latter group was flown in to the South Pole in the Twin Otter and were skiing out with kites, which sounded like far the best option, batting along with tail winds, though tough on the knees. The only non-Brits were a group of Koreans, also heading south.

For everyone, supported or unsupported, it was a huge test of endurance. But it appeared all expeditions were doing well, all a little competitive with each other and all keen to know how far the others had got. Mike was telling no one. I asked him if by any chance he had news of Polly. 'She's made it to Marambio and as far as I know she's still waiting for a weather window to fly back to Ushuaia,' he replied.

I said I hoped she didn't have to wait as long as the last time to cross back over the Drake Passage.

'Well,' she will of course have the prevailing winds on her tail and South America is less of a weather hazard, but then Marambio is renowned for having the worst visibility in all of Antarctica – that whole northern stretch is appalling.'

I remarked that it was bad luck that the winds had picked up on her attempted flight to McMurdo and that she had had to turn back.

Mike interrupted, 'The problem there was that no one could give her a wind forecast – for the entire central section of her journey there is no satellite coverage, so it's all pure assumption and guesswork. There are some 53,000 stations spread around the world, inputting information into models. Here in Antarctica there are three stations and at Patriot we have none. We input no information from here, so that means to the north, south, east and west of us for a thousand miles there is no possible forecast of winds – that's where Polly came unstuck.'

'I heard the Brits wouldn't give her the weather forecast. Was that because they were just being bloody minded?' Colin asked.

'No, I don't believe so,' he said, 'No, the people on the ground aren't bloody minded, the policy comes from higher up. The Brits have a policy of giving the current weather but not the forecast. The former is safety, the latter is deemed to be "support" and the BAS policy is not to give any support to expeditions. Governments have always been very wary of their expensive and scarce resources down here. It's not like back in the UK where you've got the RAF and they need the training. Take the Americans, they are at full stretch all the time and a lot of their stuff doesn't get done because of the weather. The weather is the big factor – I've known scientists spend a whole season here without ever getting out into the field because of weather conditions. They've gone home having achieved nothing. Anyhow,' he added with a smile, 'we can't give a forecast as such, so we call it the "now forecast"; we only have the capability here in Antarctica of getting the actual satellite image of the current weather.'

We had grudgingly to admit that the scientists had a case and the Antarctic summer is very short. Frustrating for everyone. The American policy of non-support is the same, but we were to find that although there is officially no support as such, they give all expeditions at the Amundsen Scott South Pole station, coffee, cookies and a warm welcome.

After supper, Jason and Martin Hartley volunteered to go back to the helicopter and give us a hand with our bags. Jason pointed out the loo tent and its intricacies: 'Solids down the loo, pee in a separate drum!' A rather easier operation for the men than the women. 'Solids freeze and pee doesn't,' Jason explained. Another interesting fact he pointed out was that when you washed your clothes and hung them to dry on the clothes line, they immediately went as stiff as a board, but within hours they would be flapping free and dry, all moisture literally freeze-dried out of them. Such is the dryness of the air.

It was only on returning to the helicopter for our kit that we realised we had left the two bags behind in the snow at Carvajal and we immediately blamed each other. Colin's bag full of all his clothes included his warm padded outer trousers, although he was more concerned about a change of underpants than anything else. I reminded him that Simon and Pen would be wearing the same pair of underpants for their entire trip, so felt sure he could manage for a few days until we got back to Carvajal and could retrieve everything. 'It's OK for you, you've got all your kit, I haven't even got a toothbrush,' he said. I made placatory noises while selfishly feeling vastly relieved it hadn't been my bag as this had my all-important supply of daily disposable contact lenses in it.

The problem of the padded trousers was solved by one of the engineers, Garry Middleton, who said he had a spare pair of windproof trousers that he could lend Colin for the return trip to the South Pole. 'You can give them back to me on your return,' he said. Luckily our small stove was not in the other missing bag with food and cooking utensils in it; again there was nothing that couldn't be borrowed. It could have been a lot worse, although the loss of Colin's trousers was to prove near catastrophic and we would never make it back to Carvajal. As far as we know the bags are still sitting there today.

My little tent was a joy, complete with box-spring mattress! Luxury indeed. I had to crawl in on all fours, sort of falling down and in as the snow had piled up all around. There was a minute entrance area inside the outer lining, where I could leave my big snow boots and shut the outer flap, then unzip the inner flap and crawl onto the mattress. It felt snug and warm inside with the elements going crazy outside and in sharp contrast to the memories of the frozen tent in Alaska, where we had done our survival training. There the tent had been rimed with inches of hoar frost, thanks to the extreme cold of -45°C, and darkness, while at Patriot Hills we had 24 hours of daylight and it was only -18°C. However, there had been no wind in Alaska, while at Patriot Hills it felt as though the whole tent was about to take off with the flimsy fabric structure slapping and thrumming to the wind. There were no clouds and the sun warmed the tent to such an extent that my -60°C sleeping bag was way too warm. I wrapped my computer and cameras inside my outer garments, wedged them in beside me on the windward side and set my alarm for 7am. We had been firmly told that breakfast was at 7.30am. I was asleep in minutes.

When I woke the next morning everything was much as I had left it eight hours before – the sun was still shining and the wind still slamming into the tent. The temptation was to lie there and enjoy the delicious cosiness of my sleeping bag, but the thought of breakfast and seeing Simon got me on the move and I was also dying for a pee.

Tent life is quite complicated. Putting things in findable places is key and I'd put my socks somewhere 'clever'. I finally found them in the bottom of my sleeping bag. Also putting in contact lenses with the aid of my powder compact mirror balanced on my knees was tricky. By now I had abandoned any attempt to keep up appearances – every day was a bad hair day and the only thing for one's face was sun cream. So that part was simple – and thankfully I seldom saw myself reflected anywhere.

I crawled out into a beautiful frozen world, looking all the better after a good night's sleep, and made my way to the loo tent and its intricacies – boys one side, girls the other. I thought that Fran and I had a rather exclusive arrangement being the only two women in camp at the time, until I realised the men used whichever side was empty. I won't go into all the details of the separate containers, but there was a system of bowls and funnels – and care had to be taken by the unitiated not to confuse the basin for washing your face and brushing your teeth with the one that you were meant to pee in. I got it wrong that first morning and spent some time outside in the snow thoroughly rubbing pee from the 'teeth' bowl with handfuls of snow.

Colin was already enjoying scrambled eggs, coffee and toast by the time I made it to breakfast. He said he'd had a bad night – the wind had kept him awake. He was also challenging the wisdom of visiting Simon and Pen that day. While the weather was good he felt we should push on to the South Pole. I still didn't fancy having to camp for five nights at over 9,000 feet, waiting for the 17th, and I wanted to see Simon and I wanted to rest. We had been on the go, virtually without a break, ever since we left New York – in fact I felt as though I had been going for months without a break. There had been little time for relaxation, especially for me, as at the end of each long day I had all the onward planning to handle. I had to do route checks and double check fuel availability, printing out Jeppesen's excellent 'Jeppview' airfield charts on my small printer, web updates, downloading photos and sending some back to Tamara in the UK, along with answering emails. Even during our three days in Carvajal, when we had a little time off, we had kept busy. It had been difficult to relax and, besides, when not doing 'trip things' there was so much to explore. At least I didn't have to check routes and fuel in Antarctica, that had all been done months previously, but everything else took longer.

Though there was wisdom in Colin's wish to continue while the weather was good, I persuaded him to relax and enjoy the day. I reminded him that Simon and Pen had taken the day off in anticipation of our arrival and it was possible we wouldn't be able to see them on our return journey if the weather was bad.

Just as we were finishing breakfast Jason came hurrying in to say that Fiona's Argos beacon had gone off. Fiona Thornewill was one of the two solo women. The message was, 'Situation critical, need assistance!'

All the foot expeditions carry the small, lightweight Argos beacons. They have nine settings on which you can pre-set messages, ranging from anything like 'All going well' or, 'I'm stuck but happy', to 'Immediate assistance required'.

Fiona had pressed the most critical button and immediately the camp swung into action. Doc Martin hurried off to the medical tent and Mike Sharp went to find out the status of Karl Z'Berg and his copilot Paul Rask in the Twin Otter plane. They had left early that morning to bring in a group of mountaineers from Mount Vinson. No sooner had everyone hurried off in various directions than Jason was back saying the beacon had been turned off and then on again, with another message saying 'Situation OK'. He had tried to call Fiona on her satellite phone – no reply. In such a situation Mike said that if they couldn't raise her on the satellite phone they were duty bound to go and check her location. She could be in trouble and perhaps had inadvertently pressed the Argos a second time by mistake. On the other hand, if she was in no need of assistance and the Twin Otter went out to her, that would not only cost her thousands of dollars but would also end her attempt as an unsupported expedition, as the mere act of the Twin Otter going out apparently constituted support.

As Fiona's coordinates placed her only 30 miles away from Simon and Pen's position, we volunteered to fly to her campsite, which was her last known position given on the Argos. If we could find no sign of her we would know that she was fine and had continued on. As the Twin Otter was not due back for another hour, this was the sensible option. Our one request was that Mike give us a small amount of extra fuel for the detour, for the further you get from civilisation, the more expensive it gets. Fuel at Patriot runs at US$7,000 per 40 gallon drum, at the Pole it's $24,000! Every drop counts. Mike hesitated a moment then, with a grin and a shrug, agreed.

I managed to reach Simon on his satellite phone; they had put the kettle on! It would have been nice to take them all sorts of goodies like some of Fran's banana bread, but they were strictly 'unsupported' and we were following all the rules. It was agreed that a kiss did not constitute support!

On our way over to the helicopter we met Geoff Knight the cyclist, who had been introduced to us at dinner the night before. He was heading towards a very strange contraption – a sort of Chitty Chitty Bang Bang tricycle that looked more suitable for use in a circus than as a serious all-terrain vehicle for polar travel. Geoff had a rather abstracted, professorial look in his eyes as he explained: 'I was hoping to cycle to the South Pole, but I'm having problems with the friction of the wheels on the snow. I tested it many times in New Zealand. This is my ninth prototype, but the snow is so much drier here, I'm going to try drilling holes through the wheels, and then I will thread rope through them.' He walked us around it, explaining the workings of the machine. It must have weighed close on half a ton and had a small engine to assist pedalling. There was lots of enthusiasm and he hoped, after having roped up the wheels, to make a trial run that afternoon. He had arrived five days before us on the last Ilyushin flight with the mountaineers, but so far he hadn't made it out of the camp. We wished him good luck.

Martin, Simon and Pen's photographer, joined us for our rendezvous. In his early 30s, Martin looked about as debonair as it is possible to look in Antarctica and with a week's growth of beard. He arrived at the helicopter laden with cameras and a rather anxious expression on his lean, slightly freckled face – he was worried that he had brought too much kit. Martin has accompanied numerous expeditions in polar regions and had been with Simon and Pen in the Arctic during Simon's introduction to sledging. He had then flown on with Pen to Ward Hunt Island, the last strip of land in the frozen north and Pen's starting point for his great solo trek to the North Pole. Martin told us he would be taking the next Ilyushin flight back to Punta Arenas from Patriot Hills and so it would be his last chance to take pictures of Simon and Pen.

We took off around 11am under clear blue skies. The winds had calmed down to a more reasonable 25 knots. We headed southeast in Fiona's direction. The frozen world looked wonderful – the endless ice, stretching forever in changing patterns of 'sastrugi', the waves carved by the winds on the frozen ocean – and the stark silhouette of the Ellsworth Mountains grew ever smaller behind us.

As it was Colin's turn to fly, he had chosen the music and had put on a Bon Jovi selection, but I had an ally in Martin who said, 'You can't play music like that in these surroundings, haven't you got some glorious classical music, worthy of this grandeur?' Colin was outnumbered, and we put on Beethoven's Ninth Symphony.

Thoughts and talk were a mixture of excitement for our meeting up with Simon and Pen and concern for Fiona, whom Colin and I had never met. We all prayed that she had flipped the wrong switch in error, but the niggling doubt was there. What if she were in a desperate state down a crevasse, or had had a fire in her tent? All very real possibilities. Just one small mistake can have fatal consequences in Antarctica. Whether you are on the ground or in the air you have to be constantly on the alert or the elements will get you. We had one rather short length of rope and a standard first aid kit, but we did have communications and we could probably squeeze Fiona into the back of the helicopter with Martin if she really was hurt and needed to be evacuated in a hurry.

From 1,000 feet above the ground, the snow looked flat and comparatively smooth. Only when we descended and skimmed the frozen sastrugi could we begin to appreciate the difficulty of pulling a sledge over those ridges. We talked about the comparative challenges all the expeditions faced in the hostile world of Antarctica, of crevasses and frostbite, of wind and whiteouts, but there was one thing we were all agreed on: when bad weather hit, you were far better off on the ground than in the air.

Three miles from Fiona's campsite we could see no sign of a tent or sled or Fiona – we circled overhead the area of her last coordinates, and then, yes, there were ski tracks and a flattened area where she had pitched her tent. All was OK.

I called Jason on the satellite phone and gave him the good news. He asked us if we would do a small 'grid' search pattern to the south just to be doubly sure. Which we did. Unfortunately we spent rather longer than we realised searching. We followed her ski tracks, then lost them, then found them again, finally deciding we must call it a day, and rather belatedly we realised that we barely had enough fuel left to get to Simon and Pen and back to Patriot Hills. 'And it will be a head wind on the return,' Colin said. 'We'll just have to hope the winds don't pick up any more.'

Finding Simon and Pen was a cinch. They had their red tent up and we had their exact coordinates. We were all straining for our first glimpse of a speck on the horizon. I think Colin spotted them first and then we were circling overhead and I could see Simon doing a sort of Indian war dance around the tent! Martin was taking photos and I was on the video camera and waving madly. Colin circled and then landed, completely blocking my camera view of Simon's war dance. I was complaining and Colin was pointing out that he had to land downwind otherwise he would cover them in snow. 'But you could turn fractionally,' I said – anyhow the long and the short of it was that neither Martin or I managed to record the landing, waving and dancing scene, but all was quickly forgotten in the happiness of the moment.

I leapt out while Colin was still shutting down and ran across to hug Simon and then Pen. Yet again we hadn't recorded the moment, so we re-enacted it with Martin filming me running over to Simon – only Colin decided to liven things up and charged past me and grabbed Simon first in a big bear hug – we all fell about laughing. We did finally get a semi genuine looking reunion, but when I had a chance to see the footage months later, Colin is standing in the background looking as though he had been there forever.

Simon and Pen invited us in for a cup of tea. Their tent was twice the size of ours, but even so it was a squash with five of us squeezed inside and leaving scarcely enough room to boil the kettle safely. It would have been nice if we could have at least offered them fresh water for the tea, but instead they were using up the precious fuel that they had hauled for over 80 miles to melt the snow and boil the water.

None of us could stop smiling and exclaiming about how incredible it was, with sentences constantly punctuated with – 'I can't believe it…', 'Well here we all are…' and 'Do you remember all those months ago when we were making plans…' And then we were all telling each other of our highs and lows: and they were telling us of their ground problems and we of those in the air, and possibly all a little competitive as to who had faced the greater risks! And in the midst of all this Simon laughingly remarked, 'Well, I drew the short straw, my wife got the helicopter!'

Simon and Pen's expedition was all about sheer physical endurance, the all too inherent dangers on the ice and whether Simon's 64-year-old body could regenerate the necessary energy levels day after exhausting day; ours demanded constant mental concentration with all the scenarios of airborne activities over hostile terrain. We were all up against the extremes. Two very different challenges, both demanding everything we had to give and the risk factor there for us all. But the rewards were evident: the thrill of the personal challenge, the adrenalin surges and the sheer joy of living life on the edge. I looked over at Simon and thought of all the years we had been together and now here we were, the two of us, sitting in a tent in Antarctica. How rich our lives were with our wonderful family and friends and all that we had experienced together and how, in our 60s, we were still on for it all, reaching for the far horizons and living our dreams.

I was able to show Simon some pictures of our brand new, one-month-old baby grand daughter, Talitha. We talked and laughed, but all too soon it was time to go. It was hard to believe, while sitting huddled together in the tent, that we had all embarked on one of the toughest challenges any of us had ever faced. Simon would be the oldest man by more than a decade to reach the South Pole – if he did – and Pen would be the first Englishman to complete unsupported treks to both poles, and we would be achieving a series of aviation 'firsts'. Colin brought us all back to the present by saying that the wind had increased and reminded me of our fuel situation.

To make goodbyes easier we focused on being able to drop in on Simon and Pen again on our return from the South Pole. We knew the chances were only 50–50: weather would play a deciding factor and Pen said they couldn't afford to take a day off the next time as they would be on the move and would not be able to stop for long. Anything more than a 15-minute stop and they would start to freeze up.

We agreed on a 10am Antarctic time phone-in in three days time. If we couldn't get through, then to try again every half-hour for two hours, or again the following day. Coordinating times with Pen and Simon had problems. All of the South American side of Antarctica is on GMT -3 hours while the South Pole and the New Zealand half are on GMT +11 hours.

We had been keeping a watchful eye on the helicopter. The back of the skids were deep in the snow and appeared to be sinking further – it was time for final big hugs and kisses. God willing, we would see Simon and Pen again in a few days. I phoned Jason at Patriot to tell him we would be airborne in five minutes and would phone in on the half-hour, if for some reason we were not back at Patriot. Colin had checked the radar altimeter – it was reading a somewhat worrying 90 feet out. 'Snow's softer here,' he said.

We circled once, then low on fuel set course for Patriot Hills, with me craning my head over my shoulder for a last glimpse of the two small figures and their little camp, the only sign of anything as far as the eye could see. How helpless and small and fragile they looked, dwarfed by the hugeness that is Antarctica. I remembered that it was I who had suggested the whole mad scheme to Simon in the first place. I felt such an emptiness. I realised how much I had been focused on being with him, being able to spend a few short hours together and it was over, as though it had never happened, a dream. And now we were short of fuel. All of the glory of rescuing Fiona was replaced by the stupidity of getting ourselves into such an unnecessary situation. Martin in the back was unconcerned, happily taking pictures of light effects on snow.

The wind had strengthened and Colin was reminding me that the winds would increase as we came under the influence of the Ellsworth

Mountains, until we realised that we would be flying along in the lee of the mountain range, paralleling the mountains. This would ensure we lost our head winds for cross winds and give us a much better ground speed, which turned out to be exactly the case. We landed with 20 minutes of fuel to spare and a tremendous feeling of relief.

At Patriot Hills the wind had not increased dramatically, but none the less it was blowing at a steady 35 knots off the mountain. Once more the snowplough was positioned and we secured the helicopter with ratchets to the ice screws and put the tie downs on the blades.

We had missed Fran's lunch but were able to enjoy a cup of tea and banana bread while we discussed the merits of whether to continue south that day. Tiredness was an important factor and once again I emphasised to Colin that we had nearly four whole days to do 600 miles, a distance we could cover in 5–6 hours and that we would be seriously unlucky if there were no flying conditions for that long.

'How can you say that?' Colin retorted, 'No one's been able to get off the ground here for days.'

I argued that I was just too tired and we'd have to risk it. I also reminded him that there would be no comfortable mattresses in our tent and asked if he really wanted to camp a short distance from the South Pole at over 9,000 feet for longer than we needed. I also needed to send emails.

'Well you're the boss,' Colin said, 'But I think we should go.'

Five minutes later, Jaco came in saying, 'There's heavy cloud cover at Thiel Mountains to the south and all the way to the Pole. Not flying weather.'

So that, I thought, settled that. However, after tea, as we headed off to the 'expedition tent', Colin put in one last bid for continuing saying, 'I think we should head as far south as we can – after all it's 300 miles to Thiel.'

We were still discussing whether to press on or not, when we spotted Geoff Knight and his tricycle at the other side of the camp, about 100 yards from his previous position. The tricycle was indeed sporting ropes threaded through the wheels but a rather disconsolate Geoff explained that the results were not as he had hoped. He had only managed to get about half a mile from camp, close to a wrecked DC6 transport plane, which had crashed four years previously. He said that the first few hundred yards were good, but then the snow compacted on the wheels and around the ropes and he had ground to a halt – he cleared them, but the problem persisted. I think he was rather relieved to be back in camp as he was concerned about crevasses and asked us if we'd seen any. However, nothing daunted, he said he would go back to New Zealand to start work on Prototype 10!

The crashed DC6 plane had been on the approach for the ice runway at Patriot Hills, the skies had been overcast, the light was flat, making it almost impossible to see the ground or judge distances. Everything had been white on white and the pilot had thought he was over the runway when in fact he was some two miles short and touched down on soft snow. The plane had wheels, not skis, and crumpled in the snow, but luckily no one was killed. The DC6 was irreparable unlike the DC3, which the mechanics were now racing against time to repair before the end of the season – and it was possibly thanks to that DC3 that all of us were there in Antarctica. It was that expensive asset sitting in the snow that had first motivated the McDowells to take over the expedition base at Patriot Hills. So while the DC3 looked set to fly again by the end of the summer, the poor old DC6 remained there, each year getting buried a little deeper in its snowy grave, too impractical to move.

Ever since leaving the overcast of Marsh on the northern tip of the Antarctic Peninsular we had enjoyed good visibility with little or no cloud. We had experienced the optical illusions caused by the blowing ice crystals and strange halos around the sun, but all in all we had had immaculate flying weather. We had been lulled into a false sense of optimism and safety and so the DC6 lying like a dead goose in the snow was a salutary reminder of the all too present dangers inherent in Antarctic flight. Wind, as Jim the New Zealand helicopter pilot had told me all those months ago, might be the greatest enemy, but visibility, the deceptions of light or lack of it was waiting for you too.

We met Mike Sharp in the expedition tent. He thanked us for looking for Fiona and then with a sheepish smile asked if we might help out with another expedition. This lot hadn't got an emergency, they'd got sore feet! 'The ski boots they ordered were the wrong ones and their feet are killing them,' he explained. 'Matty McNair who is leading the expedition has asked if we could get them all another pair. The new boots arrived on the last Ilyushin flight and we were planning to leave them at Thiel when the Twin Otter next goes in there, but as you should be flying over them, would you mind dropping them off?'

Matty's team still had 150 miles to go to the Thiel Mountains, by which time their feet would be a mess. We were happy to oblige and slipped comfortably once more into 'saviour' mode. 'If you can't find them, then just leave them at Thiel. Place them up against the fuel drums with some sort of marker and be sure to dig them in a bit, those winds could blow them away in no time. Jason will have their latest coordinates tomorrow morning, but I doubt you'll be able to get into Thiel tomorrow, weather's bad down there.'

I was concerned about how we could squeeze all those boots into our already full helicopter, but Colin reminded me that we would be leaving a certain amount of kit at Patriot, like the life raft and waterproof survival suits, which we wouldn't be needing until our return.

The following day was 14 December and our planned departure to our next fuel depot at Thiel Mountains, 300 miles to the south and the halfway point from Patriot Hills to the South Pole. The deciding factor would, as always, be the weather.

CHAPTER FIVE
Patriot Hills — Thiel Mountains — South Pole

'Up, up, the long, delirious, burning blue
I top the wind swept heights with easy grace
Where never lark or ever eagle flew…'
John Gillespie Magee

Left: CB at the South Pole

The next morning we woke to overcast skies; we weren't going anywhere in a hurry. 'It's looking iffy at Thiel too,' Jaco said. With those words I could feel the 'I told you so' boring into the back of my head from Colin who was standing behind me. The satellite images were still showing extensive and solid cloud cover at Thiel Mountains.

Jaco went on to say, 'There's a system coming in from the Weddell Sea, it's starting to weaken, leaving a lot of cloud cover in its wake. Unfortunately it's not dispersing the way I had hoped, although the weather at the South Pole is looking better – only showing thin bands of cloud there. I suggest you wait for the next down-pass of satellite images.' To which we glumly agreed. Jaco told us that the Twin Otter was also planning to fly to Thiel in the near future as no one had been in there that year and they needed to check out the runway and the fuel. Then he suggested we go and have a word with Karl. 'I know Karl isn't too happy with the weather – I doubt he will go today.'

We found Karl checking the tie downs on the Twin Otter. 'Don't want it blowing over too,' he remarked, nodding his head in the direction of the DC3, half-hidden behind the protective snow wall the engineers had built around it. Karl confirmed he wasn't going anywhere for the present, but for him there was no pressing urgency and he didn't really want to be out of camp for long with the other Twin Otter sitting 600 miles to the north. He said they might go later in the afternoon if the weather improved. 'Can't forecast anything here – just have to wait and see.'

We felt we had greater flexibility than the Twin Otter in our helicopter. In hindsight we should have talked some more with Karl, learned more from his extensive experiences, understood a little better the vagaries of polar weather, about light effects, about when to fly and when not to. But we had this sublime faith that piloting a helicopter we could land anywhere if the going got bad – that we would have time to make a safe landing. Such thinking had worked well during our other global flights and we thought it would hold true for Antarctica too. We thought we knew and understood polar weather. How wrong we were.

The next set of images showed a slight improvement. We decided to head south and if the weather deteriorated we would land and sit it out. Karl said he'd stay put – 'Maybe tomorrow if the weather improves.' Colin went off to find someone to help with refuelling. The drums were all stored several hundred yards away near to the ice runway, so they had to be loaded onto a heavy wooden sled attached to a snowmobile and driven over to the helicopter. An hour later we were ready to go.

Everyone wished us luck for our final push and Jason reminded us to phone in every half an hour. We were leaving the security and comparative comforts of Patriot Hills where we were surrounded by people with years of understanding of the region and the weather, and Karl, maybe the most experienced polar pilot in the world, who had opted not to fly.

My feelings were a mixture of nervousness and exhilaration as we lifted off, new boots and all. It was 6pm local time as we circled the camp, taking a few photos, and then set course for Matty's group and the south. Colin was flying so he chose the music. He finally got his Bon Jovi, Rod Stewart and Andy Williams.

The visibility was good with only slight headwinds and partial cloud cover. Half an hour later, under clear skies, we homed in on Matty's campsite of the previous night. We then started our routine of following ski tracks. We reduced our air speed from 120 knots to 70 and flew at 50 feet above the surface. It's more difficult than you might imagine to follow tracks because where the sastrugi was firm the tracks disappeared and then reappeared where it was soft. The tracks meandered all over the place where the team had searched for the best route. We began to realise that the 750-mile trek from the coast to the South Pole was in reality more like double that. We 'tracked' away for some nine miles, skimming the surface, losing and finding their tracks, and then we lost them altogether. We were about to give up when Colin spotted them. 'There they are!' Sure enough, away in the distance, way off to our left I could just see the small black dots of Matty's group.

Great excitement on the ground. As soon as we landed and shut down everyone began talking at once. They had spotted us before we saw them and when they saw us heading in the wrong direction there had been collective groans of dismay. These had changed to shouts of joy when they saw us altering course. Their joy was twofold – delighted to have their new footwear and happy to see new faces. It turned out that one of the four men of Matty's team was from Hong Kong and had seen my daughter Christy at the Country Club just a few weeks ago at their respective infants' swimming lessons!

Huddled in the minimal shelter of the helicopter, thermoses were produced and, in true British style, we all had a cup of tea. But we didn't stay long, Matty and co still had an hour's walking to do before making camp and we were anxious to get to Thiel. There were a few laughs about how long it would take them to get there versus us – about 20 days for them and three hours for us. We all took some groupie photos before wishing each other safe journeys south.

As we lifted off I laughed and commented on how great it was to see four big burly men being led by one neat little lady. Colin gave me that lopsided smile and muttered something about being a threatened species.

'Well, you'd never catch me doing it supported or unsupported,' Colin said.

'They're probably saying the same thing about helicopters and us,' I replied with a laugh.

The weather only started to deteriorate some 50 miles out from Thiel and when we finally saw the mountain range in the distance, the peaks were lost in cloud. It was a relief to spot the marker flags for the skiway and then, at the far end, the now familiar green drums of fuel, three-quarters buried in the snow. I phoned through to Jason at Patriot to say we had landed.

Just after 11pm we wearily faced the prospect of getting the tent up – which had yet to have its first-ever airing. Colin's reaction when we did pull it out was comical. He had a look of disbelief as he accusingly said, 'Why on earth did you get such a small tent?' I too was a little surprised at how small it was, but I wasn't about to let on, so staunchly defended the tent, and my judgement. I told him it was the one that Pen had recommended, that it was perfectly adequate, and that I had had long discussions with the immensely experienced Swedish manufacturers about which one and how big. Irritably I added, 'You could always have checked the kit out yourself before we left England.'

We decided to put the tent up as close to the helicopter as possible, thinking it would give us a little more protection from the relentless wind and make life easier getting things to and from the helicopter. We each had different but very definite ideas of how the tent should be put up, both claiming years of Boy Scout and Girl Guide camping experience, so it probably took longer than it should have.

The really serious problem was our little stove. It wouldn't light. Without the stove we were well and truly stuck. We couldn't melt snow, so had nothing to eat or drink and we didn't even have a thermos of tea, having shared it with Matty's group. Colin tried for hours to get it going, as I sat huddled into one corner of the tent wrapped in my sleeping bag. There was no room in the tent to be able to lay out the sleeping bags and light the cooker safely. I said that we should call it a day and try again in the morning, but Colin wanted to try changing and cleaning the jet one more time, muttering about how he couldn't understand it, how it had been fine before and how we'd had no previous problems. I began to understand why Simon and Pen had two stoves with them. Finally, at 2am, sleep won over hunger. I could stay awake no longer. So, cold, hungry and thirsty and trying to make myself as small as possible, I climbed into my sleeping bag, curled up in the corner and went to sleep, with Colin still working away on the stove.

Five dreamless hours later I woke, still curled up in a tight ball, and hungrier and thirstier than before. The wind was screaming around our fragile little tent and the light filtering through was suspiciously grey. I could feel the icy, lumpy surface through my sleeping bag as the thin foam pad underneath that was meant to help keep out the cold did a very poor job of it. Colin was awake and said he'd been awake for hours, thinking about the cooker. 'It's got to be ice, there must be a lump of ice stuck in the pipe, I've checked everything else. We've got to fix this as there is no way the Twin Otter will be coming in here, just take a look outside at the weather.'

I did just that as I was dying for a pee. I put on my boots, hat, goggles and gloves – I'd gone to sleep in everything else including my big parka. Thinking about the non-functioning stove and how hungry and thirsty I was, I clambered out into a full-blown blizzard. What if this blizzard held out for days? How long could we last with no water or food? Not for the first time I asked myself, 'What am I doing? Me, a 63-year-old mother and grandmother, battling against a blizzard in the middle of Antarctica, trying to fly a helicopter to the South Pole?' Then I realised, rather to my surprise, that I was actually enjoying myself.

I could just see the couple of yards to the helicopter. The surface of the snow was invisible and only the crunchy squeaking of my snow boots and the solid feel of the snow underfoot confirmed that I wasn't walking on clouds. It was a strange feeling. I found the shovel and headed off down the side of the helicopter, just far enough away to keep it in site and dug, what I hoped, was a little hole – although I couldn't see a thing. As I dug I thought of our survival training with Art Mortvedt back in Alaska when he had us digging snow caves on a beautiful day without a breath of wind. Then we could see easily see what we were doing. Now I was doing it blind, but at least I only had to dig a small hole, not a cave. I shoved the shovel deep into the snow and clung to it for dear life with the wind whipping up my backside. The whole process was incredibly complicated – my big padded trousers had a 'bib' front, although luckily I had thought to take the straps off my shoulders before putting on my jacket inside the tent. But all three layers of trousers had to be pulled down, unlike the nifty suits that Simon and Pen had, with a zip that unzipped through their legs. I tried to pee as fast as possible – frostbite would have been very uncomfortable. Mission speedily accomplished I shovelled snow back into where I thought the hole was and headed back to the tent.

As I crawled inside, I heard the wonderful hissing noise of a fully operative little cooker going for its life. I'd never really doubted Colin, he's an ace mechanic, but then sometimes things are beyond repair. Happily this time the cooker wasn't. 'I knew it must be ice – I checked the pipe again and sure enough, it was blocked,' he announced happily. Breakfast was served – porridge with raisins and a big mug of tea. Life was good.

With blizzard conditions outside, I said that I for one was going to get some more sleep, this time on a full stomach. Colin started to say we should refuel while the weather was foul so that we would be ready to go. I reminded him that we needed to move the helicopter closer to the fuel drums, which in turn would mean taking the tent down. In the current weather conditions it would be impossible to move the helicopter even a few feet. He poked his nose outside the tent and agreed, so back to sleep we went for a couple of hours.

You couldn't move in the tent without the other knowing about it, so when Colin clambered out for a weather check and to collect some snow for a cup of tea I reluctantly surfaced, just in time for our scheduled call to Patriot Hills to find out what the weather satellite images were showing. Jason's ever-cheerful voice came on the line, but only with the dreary news that there was little change – still widespread cloud – and that the next download of images would be in five hours time, at 9pm. I asked if that would be too late for him if we checked again then. 'No problem,' he said, 'hope you've got a good book!'

Colin reckoned our weather was improving and pointed out that we could see the base of the mountains some 10 miles away. I said I'd like to be able to see the tops too. The wind had dropped a little and there were definitely some brighter patches of cloud.

'Let's have some lunch, take down the tent, move the helicopter and refuel, then if the weather improves we should be ready to go.' I agreed rather ungraciously to go along with all his suggestions. I didn't like the weather and I was starting not to like him. I could see I was getting on his nerves and he was definitely getting on mine; we both wanted everything done our own way. So, for the most part, we both retreated into a safe silence while we got on with all the preparations.

The weather remained marginal and I was reluctant to move on.

'It's still only the 15th,' I argued.

'Not at the South Pole,' Colin quickly retorted, 'Don't forget they are 14 hours ahead of us, it's already the 16th with them.'

Graciously I said, 'You're right.'

'As usual!' came the smug reply.

Now really irritated, I bounced back to point out that we had in fact got quite a large and flexible time span. It would take hours for the aviation world to celebrate 17 December and we should make sure we were at the Pole when America got around to celebrating. I got a sort of grunt in reply. Tempers were definitely frayed.

I phoned Jason promptly at 9pm. He said Jaco was just receiving the images and that it looked as though there was a slight improvement, the cloud finally appeared to be dispersing a little, but it was impossible to say how thick it was. I told him that conditions had improved at Thiel, that we hoped we would shortly have flying conditions and would call again on departure. I think I sounded more optimistic than I felt.

Before signing off Jason gave us the news that we were expected at the South Pole and could we please arrive at 8am on the 17th! Anyone would think a message like that was for someone catching the early morning commuter train for a meeting in London, rather than instructions to two pilots, stuck at 5,000 feet with the temperature -22°C, the wind gusting up to 40 knots, not a single solitary soul within hundreds of miles in any direction and facing a 300-mile journey to the bottom of the world.

The enormity of our challenge and the reality that we were so close to our first great goal was sinking in – and contrary to all Colin's gloomy predictions we were slowly getting there. But were we going to make it on time? If we did manage to go in at 8am South Pole time, we would probably be the first aviators, or one of the first, in the world to start the 17 December celebrations.

Over the next couple of hours the weather improved. We had reasonable flying conditions and were once more on our way south. The one-upmanship continued. What with the poor weather delay, arguments over putting up tents, flyable weather, non-functioning stoves and lack of sleep, tempers remained frayed. 'We don't have any frequency for the South Pole Station,' Colin said.

'Yes we do,' I smugly replied. 'It's in the AFIM book.'

'What's the AFIM book!?'

'AFIM stands for "Antarctic Flight Information Manual". It's that turquoise blue book on the bulkhead behind you; it's got all the information on all the stations in Antarctica, I think the South Pole is listed under "Amundsen Scott South Polar Station". There's plenty of information there along with runways and the "no fly areas". I had to pay an outrageous amount for that book – over $300.'

'Oh – right,' Colin grunted, trying to swivel around and find the book without knocking the cyclic stick.

'It's not there,' he said. I told him not to worry. 'We'll have plenty of time to locate it when we make our next stop.' Which turned out to be sooner than expected.

For the next half-hour the weather remained good, the terrain was rising steadily and the temperature dropping. The outside air temperature was now reading -28°C.

We saw the tip of one last isolated peak – only a couple of hundred feet was all there was to see of what must have been a mountain of over 8,000 feet, now buried in the ice of millions of years. Beyond that last rock there was nothing, and yet the emptiness was different from what we had experienced on our journey so far. The light, the halos around the sun, the patterns of the sastrugi and the sunlight was thinner. I swear you could see the curvature of the earth, or was it the light playing different patterns? Perhaps our imagination played a part, too. As we flew ever closer to the Pole, my thoughts turned once again to the great explorers and how we were actually flying on the route they had trod all those years ago, and then of those on their way right at that moment – of Simon and Pen.

One hour out and the cloud cover began to increase. Half an hour later the cloud had thickened still further, but we continued on, agreeing that if conditions deteriorated much more we would have to put down.

'Look over there!' Colin shouted out. Several miles away to the southeast was a small black speck in our empty world and as we drew closer we could make out two tents. It turned out to be the team of 'kite skiers' on their way back to Patriot Hills!

'Our route seems to be positively crowded,' I chirped.

'At least we know we're going the right way.' Colin said with a grin.

We circled overhead. One man was standing outside the tent waving. 'They must be getting ready for bed,' I said.

'Well that just depends whose time they are on,' Colin replied. 'They could be finishing breakfast.' It was all confusing. I made one last circle then started turning back onto our southbound heading.

And then it all started to go wrong. The visibility deteriorated dramatically and what with the combination of the turn, the myriad of swirling ice crystals and the weather closing in, I became momentarily disorientated. It all happened so quickly. One moment the visibility had been flyable, the next it was marginal and I was taken unawares while making that fairly tight turn.

'I'm not going on in this,' I said, thoroughly shaken.

'OK, straighten out – take your time, I can see the ground.' Colin said reassuringly.

The whole world was on the move, I tried to shut out the swirling white mass outside the helicopter, eyes only for the instruments, fighting off disorientation and bringing the helicopter back to straight and level flight. Luckily, in spite of the blowing snow, there was fractional sunlight

– we had ground definition and were finally able to land without mishap. Unnervingly, within moments of touching down we lost all visibility. Ground and sky were one. Even Colin's normal self-assurance was clearly shaken. We should have learned a lesson from that experience on how fast conditions can change, although we did both agree that in future we would land sooner and sit it out if we thought we were close to losing visibility.

Our prospects of making it much closer to the South Pole that evening were not looking good. Time passed, the interior of the helicopter got colder and colder. For two hours we sat there, waiting and hoping for an improvement in the conditions and discussing the speed with which the weather could change. I for one felt infinitely relieved that we had landed when we did but badly shaken at what a close call it had been.

I was frozen and intermittently suggested we should make camp. Colin was all for waiting a little longer saying, 'It'll be the 17th in a few hours at the South Pole and they want us to be there at 8am.'

I didn't need any reminder, and said 'If it's later, well then it will just have to be later and besides, in many ways, a little later in the day would be better – less time to wait for the rest of the world to wake up and be able to tell them we had arrived.'

'Don't talk too soon, we're not there yet,' was his reply.

We waited and waited and then just as I'd persuaded Colin that we should call it a day and put up the tent, blue sky appeared as quickly as it had disappeared. We decided to push on once more.

As I was still feeling rather shaken by the whole experience I asked Colin to fly the next leg. We lifted off, the weather improving by the minute and found our tail wind had now increased to 7 knots. The weather and winds held until 50 miles from the South Pole when the horizon to the southeast appeared to be entirely blotted out. After our recent experience we were taking no chances and turned slightly west of our direct course to avoid the 'storm'. As we got closer we could see that it wasn't a snow storm – we could see through it, it was a localised cloud of swirling ice crystals with sunlight reflecting off all surfaces. Ice crystals, unlike other types of precipitation, can form out of a clear blue sky.

We still gave it a wide birth. The sun was shining, the skies up ahead were overcast and I was all for making camp in the sunshine. 'It's only 48 miles to the Pole, for goodness sakes, let's call it a day while we still have some good weather,' I reasoned. But Colin wasn't budging and he was in a rather strong position as he had the controls. He insisted on pressing on to the previously agreed 20 miles out, where it was dull and cloudy and the snow proved to be very, very soft. Every time we descended and gently touched down, we sank alarmingly and each time I would say, 'I knew we should have stopped back in the sunshine and now we're using up precious fuel.' Neither of us was being very nice.

We had some small blocks of wood in the back of the helicopter for sitting the generator and cooker on and I suggested that I should get out and try and place them under the skids while Colin held the helicopter in a low hover. The theory was good; the practice was not. You forget just how cold it is outside. I didn't have my jacket, hat or gloves on and the wind cut into me like a knife as I clambered out of the helicopter. It was also incredibly difficult for Colin to hold the helicopter in a stationary hover in 20 knots of wind. Each time I placed the wood, the helicopter moved fractionally forward or sideways. The wood was too small and the winds too strong. I could hear myself whimpering with cold. I gave up and leaped back on board. Colin was grinning happily for the first time that day at my frozen attempts. 'Didn't think that would work,' he said.

We flew around for some while and finally found a firmer spot, landed and quickly dug the wood in under the skids. The altimeter reading was again 100 feet out. I phoned Jason to tell him we were on the ground. 'We're 20 miles out,' I said. He was full of congratulations that we were virtually there and confirmed once more that we were to fly in at 8am New Zealand time.

We had completely lost track of night and day and now just 20 miles away it was already 1am on the 17th – and we were tired and hungry. Our tempers were on an even shorter fuse and it only took our opinionated views on how to put up the tent for both of us to lose it. This proved to be our only major row of the entire journey – though we had been fairly close a couple of times before. We weren't listening to each other – we were both too busy yelling at each other over the noise of the wind and flapping tent, shouting and swearing. I remember his furious face just inches from mine and thinking that perhaps I should back down because he was an awful lot bigger and stronger than me. But instead he stamped off into the distance waving his arms in frustration and fury while I stamped off around the other side of the half-put-up tent, which thankfully hadn't blown away during the screams and shouts and waving of fists. I can't remember which part of the tent erection we had disagreed on, but in the light of future events there was to be a certain irony in the whole situation.

The good thing was that I think we both felt better for venting our feelings and releasing all the built up tension When Colin returned he rather sheepishly apologised and I muttered something about male ego. Finally we both managed to laugh at the absurdity of it all.

By the time we had melted snow, boiled water, eaten beef stew and climbed into our sleeping bags it was 2.30am. I set my alarm clock for 5.30am. My last little nagging worry before collapsing into sleep was whether the engine would start after so many cold hours and without some added heat – I remembered being told that the big American C130 transport planes that fly to the South Pole never allow their engines to cool off fully. The temperature was -24ºC; we were now at 9,300 feet above sea level and the winds were a mild 10 to 15 knots.

Three hours later and we were once more on the move with Colin anxious to get the helicopter's battery on charge and warmed up. He too had been worrying about the start up. I peeked outside and the heavens looked good with the palest of blue skies and high ribbons of cloud, while down on the ground blowing snow streamed over the waves of sastrugi. The temperature and winds were much as they had been before we went to sleep. There we were in a tent, camped at nearly 10,000 feet, 20 miles from the South Pole. It was 17 December 2003, we were going to make it on schedule, and it was my daughter Suze's birthday!

Colin interrupted my thoughts. 'What are you daydreaming about? C'mon, we've got lots to do – we don't want to be late – hope that engine starts.' But first we needed some breakfast. The snow had to be melted, the water boiled and finally a good morning cup of tea and bowl of porridge.

Colin checked out the helicopter. With the remote generator supplying power to the battery charger, he put the helicopter battery on charge for 20 minutes before start up. This not only topped up the battery but also warmed it at the same time. Then just before starting he would turn the charger to boost and finish charging the battery. Meanwhile I packed up the tent. I didn't see the box of matches lying in the bottom of the tent. Providentially they remained there.

We need not have worried whether the helicopter would start: it powered up instantly. We phoned Jason to say we were off. We had located the elusive AFIM book so Colin had the frequency for the Amundsen Scott South Pole station. Once airborne Colin radioed through and we were cleared to land on Runway 06. 'What if we miss the base?' Colin said. 'There's nothing much else out there before Australia.'

The GPSs were showing wildly different convergence lines. We had one GPS on 'magnetic' and one on 'true'. The magnetic course went in a straight line south then did an abrupt right turn, hardly surprising as the magnetic South Pole was some 1,400 miles away in the Ross Sea. The GPS on 'true' showed a straight course. But we were on the right track and minutes later, with happy relief, we were able to make out the dim shapes of the thin sprawl of buildings of the polar station. Briefly I thought back on the 2,000 miles we'd flown since leaving Ushuaia – of the hostile waters of the Drake Passage and the unforgiving territory of Antarctica, where even the smallest error could prove fatal. We were so vulnerable and looking at the distant polar station, it too looked exposed and insubstantial against the overwhelming might of that bleak and beautiful world of ice.

I had looked at many pictures of the South Pole, but seeing it all for real and knowing we had reached the bottom of the world was incredibly special. We both had the biggest grins on our faces, irritations of the day before forgotten, as Colin looked at me saying, 'Well, I guess we're going to make it after all!'

Of all the surreal moments, this had to be the greatest. We were actually making our final approach to the geographic South Pole. We flew towards the huge runway of hard-packed snow, long enough and wide enough to accommodate the vast ski-equipped C130 transport planes. And yes, there on the far side we could see the semicircle of flags surrounding the commemorative South Pole and, beyond, a small crowd of people. It appeared as though we had a welcoming committee!

I was once more looking through rose-tinted spectacles while Colin was remarking in his usual way that we'd arrived at a construction site. The Americans were in the process of moving their quarters from the fabled dome to new premises raised well above the snow on cantilevered poles. There was construction material everywhere and an immense crane dominating the scene. 'Unbelievable that all that lot has come in on the C130s,' Colin remarked, as the air traffic controller directed us to land about 100 yards from the commemorative South Pole, close to the waiting group of people who were all waving enthusiastically.

We touched down, raising a fine cloud of ice crystals, and looked at each other, laughing and waving to the small crowd. We'd done it, we had landed at the South Pole, 100 years to the day that Orville and Wilbur Wright made those first-ever mechanised flights back at Kitty Hawke in Virginia, USA, in 1903. And perhaps most importantly for us, we had achieved what many thought impossible.

The resident scientists and station operators made us feel very welcome, clapping, smiling, patting us on the back and introducing themselves. Muffled and goggled against the cold, it was voices and beards that identified male from female. 'Hi, I'm KP,' said one beardless, smiling person, 'and this is Pete, he's station manager and will show you around.' Pete was a good head taller than KP and appeared to be quite thin with a dark beard under a dark blue fleece hat and all-encompassing goggles. 'I expect you'd like to come inside first, come to the coffee shop in the dome and I'll try and answer any questions,' he said.

The group quickly broke up. They were all on tight schedules. KP said she'd try and see us later and apologised that they could not offer us full hospitality. 'We're at full stretch, working 24/7, three shifts a day,' she said, adding, 'Jerry Marty, the head of all South Pole operations, would like to meet you later when he comes on shift in a couple of hours time. In the mean time, Pete here will look after you – see you later.' She hurried off in the direction of the new building. I asked Pete if we might reposition the helicopter closer to the commemorative South Pole to get some good photos and, on the way, do a couple of quick circuits around the world. He had no problem with that.

Pete explained the history of the commemorative South Pole. Years before, some joker had made a replica of a striped barber's pole, placed a silver orb on the top and stuck it in the ground, and there it has remained ever since, absurd and colourful, placed in front of a semicircle of flags of all the founder nations of the Antarctic Treaty. The actual geographical South Pole lies some 50 yards away. A simple wooden sign marks the spot with a series of marker poles giving each year's new position as the whole ice cap moves some 33 feet a year, and the South Pole station with it.

Pointing to a building in the distance behind our helicopter, Pete said 'That's the Clean Air Zone, cleanest air in all the world, no aircraft allowed to fly there, there's nothing for 8,000 miles in that direction,' and then swinging his arm 90 degrees he pointed to another structure. 'That is the Dark Zone, studying the stars, not much happening there right now, mostly engineering work, got to wait for darkness.' The arm continued to swing: 'And that's the new elevated section which they hope to have fully operational by 2006, and those there,' he said, stabbing the air with a gloved mitten, 'those huge cantilevered poles that the whole structure sits on, they serve a double purpose. The snow can blow freely, unobstructed under the building, so there's no danger of drifts, and the whole building can be jacked up periodically as everything here slowly, inevitably, sinks deeper and deeper into the ice. That's the problem with the dome, it was built in 1975 and has been sinking ever since. It's being crushed by the ice – what you see now is the top quarter, the rest is all under the surface.'

I said that I imagined everyone was delighted by the prospect of moving out of the windowless dome into a building where they could see out. Pete grinned and said, 'You bet, but for some of the folks like Jerry Marty, who have spent their entire careers here, there's some sadness.'

We crunched across the hard-packed, squeaky dry snow to the geographical South Pole where we did a little dance around it and completed a couple more world circumnavigations. We took more photos and then headed onwards down the ramp leading into the dome, the thought of coffee and cookies, and the chance to sit on a proper loo, spurring us onwards.

Walking into the dome is like walking into a freezer. You leave the wind, to enter a frozen, silent world and a building where the great domed ceiling is covered in thick frost, the ground is hard-packed snow and the three two-storey 'buildings' inside looked like overgrown containers.

Pete opened a door into a different world. We moved into the warm gym where a couple of scientists were enjoying a short coffee break watching an astrophysicist from Utah on the running machine. He was warming up for the 'Christmas Polar Marathon' the following week – a two-mile race, twice around the world.

Pete led us onwards and upwards into the second level of the container, past the post office and general store that looked like your average village shop-cum-post-office, and into the coffee shop, which didn't quite live up to expectations. After the previous rooms we were fully expecting Starbucks. The room reminded me of school with its cream coloured walls in need of decoration and one long table in the middle of the room where a thermos of coffee, three mugs and a plate of assorted muffins covered in clingfilm sat waiting for us. But who were we to complain? These guys made us welcome and were giving us a lot of their time despite their tight programmes.

It was still hard to believe we were actually there, sitting with our cups of coffee and eating blueberry muffins, in the dome at the Amundsen Scott base at 90 South. There was an overwhelming sense of history all around us, of all the expeditions that had made it there and of all the adventurers who had sat where we were now sitting. I felt a bond of camaraderie with them having now made it there too. We talked of the Wright brothers and of our own auspicious landing at Kitty Hawke during our solo flight around the world in 2000 – a day that Colin and I will never forget because he nearly died twice in his microlight. The first time was on final approach to the small landing strip at Kitty Hawke where he encountered near catastrophic wind sheer. I was following close behind in my helicopter and, as I watched, his small craft tumbled out of the sky. Somehow he managed to regain some semblance of control just before hitting the ground and careering sideways across the runway on one wheel. Having nearly killed himself once, he had another try later that afternoon on the approach to the airfield at Norfolk, 50 miles to the north of Kitty Hawke. Seven miles out from the airfield, over the downtown area, Colin's engine failed. I radioed out the May Day distress call; there was nothing else I could do but watch and pray. Colin somehow managed to land in a small, empty school playing field. These were heart-stopping moments and now the memories came back. We regaled Pete with our daring-do while thoroughly enjoying the luxury of sitting on chairs and clinked our coffee mugs together as we toasted being there, 100 years of flight and a happy birthday to Suze!

Out of the blue, Pete asked us what we thought of the Australian pilot's attempt to fly to the South Pole. This was news to us, we had no idea anyone else was flying to the Pole. Pete explained that a young Australian pilot had built his own small plane and had set off from Australia in an attempt to fly non-stop across the Southern Ocean, across Antarctica, over the South Pole and finally land in Ushuaia. He ran low on fuel over Antarctica and had to turn back and land at the American scientific research station at McMurdo – the base that Polly Vacher had tried to reach. The Americans were not amused. It appeared that no one in Antarctica knew he was coming and he had no Search and Rescue in place. 'How incredibly, wonderfully brave' was my immediate reaction, while Colin's was more prosaic: 'Daft. It's guys like him that give aviation a bad name. Think how tough he makes it for anyone else wanting to fly in here.' I had to agree, but the adventurer in me still thought it was marvellous – like the crazy pilot who landed his small plane in Moscow's Red Square.

'So what's happened to him now?' I asked.

'He's stuck at McMurdo and no one is offering him any help. He's been told he will have to leave his aircraft there and will have to pay for a seat on one of the American transport flights out to New Zealand.' Frustratingly Pete didn't have any more details.

'What a dreary ending,' I said, disappointed for him.

It looked after all as though we were the only private aviators to make it to the Pole that year. Quentin and Steve had ditched in the sea, Polly had had to turn back because of head winds and now the Australian appeared to have had the same problem.

We stayed sitting there for a while sipping our coffee and discussing polar stories and disasters. Pete told us the story of the camera crew that had been there a few years previously making a documentary at the South Pole. One of the poor camera men on the trip had parachuted in from a DC3 but had been so engrossed in filming that he forgot to open his chute until it was too late. Next he told us about the Russian Antonov plane that was still lying at the end of the runway. The pilot had made a heavy landing having failed to take-off because he hadn't taken into account how thin the air is at the Pole. The thin air doesn't just cause occasional take-off problems, but often leads to people at the Pole suffering with headaches and tiredness. Luckily Colin and I seemed to be faring pretty well, but I suspect the adrenaline high we were on was helping that.

Colin asked Pete about the shop: 'Any chance of getting some underpants?' he asked.

'Underpants? You mean fleece liners?'

Colin looked first surprised and then rather interested. I explained to Pete that Colin meant shorts. Pete was doubtful, 'Haven't seen any, but then I brought enough with me, best go and check it out.'

We went shopping. We bought T-shirts, sweat shirts, caps and postcards, but, much to Colin's indignation and protestations of disbelief, there was obviously no demand for underpants at the South Pole, so he remained a one pant man.

Jerry Marty appeared as we were sitting writing the postcards we had just bought. Jerry was a tall, good-looking man in his early 50s. He had a rather sexy, craggy and weathered face and sported a shaggy blonde head of hair and an equally shaggy moustache. He would have looked very much at home in a Hollywood Western movie. Jerry welcomed us to 90 South – and took over from Pete, who wished us safe flying before disappearing. Jerry gave us a brief overview of operations then asked if we would like to see the greenhouse. We went back out by the gym into the freezer-box dome, up an outside staircase and onto the roof of one of the 'containers'. As we walked over a series of box spring mattresses, Jerry explained, 'We put those here to deaden the noise of people walking overhead. Working three shifts a day, there are always people sleeping, so we put out the mattresses. They work, I know,' he said with a smile, 'my room is underneath these ones.' He led us over to a small, plastic-sheeted structure – and inside we could see lettuces and tomatoes and various other salady-looking leaves growing.

'About 10 years ago', Jerry said, 'someone had the idea that it would be good to try and grow our own salads. It started on the surface, but it proved so popular that we moved it in here. We now produce enough for two salads a week and more in the winter – fewer people here then. Folks like to just come and sit in the vestibule area here and enjoy the oxygen and the greenery. We're putting in a real big growth chamber in the new elevated section. It's been designed by Nassau and the University of Arizona and is due to be flown in here in the autumn. We'll have 300 square feet under production and a large vestibule area where folks can just come and sit and enjoy seeing veggies growing at 90 South.'

We went back over the mattresses and down the stairs with Jerry pointing out the trap door in the ceiling. 'All buildings have two departure points, fire is a real concern here. In the past if the dome had caught fire, there would have been no place else to go. Everything happened right here in the dome, food service, science, housing, recreation, communications, administration. Well, we've outgrown the Dome now, we're slowly transferring sections to the new elevated area – we expect to have it fully completed in 2006, so we're moving the buildings here. Finally the Dome will go too. We're all about the environment here in Antarctica – nothing stays that isn't being used.'

Colin remarked on what a big job that would be and how incredible it was that every last item had come in by air, and Jerry said with a grin, 'Well, it came in and it can go out – the C130 transport planes will be making 923 flights in here this season. Mostly they go back real empty, so taking this lot out isn't a big problem.' He then returned to his subject: 'It's all real quiet here now in the dome. The food service has moved over. This place used to be full of 200 some people going backwards and forwards, standing around, drinking cups of coffee, real busy – and for those of us who've spent nearly all our careers here it's kinda sad. But this has had its day, it's old-fashioned, dark and dingy. Now it's so great, you can sit there in the elevated section, have a cup of coffee, look at 90 South and see airplanes taking off,' and with a grin at us, he added, 'and helicopters landing.'

He apologised that he couldn't take us into the new section, explaining that as it was still under construction the safety regulations wouldn't permit any visitors. Even at 90 South you couldn't get away from red tape.

We had reached the dome entrance and Jerry had things to do and suggested that we might too. But first he wanted to present us with South Pole certificates and have us meet some of the programme heads: 'We want the folks out there to know what we are doing down here.' We told Jerry that we planned to stay at the Pole till the following morning as there was so much to see and we wanted to still be there when the UK and the US aviation world were celebrating 100 years of flight. We also wanted time to talk to family and friends from the bottom of the world. We arranged to meet up again with Jerry towards the end of his shift.

The following hours raced by. We got our tent up – amicably. We visited the building holding the communications room, a crowded, comfortable place, full of high-tech equipment and festive Christmas decorations along with a comfortable, worn leather sofa where we sat and finished writing our postcards. We then made our way back to the post office where the 'postmistress' duly stamped them with a polar stamp. I was allowed to bring my computer indoors into the coffee shop and sent off happy messages and triumphant photos of us and the helicopter beside the commemorative South Pole. Colin chatted with scientists taking coffee breaks.

We met up again later with Jerry who gave us our certificates, signed and stamped our navigational chart of Antarctica and took us off outside to meet the group of departmental heads who were waiting for us in the freezing cold close to the commemorative South Pole. We were flattered to be given such VIP treatment. We listened to the head of the Astrophysical Research Department and began to appreciate what a unique environment there is at 90 South for scientific research: 'For our observations,' he said, 'the clean thin air and the lack of moisture here at the South Pole is as close as you can get to space while having both feet firmly planted on the ground.' Incredible! He went on to explain that it is this thin, clean air and the lack of water that also makes the South Pole one of the premier places in the world to study and research the 'Big Bang'.

Thanks to the new telescope at the South Pole, cosmologists have also been able to get a 'snapshot' of the universe in its infancy, which apparently helps to explain all the current theories around the Big Bang. Their research shows that only 5 per cent of the energy in the universe takes the form of familiar matter, matter – which makes up our planets and stars. Some 30 per cent of all energy is a strange form of dark matter that doesn't interact with light, and 65 per cent is in an even stranger form of dark energy, which appears to be causing the expansion of the universe to accelerate. I was fascinated by what was being said but Colin, who was filming with our video camera, was clearly getting cold and bored.

Next to speak was Julie Pallais, the manager of the glaciology programme. Julie Pallais told us about the ice cores and how they were able to study nitrates in the atmosphere to gauge the ozone levels going back hundreds of years, and see the natural variations. She went on to speak about the South Pole remote earth science observatory located five miles from the South Pole station: 'We've installed new seismometers 1,000 feet beneath the surface of the eastern sector ice cap in specially drilled boreholes. These can now recall some of the smallest vibrations on Earth. Being at the Earth's axis, the South Pole is an unrivalled seismic laboratory, not only are vibrations free of the effects produced by the spinning globe but Antarctica is also the quietest continent on the planet, which means fewer earthquakes than anywhere else. Large earthquakes make the Earth ring in much the same way a bell does after being struck. Analysis of these vibrations reveals invaluable information about the Earth's composition, the study of tectonic plates and predictions on future movements.' Facts and figures were coming thick and fast. Apparently the South Pole seismic data has helped to prove that the Earth's solid inner core spins at a slightly faster rate than the rest of the planet.

Our third manager to speak was Kris Perry who had greeted us on our arrival that morning. Kris's area was meteorology, but she was also the representative for the construction company building the new facilities. It seemed that all the scientists wore 'two hats' during this big construction phase and in the case of Kris, during the summer months she had her hands seriously full with the massive task of overseeing 200 plus workers and eight C130 transport planes arriving and departing every flyable day.

Kris explained to us that the primary function of the meteorological staff was to collect and distribute data throughout the year. Her team were collecting information on temperature, wind and pressure from both the surface and the upper levels of the atmosphere, to be used to support scientific research, based at the South Pole as well as international research projects elsewhere. Their invaluable database spanning 40 years is routinely used by researchers studying global climate change. They also support aircraft operations in Antarctica, sending information twice daily to their coastal station at McMurdo.

By this stage we were all stamping our feet and banging our hands together in a vain attempt to keep warm – it was time for everyone to move on and Colin was obviously well passed 'saturation-of-information' point. We thanked Jerry and the other scientists and they wished us a safe journey the next morning. It would be their sleep shift when we left so we wouldn't be seeing them again. They went off to their nice warm offices and we hurried over to our tiny little tent, a small red blob some 100 yards away. It is company policy that no accommodation is ever offered to expeditions. It was by then around 9pm, so time to make those phone calls to people in England to tell them we'd made it.

First I called my daughter Suze in London and wished her a happy birthday. She was thrilled to hear we were at the South Pole. Neither of us could believe that we were talking to each other while she was having a birthday breakfast with friends in a coffee shop below her apartment on the King's Road in London and I was standing at 90 South. Suze quickly brought me up to date on all her news and I was reassuring her that we were fine and being very careful. Then she was anxious for news of her father, and why hadn't he called her? And was he really all right? I reassured her that he and Pen were on great form, that Simon's shin splints were much better and explained about the solar power limitations on their satellite phone and their exhaustion at the end of each gruelling day meant they rarely could phone. Then we were both saying goodbye and that we'd talk again on Christmas day. Suze and London were gone and I was still standing in the snow holding an empty satellite phone – and so it was with each call.

Next I called my younger daughter Chris in Hong Kong. She was busy packing up the family for departure to Phuket where they were all going to be for Christmas. Suze would be joining them there. I could hear two-year-old Domingo in the background and then he came on the phone with happy chatter about helicopters – he's gratifyingly nuts about them. Then it was back to Chris with news that baby Talitha was gorgeous and for a few wonderful moments they all felt very close. Like Suze, Chris was voicing concerns for us both, begging us to be careful and saying how absurd it was to have both parents in Antarctica. As a parent I had to agree, as an adventurer it was different.

No sooner had I rung off than the phone buzzed and it was Tamara back in the London office. She was squeaky with excitement and full of congratulations. Apparently various newspapers wanted to talk to us and an Australian radio channel wanted to interview me. It turned out that all the Australians were interested in was my views on the young Australian man who had run out of fuel and was by then stranded on the coast at McMurdo.

I also managed to speak to Simon, who was happy and relieved for us, but most especially anxious to know where we had put the food package for them at the South Pole. Had we marked it in big letters with his name? He was worried others would take it otherwise. As it turned out, weeks later, when they reached 90 South, they didn't need the food package as rather than having to wait for days for the Twin Otter, it was already there to pick them up. They only had a brief two hours at the Pole before heading back to Patriot Hills. Pen had wandered around the base taking photos and making the most of the great moment while Simon made an immediate beeline for the coffee shop and was recorded saying, 'I never want to see another f…g snowflake!'

Phone calls made, we managed to get a couple of hours of sleep, but night and day had merged long ago and it's strange how the adrenalin goes on pumping and keeps you alert and focused. It's only when you have some real time to relax mentally and physically that you realise just how tired you are.

At 6am we packed up our tent as fast as we could, the icy wind spurring us on. Then with everything stored once more in the helicopter we made a quick dash to the dome to enjoy the relative luxury of the loo facilities and fill the thermos with hot water.

The weather was flyable, with the palest of ice blue skies, encouraging us north. The visibility was a good three miles, but beyond that sky and ice were difficult to distinguish one from the other. At 90 South they seldom experience snowflakes, instead they get snow grains and usually in blizzards. Precipitation, like elsewhere in the interior of Antarctica is light, only a few centimetres a year. What we were seeing ahead were ice crystals forming in a clear sky meeting and mixing with surface snow being whipped around.

The helicopter, with Colin's tender loving care, started immediately, once more making light of the cold – -26°C – and our altitude nearly two miles up.

A small crowd had turned out to wave us off. One of the girls we had met in the gym the day before came hurrying over with a CD she had made especially for us, with the title – 'Helicopter Music from the South Pole'. This would make a change from Colin and me arguing over rock or classical music.

We thanked them all for their hospitality and they wished us a safe flight north. Then with a final salute we lifted off – it was goodbye to the South Pole, to 90 South, to the Amundsen Scott South Pole station and the earth's axis, where for a few short hours we had all but ceased to spin.

APHIC

CHAPTER SIX
North

'No step backwards.'

Horace

Left: JM & CB at the geographic South Pole

The weather improved every minute as we headed north and the beautiful ice crystals known as diamond dust were everywhere, at one point hitting the sun's rays to create a secondary sun – a 'sun dog' – that touched on the ice below. 'It looks like the gates of heaven,' I said.

'I hope not,' was Colin's reply as he glanced up quickly at the horizon. He was preoccupied trying to pour out a cup of tea from the thermos without spilling any or knocking the sensitive cyclic lever.

'Here's a cup of Earl Grey tea,' he said, and then produced the rest of the uneaten, rather the worse for wear, muffins that we had been given the day before, announcing, 'I've got the buns, or do they call them scones?' I had no idea that he had saved them.

We were hungry, which was hardly surprising, as other than a muffin apiece we had eaten nothing since the porridge at our '20 miles out' campsite the previous day. Neither of us had felt hungry until then, no doubt a combination of adrenalin and altitude: 'Do you think that's why people at sea level are fatter than those who live in the mountains?' Colin asked with a laugh.

That first day going north we had sunshine all the way. The helicopter was like a hot house as we had the heater on full blast to keep frost from building up on the windows. It hadn't been a problem going south, perhaps because we had had the sun behind us, or maybe because there had been so little of it. I remembered our New Zealand pilot's advice that we should keep the cabin heat as low as possible at altitude to reduce the risk of hypoxia, a condition that results from a lack of oxygen to the brain, and is a real risk for pilots flying at altitude. But with the windows frosting up we had little alternative than to keep the heat high, albeit in the knowledge that warm air is even thinner than cold air so the risk of hypoxia was even greater. We just needed to monitor each other.

We were more than 30 minutes into our flight and Colin had been unable to reach Jason at Patriot Hills on the satellite phone for the standard half-hour 'flight following' check in. We started to get concerned that they would be worried, so it was a relief when some minutes later Colin managed to get through and report: 'flight normal' and give Jason our coordinates: 'South 88'.37, West 108'.00'. Jason asked for our fuel endurance and Colin reported, '2 hours 40 minutes and estimated Thiel Mountains, 2 hours and 10 minutes'. A fine 30-minute margin. We were thankful for the favourable winds we had had on the inward journey, thus avoiding having to purchase an extortionately priced drum of fuel at the South Pole.

Colin then tried to reach Pen and Simon; it was also past our agreed time. For the next half an hour, at 10-minute intervals, he tried to raise them. If we couldn't get their coordinates we didn't stand a hope in hell of finding them. Then suddenly the satellite phone buzzed. It was Pen. He had been trying to get through to us but the line had always been busy.

Colin told him, 'The weather's good, got tail winds, outside air temperature, -28°C, but ground elevation is still 9,000 feet. With a bit of luck we'll be there in about four hours, in fine time for a cup of tea.'

Pen reported that the weather with them was good too, 'Usual bloody wind, but the sky is clear.' He gave Colin their coordinates.

I handed over the controls and had a brief talk with Simon – I could hear Pen in the background telling him to make it quick and 'Keep the jokes for later!'

I told Simon that everything had been terrific at the South Pole. That the weather with us was good too and Jason had told us the skies were clear en route.

'Have to forget the tea this time,' he said, 'we're on the move.'

'Don't worry, we've got our own thermos.'

'Hope its Tetley's! [their major sponsor]' he said, 'Bye now, safe flying!' and he was gone.

I handed the phone back to Colin and said, 'Four hours? That's pushing it a bit isn't it?'

'Well, we're 150 miles from Thiel, we've got a ground speed of 130 knots and that'll increase as we get lighter. Then I reckon it will take an hour for refuelling at Thiel and we can expect the tail winds to strengthen as we get further from the Pole.'

Now Colin was being the optimist.

It all sounded so easy, but we still had 400 miles to go and an awful lot can happen in Antarctica in 400 miles. On top of this and to generally confuse us we then had to jump back in time again. We left New Zealand's 8am time on 18 December and tried to adjust our thinking to it being tea-time on the 17th. The 24-hour daylight helped the flexibility when deciding what day it was: you could make it any time you wanted. We were having a very extended 17 December.

The effects of the diamond dust and blowing snow continued to create strange and glorious illusions all the way to Thiel Mountains. At one moment the surface appeared to be sloping upwards to our right, while the next there would be the appearance of a ridge that wasn't even there – and all the while the ever-changing patterns of the sastrugi, a confusing world of ice mirages. But luckily the sunlight gave us good visibility and on that day, importantly, there was always definition of the surface. We were tracking 306 degrees, the visibility remained excellent and the tail winds held. An hour later we were skimming the peaks of the Thiel Mountains and looking for our fuel drums.

Positioning the helicopter close to the drums proved a harder exercise than on the way south. We had already used the drums on the windward side of the dump where the snow was firm – the snow on the lee side lay in drifts and proved to be very soft. I kept testing the helicopter on the surface, but every time we sank in alarmingly. We needed to get close enough for the hose of our fuel pump to reach from drum to helicopter; digging the drums out was not an option because of the time and effort it would take. Then Colin spotted two long planks of wood that had probably been used for rolling the drums from the Twin Otter to the dump. He was able to line them up and we parked right up against the nearest drums, so all we, or rather Colin, had to do was unscrew the tops and put the standpipe of our electric pump into the drum and pump away.

We had thought we might see the team who were skiing and kiting to Patriot from the South Pole, but there was no sign of them. Then we spotted some ski tracks close to where we had landed and realised they must have already gone through, having picked up good tail winds. It was only later, on arrival at Patriot, that we heard they were still well to the south and that those tracks must have been from the year before! It didn't seem possible, but Mike Sharp told us that it was entirely possible: 'Without an obstruction, the little snow that does fall will blow away, and of course, nothing melts.'

I got busy with the cameras and then tried to phone through to Sarah Ferguson, the Duchess of York, who was our expedition patron. I had been calling her regularly throughout our journey for she was always keen to know how we were getting on but I had disappointingly failed to reach her from the South Pole.

I failed again now and only got the answering machine. I then tried to call my mother and was more successful. She sounded very happy and relieved to hear my voice and to know that all was well. She has always been a great supporter, but, like most mothers, she naturally loved, worried and cared about all her children, especially when her younger daughter kept on flying off around the world in helicopters. She said she had seen a picture of us at the South Pole in the *Daily Telegraph*, and I appeared to have bandages on my fingers. She was worried I had frostbite. But I reassured her I was fine, that we were constantly checking for frostbite and that it was only the intense cold and the dry atmosphere that was splitting the tops of all my fingers. I told her that Simon had the same problem but had found that if he taped them up they healed under the tape and so far, since taking the plasters off, he'd had no more splits. I was hoping for the same results. I asked how everything was at home. All was well, she had played 18 holes of golf the previous day and was in the middle of making up beds for a family invasion. Everyone was due to arrive the next day, stay the night then drive on south to somewhere in Bedfordshire for the wedding of my brother William's daughter Sarah.

Listening to my mother talking about life back home brought on all the same feelings of distance and closeness that I had felt talking to the girls the day before. To be able to talk about normal, happy, everyday family things had a lovely and yet surreal quality. I missed them all so much and yet I wouldn't have changed what I was doing for the world. I looked around and tried to describe the scene to my mother. I knew that she, as an artist, could appreciate all the glory that I was seeing. She talked of how proud my father would have been if he were still alive, and I told her how close I often found his presence, especially in the wild and lonely places we visited. We talked a little more and said our goodbyes – 'I'll call again soon,' I said before hanging up. How different the circumstances of that next call were to be.

By the time I got back to Colin he was nearly through refuelling and complaining good naturedly about someone having to do all the work and how, as usual, he was splattered with fuel, despite his disposable rubber gloves. Thankfully we had brought stacks of them. The last thing in all the world you want is to have your fingers frozen onto the cold metal, and neither do you want your warm gloves soaked in fuel, as you never get rid of the smell. Nonetheless, Colin had to keep a close watch for frostbite and had to make frequent stops to warm up his hands, at which point I took a turn. Generally though I continued on camera duty as he refuelled – we both preferred our own tasks. He did a much better job refuelling than me, and I like to think I had the edge with the cameras.

Back in the air again and Colin's time prediction was very accurate. Four hours after talking to Simon and Pen we were 10 miles out from their last coordinates, and then, in the middle distance, a little to the right of our track, we saw a flashing light! It was boy scout Simon waving his small 'survival' mirror, tickled pink that he'd thought of it. We landed and hugged, all of us laughing and asking questions, then sat down with them on their sledges as they got out their bags of chocolate bits and nuts, their daily staple diet when on the move.

'We walk for two hours,' Simon explained, munching away on his goodies, 'Then rest for five minutes, then on again. At lunch time we eat this bag of nuts and chocolates and then on we go, pulling these sledges – that's our mule-like existence.'

Pen continued the programme, 'We rest for a total of one hour and 20 minutes a day,' he said, through desperately cracked and swollen lips. He had developed cold sores almost as soon as they had started their trek and they looked even worse than when we had seen them just four days before – four days? Incredible to think that that was all it had been – so much had happened.

Simon wanted to know if I had any idea how business was! I hadn't a clue. He thought that when I had talked to Chris I might have spoken to our son-in-law, Nick, who works in his company. I told him I hadn't and laughingly said that even if I had I doubt we would have talked business. I told him how anxious the girls and Justin were about him and to please try and phone them. He said he'd talked to Justin and Suze on her birthday but hadn't got through to Chris.

It was wonderful to see Simon and Pen again, but this time there was a poignancy that it would be the last visit and there was no relaxed time, it was a working day. They needed to keep on schedule, putting in another three hours' walking before they could stop and put their tent up, and they were already getting cold from a longer than usual stop. Their polar gear was nothing like as warm as ours; theirs was for strenuous exercise.

It was time to go again. It was always time to go and I was feeling sad and hugging Simon and saying 'Goodbye darling' when Pen leapt forward, grabbed Colin and said, 'Goodbye darling!' And of course we all laughed and it lightened the moment before Simon and Pen once more put on their skis and Colin and I climbed back into our helicopter. As Colin and I lifted into the air I had tears running down my cheeks as I watched them hauling their sledges southwards, slowly getting smaller and smaller.

It was many months later that Simon told me that he too had watched our red helicopter getting smaller and smaller against the deep blue of the sky, and that he'd had a deep sense of dread as we became a mere black speck on the far horizon. He'd tried to shake off the dread but it had returned to haunt him through the night as he lay in his sleeping bag with the tent vibrating to the great winds and in the morning the feeling of foreboding remained.

Half an hour later we were at Patriot Hills where everyone was happy to see us safely back and indeed we were relieved to be there. For all the spiritual beauty of Antarctica, you are constantly aware of the perils and constantly on your guard. To be once more in the comparative safety of that small tented camp and able to relax, free from tension, was a joy, but it also made me aware of how very, very tired I was. I no longer even felt hungry. All I wanted to do was sleep. We had slept little since leaving Patriot for the South Pole and only two hours in the last 24. Despite this, Colin announced he was definitely going to wait up for supper, and persuaded me that I needed something to eat, too, reminding me that we could sleep in the next morning. The glorious thing was that the pressure was off. For the first time in months I felt I could relax – or so I thought. We had no deadlines and it was, unbelievably, still 17 December, giving us seven days to get to the Argentinean's Marambio base on the northern tip of the Antarctic Peninsula for Christmas Eve, and even that wasn't essential.

The camp was quiet. We were the only expedition and while we had been away Geoff Knight and his tricycle, along with some mountaineers, had departed on the Ilyushin back to Punta Arenas. Only Martin Hartley, Simon and Pen's photographer, remained. He had decided to stay on to get more photos. Once again he said he would be taking the next flight out.

I had a comforting, belonging feeling when I walked into the canteen, with all the familiar faces and surroundings; the wooden trestle tables, each with their tin can of cutlery, salt and pepper; and Fran at the far end dishing out generous helpings of shepherd's pie. Once again, those gathered looked more like itinerant travellers than the highly qualified men that they were, all tried and trusted leaders in their respective fields of expertise.

Everyone wanted to know about Matty's boot drop-off, our over-flight of the skiing party and what sort of reception we had received at the South Pole. Karl asked about the state of the drums of fuel at Thiel Mountains, as they still hadn't been in there, and asked if we had used the older fuel as requested. All their drums have a date stamp and so we had to admit that we'd used both old and new, opting for the more accessible ones, the ones we could reach without digging.

After many questions, shepherd's pie and a glass of red wine, we wrapped up warmly and headed for our respective tents, via the loo. We learned rather belatedly that the common and sensible practice was to have a bottle in your tent to avoid the need for middle of the night sorties. On my solo flight around the world in 2000, I had had what was delicately called a 'Lady Jane', an interestingly shaped plastic bottle. I never used it then but I could certainly have done with it there at Patriot Hills. That night the wind was whipping up the surface snow – tents were just visible and yet if you looked heavenward, the skies were blue. My small yellow tent over on the far perimeter of the camp was just visible and most welcome.

When I met Mike at breakfast the next morning, he was holding a strange black rubber bag that looked a bit like a long hot-water bottle with a hose attachment. 'I've just had a shower,' he said. 'Do you want one?' I couldn't think of anything more exquisite and the prospect of washing my hair was pure heaven. Mike explained that the facilities were in the 'expedition' hut, the one where Martin and I had previously worked on our computers. 'There's a stove at the far end with a hot water container similar to this one,' he said, pointing to the one in Fran's kitchen area. 'You can fill this bag up from the stove and then hang the bag off the central beam with this piece of string. There's half of a big blue plastic drum sitting beside the stove – just place that underneath your shower and stand in it...and good luck!' he added as he handed me the bag.

It all sounded fairly straightforward. I asked Mike if he'd seen Colin – he told me he had already finished breakfast and thought he had gone over to check the weather with Jaco, to which I said, 'I hope he's not thinking of leaving today – because I'm not.'

'Quite right, you both need a rest,' Mike said and looking out the window added, 'Besides the weather isn't looking too good.'

I agreed, thanked him for the shower bag and hurried through the cold vestibule where I quickly put on my jacket, retrieved my hat and gloves from one of the wooden pigeon holes and then made my way back across the camp, now half-obscured in blowing snow, to my tent to collect my towel. Then I headed off to the expedition tent and the delicious prospect of a hot shower.

The hut, although warmed by the stove, was not that warm and showers were obviously rather a public affair – anyone could walk in at any time or see through the windows, of which there were several. However the hut wasn't in the centre of camp, and the prospect of a shower far outweighed any brief thoughts of modesty.

Having the shower wasn't quite as simple as I had been led to believe and I quickly began to understand the significance of Mike's 'good luck'. First, I had to fill the bottle without burning my fingers with the near-boiling water. Next I had to get the temperature just right by adding a little cold water from a large tub full of semi-melted snow. I decided to keep the water on the extra hot side as it was bound to cool off quickly. That was the first mistake. The next was filling the bag a little too full as I naturally wanted lots of hot water, but I found I hadn't got the strength to tie it onto the beam. It's not easy holding a bag full of water and trying to tie the string around a high beam. My first efforts were unsuccessful, I couldn't hold the weight of the bag by the two ends of the string and tie a knot. I defy anyone to tie, one-handed, a string above their head while holding the bag with the other. Finally I got a chair from the other end of the hut, stood on it, balanced the bag on my head and somehow managed to tie the string in a neat little bow without falling off the chair. You might think that by the time I had done all this, and placed the big blue container underneath, stripped off and climbed into the container, that the water might have gone cold, but it hadn't, it was too hot. I stood there shivering for a good 10 minutes before the temperature had cooled enough to be able to turn the little plastic tap and let out a small trickle of water, but once the temperature was bearable it was worth all the hassle – my first shower in 10 days.

Still feeling slightly damp, having only had my pocket-sized towel with which to dry myself, I hurriedly dressed and washed my underwear and a T-shirt in the tepid water in the bottom of the bin. Then once more fully rugged up with the sodden towel around my hair and my hood pulled over the top, I ventured outside, first hauling the blue bin out to tip the water down a specific 'waste water' hole, then to hang my clothes out to dry.

As I was making my way back to my tent I met Colin coming from the direction of the canteen. 'I've been looking everywhere for you – where have you been?'

Feeling rather pleased with myself, I told him I'd had a shower.

'Why didn't you tell me we could have showers?' he said. He looked so indignant I had to laugh.

'You weren't around,' I said, 'and anyway I'm telling you now, and there's plenty of water.'

'I'll have one later,' he said, looking somewhat mollified. 'I've been looking for you – Fran said she would show us her freezer.'

Fran's food freezer was an underground network of passages and caves accessed through a wooden trapdoor in the snow some 50 yards from the canteen. For some reason the whole camp was spaced out, although the principal ALE member's personal tents rather sensibly hugged the canteen, and also rather sensibly were big enough to stand up in. Fran arrived, pulling her food sledge, and we headed off to the caverns. I made some remark about the comfortable ALE tent to which Fran laughed and said, 'Well, we're here for months, and I'm telling you, you are getting preferential treatment. All the other expeditions have to sleep in their own tents without box spring mattresses and, more especially, they have, for the most part, to prepare and eat their own rations in the expedition tent.'

I think there were various reasons for us being given preferential treatment at the camp – for which we were very grateful. There were no other expeditions in camp, we were the camp's first ever helicopter, and it was probably thanks to the commitment and huge cost of our expedition that ALE had had the basic funds and confidence to say they would be operating that season.

Colin helped Fran swing the trap door back and, one by one, we went down the flight of wooden steps into the icy depths. Fran flicked a switch – there was even electricity – and light bulbs encased in wire cages dimly lit up frost-covered boxes, bags and cartons. Some sat on shelves carved out of the ice; the rest were piled high from the floor up, and all coated in hoar frost. How Fran could find anything I don't know, but she knew her way around and was soon loading us up with unidentifiable hunks of frozen meat, fish and peas, as well as flour and cheese.

'Most of it has been here for a couple of years,' Fran said as she handed Colin what looked like half a cow, 'and there's enough here for another couple of years, so we're not in any danger of going hungry.'

Laden with assorted frozen goods, we made our way back up the steps to the windswept surface where we dumped everything on her sledge. We passed Mike, Doc Martin and Jason who were helping the two young mechanics to erect the large 'service' tent, where they could carry out maintenance on the snowmobiles, tractor and snowplough in some degree of comfort. To Colin's comment that they were already halfway through their summer and would have to be taking it down almost as soon as they had put it up, Mike gave a rueful laugh: 'You can't get a big tent like this up if it's blowing much above 20 knots. It's no more than 15 knots today, but as you can see, the snow plough is banking up snow on the edges of the tent as fast as possible, the wind is treacherous. If that wind gets a chance to get underneath this lot we won't have a service tent. It'll be at Hercules Inlet, 30 miles away, before you can say knife.'

Glancing at the sledge, Mike asked us if we would like to see the other underground depot holding the Cessna plane. As we made our way over to the next trapdoor Mike told us that 10 years ago the Cessna hangar was on the surface. 'It's been slowly sinking. ANI, the previous company, had planned to dig a slipway to get it out, but it's too deep now. Next year we'll try and get it back on the surface before the ice crushes the walls. We now have the big new tractor and snow plough so it won't be much of a problem.' Mike explained that they had only brought the big snowplough in that season. 'You probably saw the smaller one outside. That's all we've had up until now. You can imagine how long it used to take to clear the runway after each blizzard. This one takes a fraction of the time.'

Colin said he thought that the winds always kept the ice clear.

'Pretty much, but there's always an unevenness and drifting.' Mike explained. 'It's not a problem for the Otters because they don't use the ice runway, but the Ilyushin, as you know, is on wheels and we want to ensure the ice is as clean and flat as possible. It's all about safety.'

The entrance and corridor to the Cessna hangar was way bigger than the food depot and opened into a large room stuffed with some 50 mattresses, in the middle of which, cosily, sat the cheerful little yellow plane.

'Why so many mattresses?' I asked.

Mike laughed: 'There used to be a lot more, I think ANI must have over-ordered. We decided to ship some back to Punta Arenas and so we had them all tied up in piles on the surface, but the Ilyushin was delayed, the winds picked up and the whole lot blew away!' He told us that they would wedge all the mattresses that were above ground back in and around the plane at the end of the season. 'One of the good things with storage out here is that you don't have to worry about damp or airing stuff,' Mike explained. 'Everything stays in excellent nick. At the end of the season we dismantle the tents and bury them on their sites. We cover the vehicles and leave them parked into wind over by the ice runway. We all hope to leave at the beginning of February in the Ilyushin – last to leave are the two Otters.'

It was all a lot of work – the first half of the season was spent getting all the tents up and the second half in getting them all down again. But Mike reminded us that this was their first season of operations and it was something of a miracle that they were there at all – a factor we appreciated only too well. It was a miracle for all of us. They eventually hoped to have several permanent 'above ground' structures but in the meantime they would bring in some wooden crates in which to store things like the snowmobiles. 'That way, the Otters, who are the first to arrive at the beginning of the season, will have immediate transport and somewhere to camp until the tents can be dug up,' he added.

While Mike had been talking, we had made our way back to the surface and clambered out. We thanked him and asked if he'd like a helping hand with tent rigging, but he said they were done for the day: 'The snowplough can finish the job now, banking up the snow.'

We headed off to the helicopter to collect the generator, computer and satellite phone so that I could get on with sending the latest updates and photos. Running the computer off the generator in the expedition tent was a chilly business. The generator had to remain outside the hut otherwise we would have been asphyxiated by the fumes, which meant the electric cable had to be fed through the door making it impossible to completely shut it, and the door was on the windward side. The nice, protected door on the lee side was where the bath and shower operations and stove were. As a result there was a continuous icy blast of snow-laden, freezing air whistling around the edges of the door, and all the time I would be praying that I wouldn't lose satellite connection halfway through attempting to send out information. Only about 50 per cent would make it on the first attempt. I could be 10 minutes into the transfer and then I'd lose the connection and have to start all over again. I had to remind myself to appreciate the magic that we were able to send anything at all.

That was to be the penultimate day of our expedition. It was a reasonably restful one, apart for the short night. I had agreed to do a live radio interview for BBC Radio West at 11pm. Colin generously said he would keep me company until the allotted time. We played computer scrabble. He nearly always won. By 10pm I was dying to go to sleep, but having agreed to the phone-in I felt obliged to honour the commitment. At about 10.45pm I once more checked the details that Tamara had sent through to me and saw to my dismay that the interview had been scheduled for 11pm GMT, not 11pm local time. I'd not only missed the slot but we had stayed up for three hours in vain. 'Don't worry,' Colin said, 'they probably only half-believed they would get through to Antarctica.' I felt bad for keeping him up, too. He was very nice about it, but then he'd won three games of scrabble off me.

CHAPTER SEVEN
Last Day, Patriot Hills — Ronne Ice Shelf

'Man must strive and, in striving must go wrong.'
Goethe

Left: Farewell to Patriot hills

I woke to whiteout conditions. Wonderful, a day of rest! It reminded me of the last time I had woken to a whiteout and been delighted. Simon and I were skiing in Switzerland and Suze had given us the first of the drama series *24*. We'd stayed up until 3am watching the first two DVDs, unable to tear ourselves away. When we woke up the next morning and found we had whiteout conditions, we'd given a whoop of joy and dived back to the television for the rest of the series. The feeling was much the same that day, except I turned over and went back to sleep.

It must have been about an hour later that I finally surfaced, hungry and thinking about breakfast. I had got 'Antarctic-tent-living' down to a fairly fine art by this time. Top priority was either to wear or put all inner layers of clothing inside the sleeping bag with you the night before, that way you had soft and warm gear instead of rigid frozen kit when you clambered out to face the day. It was also a good but uncomfortable idea to accommodate slightly less comfortable items, like assorted batteries, toothpaste and cameras – but I found that if I shoved them down to the very bottom of the bag it worked quite well.

I retrieved all the clothing, got my top half as fully clad as I could, then went through the complicated procedure of getting my contact lenses in, before having to release the rest of me from the warmth of my sleeping bag. Last items on were my boots; I'd put them against the slap-slapping, windy side of the tent by my head, giving me a somewhat tenuous feeling of protection and – more importantly – ensuring that I didn't have frozen boots. The first day at Patriot I'd left the boots in the outer area between the 'zips'. It had not been a nice start to the day.

Fully kitted-out, with toothpaste and toothbrush in my pocket, I unzipped the inner lining, got myself half through it, and then undid the outer lining. At that point it became necessary to turn around somehow and back out feet first uphill, zipping shut all the zips as I went into the all-white world of blowing snow and some 20 knots of wind.

The cloud was not down to the ground and the blowing snow was not thick enough to obliterate the sight of the nearest tents but there was definitely no ground. It is the strangest sensation walking in those conditions as you have no idea where or what you are walking on. I made it without incident and arrived in time for home-baked bread with butter and honey and a big mug of coffee. I joined Karl Z'Berg who was sitting hunched over his cup of coffee, puffing on his first cigarette of the day. Karl, aged 63, is of Swiss descent but emigrated to Canada as a young man. A small, chunky man, his face is lined and weathered from the polar winds and years of sun reflecting off snow. Tufts of snow-white hair protruded from under his habitual navy-blue knitted hat. He looked more like Smiley in the Seven Dwarfs than one of the greatest polar pilots of our time. But when he starts to talk in his quiet, unassuming voice, with his Swiss–Canadian accent, you begin to appreciate the man you are talking to. I wanted to pick his brains about the whole Arctic set-up and flying conditions up north. If anyone could tell me, Karl was the man, with his vast experience of the ice, both in the extreme south and north. He told me about Ken Borek Air, for whom he worked, the only commercial operators in the extreme north and then about fuel availability and many of the dos and don'ts. Some I already knew, many I didn't, but you can never learn enough and it is always best to get a personal angle.

I asked Karl which he thought was the more dangerous of the two polar regions. He sat for a short while chewing his lips and puffing on his cigarette, then said he reckoned the north was the toughest: 'Fewer places to land,' he reasoned. 'It's colder too if you go at the best time, which is the beginning of April; more ice and less fog then.'

I asked him how many times he had been to the North Pole.

He smiled, 'I've lost count, I've been flying there for 40 years; it's my job. We have a fairly good reputation for helping people out. Some people shouldn't be there; they push themselves too far and they just think that if they get into trouble the pilots will get them out.' He sat there shaking his head and went on to say that he didn't really understand the adventurers and didn't understand their desire to plod along day after day.

I said something about all of us being here for much the same reason – the challenge, the adventure – and how he was the smart person. He was actually getting paid for doing it. He chuckled and nodded saying, 'Yeah, maybe.'

I asked Karl whether he had got the latest weather from Jaco and if he thought there was a chance of us getting away that day. Karl reckoned it wasn't looking too good, then lighting another cigarette reminded me, 'But we can only get the actual, and well, then you've got to try and make decisions. We can see cloud cover and get some information on areas of high and low pressure, but there aren't the satellites down here to give any real accurate forecast. Weather, it can change fast in the extreme latitudes; whole areas sock in within minutes with no warning. Visibility and wind, they're our two biggest enemies.'

I wish we had talked more about the weather right there in the Antarctic, more about judgements on safe flying conditions, on when to land, and when to continue and discussed more of his personal experiences. But at that moment, Jason and Martin Hartley joined us and I asked Jason if he had heard from any of the expeditions, most especially Simon and Pen. So the conversation turned to expeditions and I never did talk again to Karl about his views on the Antarctic.

Jason said all the South Pole expeditions had been in touch – Simon and Pen had phoned in, so had Fiona, while Rosie, Matty and the kiters had all sent the Argos message, 'All Well'. The kiters' coordinates showed them to be just to the north of Thiel Mountains: 'If the winds hold good they should be back here within the next couple of days.'

Jason reckoned that if he were ever mad enough to attempt a polar expedition, kiting would be the way he would do it. I wasn't as convinced and said, 'Since flying to and from the Pole and seeing the terrain, I've rather changed my views on that mode of travel. Imagine being strapped into a kite harness over which you can have little control and hurtling along over frozen waves of sastrugi and the odd crevasse, as well as having a sledge with a mind of its own careering along behind.'

'But the plus side is it's downhill all the way,' Martin interrupted with a grin.

Karl, puffing away on his cigarette added something about all of them being mad, and then, smiling at me, chuckled, 'Especially your husband!'

'Oh, by the way,' Jason said, 'Simon said that if you are able to call just before 11am, you should get him before they set off – if not, then try the same time tomorrow.'

We talked some more and Colin came in having had a shower and washed his long johns. He was feeling like a million dollars. He had gone via the radio tent and reported that the latest satellite pictures had come through and were still showing extensive cloud cover, though Jaco thought there might be some improvement later in the day.

Karl then chipped in saying, 'Let's hope it breaks soon. I know you guys would like to be on your way and we need to get the crew back from Bravo. Only having one Twin Otter here in camp is not so good if we have an emergency.'

Towards midday the skies at Patriot began to clear and it was decided that we would wait to see the next set of satellite images, which would come through at 6.30pm. If the route to the north looked good then we would leave after supper. Colin and I were keeping our fingers crossed as it appeared it might be the only possible weather window for some time. There was an extensive area of low pressure heading our way, which would almost certainly bring bad weather and blizzard conditions.

Martin Hartley assured us again that he would be leaving on the next Ilyushin flight to Punta Arenas and offered to take all our video film and CDs of digital photos back to England. He suggested he take some photos of us in and around the camp and helicopter. Suddenly there was a lot to do if we were to leave that day. We took the photos and then I headed off to the expedition tent to burn CDs of all our pics for Martin to take back. I then downloaded and sent final emails and last messages, a task that could have been done in half an hour back in the big cities, but took me nearly three hours in all. Inevitably, the more the hurry, the more times the satellite connection was lost, and always just before completion. However, I did finally get three pictures and about 10 emails out.

Colin in the meantime had packed up the helicopter, collected all my belongings from my tent and was pressuring me to finish so that he could load the generator on board the helicopter. He told me that he and Karl had checked the weather with Jaco and Mike Sharp. The latest satellite images showed a marked improvement with minimal cloud cover along our route, although there were some slightly larger areas of cloud near to Fowler where Karl in the Twin Otter would be caching the fuel. Colin reported, 'Karl says that if there is cloud when he gets to the allocated fuel dump, he'll position it in the nearest clear area and give us the new coordinates.' And then, concerned that I was about to send another email, he said, 'Come on, we've got to get a move on, it's supper time and Karl is ready to go. It's going to be a late night for everyone.' Little did we know just how late – there would be no sleep for anyone that night. I hadn't managed to get through to Simon, or he to me. At supper I asked Jason to say hello from me and that I would try and phone him from Carvajal in the morning.

It was time to go. We coordinated movements with Karl, agreeing on 123.4 radio frequency, then he and his copilot John Lekich headed off to the Twin Otter, which was parked on the skiway to the northeast of the camp. I had given Karl my big video camera so that he could get some air-to-air footage of us and had agreed that if weather prevented us from reaching the dump, Karl would leave the camera bag in a bin bag, half-dug into the snow beside one of the fuel drums. I had also asked Colin to fly the first leg to the Fowler cache – it was officially my turn to fly, but I wanted to be in charge of cameras.

We gave Martin Hartley all the CDs and videos and Colin returned the windproof trousers to Garry Middleton.

Garry tried to persuade him to hold on to them.

Colin reassured him saying, 'Thanks mate, I'll manage. I've got mine waiting at Carvajal. I'm tough, I'm used to flying in open cockpit microlights!'

But even as we were taking the tie-downs off the rotor blades Colin began to regret that decision and he said that his legs were freezing. 'My long johns that I washed this morning, they were still damp, so I've only got my middle layer of trousers on.' I was only just warm enough with all three layers of trousers that I had on. How desperately Colin was to regret the decision not to have accepted the extra layer of trousers.

Everyone had turned out to wave us off. I was both sad and happy to go. Mike, the two Martins and Fran were standing a little distance away, braced against the down-wash from the helicopter and the 30 knot winds cascading off the mountains, and as we lifted into wind and circled the camp we could see Jason outside the radio tent and the engineers down by the DC3 all waving us goodbye. We were airborne at 8.47pm local time (11.47 GMT).

After filming for about five minutes with Karl, I thought we probably had enough footage. Karl's plane then climbed away to a cruising altitude of 6,000 feet above the ground (AGL), while we remained low level at 1,000 feet AGL.

So by choice on this journey, Colin and I stayed low – we did not want to find ourselves flying above solid cloud cover, low on fuel and with nowhere to go; the closer we got to the coast the greater would be the chance of the aircraft icing in cloud as the moisture content would increase.

For the first 50 miles we had the Ellsworth Mountains to the west and a low range of mountains directly ahead of us to the north. Beyond stretched the Ronne Ice Shelf, with the nearest open water 360 miles to the northeast. We had 30 knots of tail wind, giving us a ground speed of 140 knots and the outside air temperature was showing -20°C. If the tail winds held, we estimated meeting the Otter at our fuel depot in a little under three hours. I made the first of the half-hourly calls to Patriot Hills and took photos as we passed over the mountains. It was all systems go and we were in good spirits.

Colin was all for pushing on all the way to Carvajal to take advantage of the weather window which Jaco thought was unlikely to last. I laughed and said that he could justifiably say that all the way to Marambio. 'Let's see how tired we are when we get to Bravo and make a decision then,' I suggested, and added, after a quick bit of mental arithmetic, 'we won't be at Bravo for at least another six hours, and then we have to refuel and fly on for another two hours to Carvajal. It will be breakfast time tomorrow by the time we get there.'

Colin's argument was that the Bravo team would be only too happy to see us on our way, especially as they couldn't pack up camp and head

Instrument flying

I have been asked many times, 'Why didn't you fly at 6,000 AGL, the same as Karl?' The answer is that helicopters don't perform well at altitude. The Otter has better fuel endurance at altitude, but importantly it has an autopilot allowing the plane to fly a straight and level course in zero visibility and is 'instrument rated'. This means the aircraft also has all the necessary avionics to be able to fly the aircraft manually without looking outside the window. Our Bell 407 had no autopilot and is not instrument rated – few single engine helicopters are. This has never been a major factor for either of us. We have both had extensive experience flying on instruments and have 'night ratings', which requires a reliance on instruments rather than visual references outside the helicopter. It is near impossible to fly around the world several times as we have done and not find yourself in cloud from time to time and experience the unpleasant sensation of being on the fringes of disorientation. The cardinal rule is, believe your instruments, don't panic and do everything slowly.

But you don't even need to have cloud to get disorientated. Haze over water with no horizon is a classic example of conditions in which you can experience disorientation. In fact, haze anywhere can do it and some light effects can bring it on too. I've experienced all of them! I remember once, flying over the English Channel when the afternoon sun was behind me, shining through my spinning rotor blades and created a flickering, sparkling light on the instrument panel. I felt disorientation coming on, but knew the signs and went into my standard routine: total concentration on the instruments, backwards and forwards between the attitude indicator, altimeter and the turn and bank indicator with frequent references to the air speed indicator and vertical speed indicator, and then looking down into my lap. I find focusing on something helps me to restore equilibrium. In a helicopter you have 270 degrees of vision, the window area is huge and the instrument panel is surrounded by window, so even if you are focusing on the instruments, you still have movement in your peripheral vision, all playing a part in the disorientation factor.

The longest I have ever had to fly alone relying entirely on instruments was on my solo flight around the world in 2000 when I had to make a 7,000 foot descent through cloud coming in to Magadan on the east coast of Russia. The cloud had slowly built up underneath me during the 470 mile crossing of the Sea of Okhotsk – the scenario I had always dreaded. There was only one way to go and that was down through the cloud. A big advantage then had been that I was able to prepare myself and knew what was ahead. Even so it was an unnerving experience, flying along in the sunshine in a deceptively warm and friendly world, then slowly descending into the all-enveloping cloud, which got darker and darker, until finally breaking out of the cloud just 500 feet above a grey and choppy sea. It is trickier when you find yourself unexpectedly disoriented, as I had only too recently on the way to the South Pole, but the more times you have experienced disorientation, the better equipped you are to cope.

back to Patriot Hills until they knew we had landed safely at Carvajal, which was the limit of their Search and Rescue coverage.

'Well, as I said, let's wait and see.'

Sadly, none of this was to be of any importance. Even as we spoke the cloud cover was slowly building. At 100 miles out from Patriot we had near solid cloud cover, but it was thin and the ground definition remained good with a tantalising strip of blue sky on the far eastern horizon that never seemed to get any closer. We discussed the possibility that we might have to land if conditions worsened. Around 110 miles out the cloud cover had thickened still further. We descended a couple of hundred feet to check that we could still see the ground and were reassured that the visuals were good.

We regained altitude and continued at approximately 700 feet above ground level, the height based on the barometric pressure reading taken at Patriot Hills and the radar altimeter – but neither of these could be relied on for any great degree of accuracy. To have an accurate reading of height above ground level from the barometric reading you need to know the height of the ice above sea level and the current pressure reading in the area. We already knew we would not get an accurate reading from our radar altimeter until we neared the coast and there was moisture in the air once more. With the dry conditions in the interior of Antarctica we could only get a very rough estimate having had readings varying from 50 to 100 feet.

It was essential that we remained in sight of the ground at all times. Karl came on the radio from the Twin Otter. 'How are things with you folks down there?' he asked.

'Pretty lousy,' I replied.

Colin interrupted me saying, 'Tell him that we're continuing.'

I asked Karl how it was looking with him and he reported that the cloud cover was extensive, but that he would carry on for the time being. I told him that we would, too.

I was not feeling good about the situation: everything was marginal with memories of our last difficult landing still all too fresh, and all the time we were being pushed further and further off course to the east because of the poor visibility to the west. Then, with no warning, the strip of blue on the far horizon disappeared. Colin agreed that it was time to land, that it would be foolish to continue and if necessary we would put up the tent and wait for better weather. I thought briefly about how much more comfortable we would have been if we had stayed at Patriot Hills, rather than stuck out on the Ronne Ice Shelf in our small tent.

We started our descent. I read out the altimeter settings while Colin checked his instruments, confident that we would shortly see the ground.

There was no sense of alarm or panic. We were making what we thought was a sensible, cautionary landing. I continued to read out '600, 500, 300, 200 feet, 170, 150' – and then, as I said '140', there was the most God-awful grinding, crashing noise and swirling whiteness. I heard Colin shout something and then all went black.

The local time was 21.35 on 19 December (00.35 GMT 20 December).

CHAPTER EIGHT
Survival

'I'd rather give my life than be afraid to give it.'

Lyndon B Johnson

Left: N44EA one month after the crash

Pain, I remember the pain and the blowing snow that was stinging my face and hands; snow was everywhere and it was desperately cold. The utter disbelief, 'This can't have happened. I'm going to wake up. Everything will be as it was, this is all a mistake.' My senses were in chaos and yet numb and always the searing pain. My left arm was in agony and every little movement hurt. I could feel blood dripping down my face and was aware of the constant whipping wind and snow. I could see the shattered remains of the front of the helicopter through the driving snow, the plexi-glass was all gone and directly in front of me I could see the smashed yellow emergency locator beacon, some small parts of it still clinging to the side of the helicopter. I stared blankly at it, seeing it vividly, yet registering nothing. Off to one side I could see the instrument panel all lop-sided and broken. But I couldn't move. I felt paralysed.

I must have blacked out but for how long I don't know, probably no more than a few minutes. Whether I had been knocked out as well as blacking out with the G-force, I don't know, but the G-force alone was huge. We had hit the ground with a speed of some 50 knots, which was like hitting a brick wall at 60 mph.

The helicopter was upright, but the front appeared to be missing. I was still strapped in my harness, still in my seat, and then I saw Colin in the seat beside me. I could hear him moaning, a low and agonised sound as he levered the shattered remains of the instrument panel off his knees and attempted to climb out of the gaping hole in the front of the helicopter, only to collapse back again saying, 'My back, my back's broken – I'm done, I'm done for.' Then between groans of agony he was telling me to get the satellite phone, to call to Patriot Hills. I looked at my gloveless right hand, almost as though it belonged to someone else. I saw the snowflakes around my fingers and everything was in slow motion. I reached out to the small pocket between our two seats where we kept the satellite phone, and by some miracle the phone was still there. All I had to do was press the recall button. I heard the buzzing tone and then Jason's cheery voice saying, 'Patriot Hills!'

I managed to stutter, 'Jason, we've crashed.' Those were the first words, the first sounds I had uttered since the crash.

Hearing me say that we had crashed was, in Jason's words, so 'Wow' that he said, 'Sorry Jennifer, could you repeat that?'

I stuttered again, 'We've crashed, we've crashed. Jason we've crashed.'

And then Jason's anxious voice was asking, 'Are you hurt?' I told him that Colin's back and insides were bad and that I thought my arm was broken.

Then he was asking, 'Where are you?'

'I don't know,' I replied weakly.

But Colin had already found our hand-held GPS, which we always carried in case the electrics failed. It was on the floor where his feet would have been, jammed up against the crushed front of the helicopter. Colin interrupted me saying, 'No, no – I have the GPS, I'm getting the coordinates, here they are,' and he read them out to me and I relayed them to Jason. What we didn't know then was that they were incorrect. Colin said later that his vision was milky and perhaps he had read them incorrectly, or maybe I hadn't relayed them correctly, whatever the case, they were the wrong coordinates. Jason in the meantime had quickly put his hand over the phone and said just two words to Jaco – 'Get Mike.' He then told me not to leave the helicopter, perhaps he said more, I don't know – the phone went dead and we were once more alone.

I remember Colin then attempting to climb out of the front of the helicopter, where there had once been a window. With enormous effort he somehow managed it. He was standing there, holding on to the shattered and twisted door, half bent over, gasping in pain and repeating, 'I'm done, I'm dead, my back's broken,' and then, through gritted teeth he was saying, 'My gut, my gut's leaking.'

I don't know what I thought, or if I thought at all, perhaps shock precludes all normal thought processes, but I believe my subconscious decided that I was in a worse state than Colin, justified by the fact that he was actually standing up and had been able to get out of the helicopter. The reverse was true. Colin had indeed broken his back, had suffered a crushed lumbar one vertebra, a split liver, had massive internal haemorrhaging and broken a couple of ribs, while I had only dislocated my elbow, broken several ribs and had superficial cuts. But, much to my chagrin, I went fast into deep shock and Colin didn't. He remained totally, obsessively focused in spite of his horrific injuries.

The following account I pieced together later. I have areas of clarity, but much was and still is missing.

When Colin came to, his first reaction was to look over at me, to see if I was still there and in one piece. To his relief I was there, blood was dripping down my face and I was saying, 'My arm, my arm.'

We were 2,000 miles from the nearest hospital. The temperature was -22°C, but with the wind chill factor it was around -50°C, and it was unlikely that anyone would be able to reach us in time to save Colin's life. Having decided his own chances of survival were nil, he calmly accepted the fact and turned his entire focus on trying to save me.

Colin saw me going into complete shock: I just sat there, staring into space, in limbo, ice crystals were everywhere and they were beginning to cover me. I for my part had zero constructive thought, somehow mesmerised by the ever-driving snow, the whiteness, the cold and the snowflakes, which all seemed to be heading for my face, for my eyes. All I could do was stare detachedly as they swirled around my bare hands. Colin said later that I looked as though I was staring at death, my eyes unblinking, unfocused, somewhere far away. He saw that the ice crystals were beginning to cover me. He had to find the tent, he had to get it up. Meanwhile all I could say obsessively was, 'My boot, my boot.' One of my boots was missing.

Neither of us had any of our outer upper garments on. You can't fly a helicopter comfortably wearing big puffy down jackets and of course we didn't have our gloves or hats on, they were in the back of the helicopter. But we had been wearing our large snow boots and one of mine was missing.

Colin was by then on all fours in the snow, the pain was appalling and he could feel his back grating, bone against splintered bone. He knelt up, looking in vain for the boot on my side of the helicopter – and then he saw it some 30 yards away, sitting upright in the snow on his side of the helicopter. He says he thought of the forces that had thrown it so far in that direction and how difficult the boots are to take on and off at the best of times. The impact of the crash must have been huge.

Slowly he crawled over – it took him a long time, willing himself to make every move, knowing that every small movement would bring another searing blast of pain. He had to make many stops as pain overwhelmed him, frequently lying in the snow not knowing whether he was going to make it. Rather bizarrely, but given the nature of the impact of the crash perhaps naturally, he thought my foot was inside the boot. Thankfully it wasn't. He brought it back, knocked the snow out, levered himself up on his knees and put it back on my foot. How he did even that I'll never know.

Patriot Hills 01.05 GMT

Mike was having a cup of tea with Fran in the near empty canteen. The only others present were two of the engineers enjoying an after supper beer at a table near the door. Mike and Fran were at the far end by the kitchen. Mike was facing the door when Jaco came in, urgently beckoning him to come. He quickly got to his feet with a muttered, 'Gotta go.' Fran turned round and saw an anxious Jaco holding the door open for Mike as he hurried out, shutting the door behind him. Fran realised that something was seriously wrong. There were so many things that could go wrong just in the camp alone, things that would be no more than a nuisance, an inconvenience back in the civilised world, but be far more serious in that lonely outpost deep in the interior of Antarctica. But her first thoughts were for the expeditions, of the some 30 mountaineers attempting to summit Mount Vinson, of the foot expeditions – and then there was the helicopter.

Mike grabbed his hat and gloves in the vestibule area while Jaco told him that Jason had received a call from the helicopter outside the scheduled time. As they hurried over to the radio tent Jaco continued, shouting to be heard over the wind: 'Jason was talking to Jennifer when he signalled to me to go and find you. I heard him say, 'Sorry Jennifer, could you repeat that," then he covered the mouthpiece and told me to come and get you, so I didn't hear any more.' Thirty seconds later they arrived back at the radio tent, Mike lifted the door flap and they ducked inside.

Jason, in the meantime had been trying without success to call us back. He swivelled round in his seat and told Mike and Jaco all that he knew. He ended saying, 'I can't get through, I don't know if the problem is with the sat. phone or with Jennifer and Colin, but seconds after Jennifer gave the coordinates, the phone went dead. Jennifer didn't sound too good, but at least we know they are both alive.'

'But for how long?' Mike said. 'It's cold out there and with shock and possible injuries that cold is a killer.' Turning to Jason he said, 'Get on the radio to Karl, we need to get him turned around. Tell him the helicopter is down and give him those coordinates. Keep lines open to Karl and the helicopter.'

'I'm worried about these coordinates,' Jason said.

'I believe Colin was reading them out to Jennifer and she was relaying them to me. But they don't look right, they put them miles off track to the east and only 80 miles from here.'

'Mmmm, well, can't do much about that, right now let's get Karl turned around. You call him, I'll notify Punta Arenas.' He then told Jaco to go and alert everyone in camp.

Punta Arenas 01.12 GMT

With 68 people 'on the ice' it had been a busy day back at the ALE headquarters in Punta Arenas. At 10.15pm Peter McDowell and Rachel Shepherd had finally called it a day. Peter had closed the office door and they had headed into town for a bite to eat and a well-deserved drink at a nearby hotel.

The waiter had just poured them each a glass of Chilean red wine and glasses were raised when Peter's phone rang. The only cell phone he carried outside the office was the one with the emergency number. He hastily put his glass down and reached into his pocket for the phone.

Rachel took a quick sip of her wine and paused, glass in hand, eyebrows raised. Mike gave him the bad news. 'Jeeesus!' Peter exclaimed, 'Well...but...well they're alive?'

'Yes, but the phone went dead. Colin apparently relayed the coordinates to Jennifer and she was giving them to Jason, then we lost contact. But those coordinates don't look right. Jason said she didn't sound too good; don't know what state Colin is in, but at least we know they both survived the crash.'

'You got through to Karl?' Peter asked quickly.

'Jason's talking to him now, he's turning round.'

'How's the weather at Patriot?' Peter wanted to know.

'It's good here, blowing a bit, but plenty of blue sky, cloud to the north though.'

'Any idea what happened?'

'Think it must have been the weather,' Mike said. 'Karl was talking to Jennifer only minutes before they crashed; she said the weather was bad but that they were going to carry on for the present.'

'Strange that, they had some pretty iffy weather going south, seemed to manage that OK.'

'Yeah, well, we all know how fast it can sock in, but those two, they're pretty new to Antarctica and when the light has gone you can't see zilch.'

Peter said that he and Rachel were in town but would get back up to the office immediately. 'I'll be keeping this line open for you. Update me as soon as you know anything. We'll call the Ilyushin crew, let them know that they may be needed for a Medivac [medical air rescue service].' Rachel was already picking up her phone to alert the crew as Peter said goodbye and signed off.

The Ronne Ice Shelf 01.15 GMT

After putting my boot back on Colin braced himself to set off to find some outer clothing for us. Every movement was pure agony. He wanted to find my jacket or a sleeping bag to wrap around me; he knew I wouldn't last long without some sort of protection. And then he heard the beeping of one of our hand-held ELTs, which had self-activated with the impact. He found it lying in the snow beside the helicopter. First he stood it upright in the snow, with the antennae pointing to the sky, then – realising it could be the difference between life and death – to optimise chances of the signal being picked up he knew he needed to try and place it on the roof. It was only his stubborn refusal to accept defeat that enabled him to force himself into a kneeling position and haul himself upwards, high enough to be able to place the ELT on the roof with the antennae pointing upwards to ensure the beams would be picked up by satellite. Thank God he did, because while doing so he saw our D1000 tracker box, one of the few items still in place in the back of the helicopter, and thought to trip the blue emergency switch, which would then send out a 911 text message to previously selected mobile phones. The box would continue transmitting our position every 30 seconds and would continue to do so for the next 36 hours.

We had four ELTs on board, the smashed one in the nose of the helicopter that was a fixed installation with a 121.5 frequency, two 'hand-helds' that transmitted on a 406 frequency – one of which was the one that had self-activated, which Colin had put on the roof of the helicopter – and the D1000 tracker box.

The D1000 was fastened onto the middle partition between the two backward facing seats in the rear, up against the helicopter's bulkhead, and was mercifully untouched when the rotor mast, transmission and gear box smashed forwards and downwards through the roof of the rear cabin, jamming up against the bulkhead behind my head. The remote generator had ended up behind where Colin had been sitting, also jammed up against the bulkhead. But for that bulkhead behind our seats, which few helicopters have, we would both have been decapitated.

Many had been the time when we had cursed that bulkhead, which is similar to the roll bar in a car, as it was difficult to access anything in the back from the cockpit and restricted the view for anyone sitting in the rear, but the Bell 407 was built to military specifications and made of the toughest material. As a result, the composite body of the helicopter, though twisted and dented, was virtually intact and, unbelievably, none of the fuel tanks had ruptured, not even the large auxiliary one positioned on the forward facing rear seats – but that too had been built to the highest Federal Aviation Authority standards and was secured with heavy duty straps.

Colin was once more back on all fours. He looked around for my jacket, but nearer to hand was a torn sleeping bag, its feathers blowing in all directions. He picked it up and dragged it back to where I was sitting, still staring out into space. I hadn't moved. He once more levered himself up and wrapped it around my head and upper body. He said nothing, or rather neither of us recall saying anything but perhaps he did mutter a few words to the effect of, 'Here, wrap this around you.' All I remember was trying with my one good arm to close the chinks where the wind was howling through, which was not made any easier by my uncontrollable shivering. Deep shock alone forces your temperature to drop, but combined with the extreme cold and the wind, my body was rapidly going into hypothermia.

Then Colin was gone. Time passed, how long I don't know. I kept calling his name but there was no reply and I felt terribly alone. In my lucid moments I thought he was dead. He wasn't, but he was close to it. Having clumsily wrapped the sleeping bag around me, he had given in to his pain, slipped down into the snow within feet of where I sat, and faded into unconsciousness.

RAF Kinloss, Scotland 01.35 GMT

Corporal Craig O'Reilly sitting in his office at RAF Kinloss in Scotland read the message that had come through from the Falklands. A British-registered emergency locator beacon had gone off in Antarctica – it was registered to Jennifer Murray. His counterpart in the Falklands confirmed that it appeared to be a genuine signal. He knew there was an American-registered helicopter in Antarctica piloted by me as I had contacted Tom Karsten the captain of HMS *Endurance* some months previously to advise him of our flight. Back then I had hoped they might be operating near King George Island at the northern end of the Antarctic Peninsula and be able to provide Search and Rescue for that area. I was told that unfortunately they would be in the Falklands during December and that they wouldn't be going south until January. He had wished us well.

The operator in the Falklands said the signal indicated a location on the Ronne Ice Shelf. 'Antarctica,' continued the man in the Falklands, 'this is a tough one. There are so few stations out there and we only get a down pass every six hours. We're looking at some 12 hours before we'll have a search area down to a matter of 100 yards. We've alerted the Chilean base at Marsh and the Argentine base at Marambio.'

He then told Corporal O'Reilly they were trying to get in touch with Antarctic Logistics and Expeditions. 'Jennifer will almost certainly be registered with them. They'll be covering Search and Rescue for the pilots. They're the only people handling expeditions in the interior of Antarctica. Don't know if they even know of the alert yet. We'll get back to you as soon as we have any more information.'

Corporal O'Reilly thanked him and said goodbye, then swivelled round in his chair and updated Squadron Leader Nick Phillips and Sergeant Gavin Thornton. 'Isn't she the lady who flew solo around the world the other way a couple of years ago?' asked Squadron Leader Phillips.

Sergeant Thornton replied that he thought she was, then asked, 'Is Jennifer on her own this time?'

'No, I think that guy is with her, the pilot who flew his microlight solo around the world when Jennifer was soloing her helicopter.'

Corporal O'Reilly turned back to his computer and started to type a message, 'I'll get this out on the wire services. Poor sods, don't suppose they stand a chance, not the best place to go down.'

La Jolla, California 01.38 GMT

Jon Gilbert and Jonas Olsen at the BlueSky Network offices in California had received the emergency alert text message from the D1000 tracker box. With murmurs of disbelief they hurried over to turn the office computer back on. Immediately they saw that the helicopter had, in a very short space of time, gone from 120 knots to zero.

'Oh dear Lord, I think this one's for real, I think they've gone down,' Jon said. 'We gotta call the ALE offices right away.'

They had the ALE phone number. Just two days previously Jon had realised that he didn't have a contact number over the Christmas season in case of emergency. He had called Tamara back in London and got Peter McDowell's number at ALE in Punta Arenas. He quickly accessed his contact numbers, found the ALE number and dialled. There was no reply, the office was closed but the answering machine gave an emergency number. He tried that – the line was busy.

'I'll send off an email,' Jon said, then turned to Jacob and urged him to be on his way. 'There's nothing you can do, just get your ass out of here or you'll miss your flight to Palo Alto, I'll call you the moment I get any news.' Jon returned to his desk to send an email to Peter McDowell in Punta Arenas.

Punta Arenas 01.40 GMT

Peter and Rachel raced back up the hill through the still busy streets in the old ALE Land Rover to their recently vacated office. Rachel drove as Peter got out his mobile phone to call Tamara back in London. There was no reply and he quickly sent her a text message. Back at the office, Peter picked up John Gilbert's message on the answer machine, to the effect that both he and Jacob had received 911 calls on their cell phones, that they had checked their computers and seen that we had gone from 120 knots to zero in a very short time. John had left his cell phone number asking Peter to call back.

The moment Peter hung up, the phone rang again and it was Jon Gilbert. Jon repeated his earlier message and added, 'I've got their coordinates.' Peter thankfully jotted them down. He then read them back to Jon. Very briefly he gave him the news from their end saying that I had called in, that we had indeed 'made an unscheduled landing' and that the coordinates I had given appeared incorrect. He thanked Jon and said he'd appreciate it if Jon didn't call back for updates as he needed to keep lines open. They said goodbye.

Immediately Peter called Patriot Hills to give them the D1000 coordinates. Mike Sharp answered, noted down the new coordinates and quickly checked them against the ones I'd given. They were not the same.

The D1000 coordinates were 40 miles away from the ones I had given. The new ones had us over 120 miles north of Patriot and only five degrees off track. Silently Mike passed the slip of paper over to Jason who had his headphones on and was already radioing through to Karl on the Twin Otter's short-wave radio. Karl reported that he was close to the area of the new coordinates and would call back when overhead. He added that the cloud cover was solid and doubted that he would be able to land.

The Ronne Ice Shelf 01.45 GMT

A distant sound penetrated Colin's subconscious state. The pain had returned and yet he was strangely warm. There was the sound again. His face was pressed into the snow. He knew he must move, he had to move, death comes with sleep...and there was that sound again, louder and louder...an engine. And with that knowledge came hope. He need do no more, someone was there, help had arrived. He listened and he waited; he rolled painfully onto his side, to stare upwards to the glorious sound of the engines. The driving snow bit into the exposed areas of his face, but all his focus and concentration was on the approaching machine. The plane was circling overhead – once, twice, three times it circled, then he caught a momentary glimpse of the silver undercarriage as it made a low pass directly over where he lay in the snow, and then the engines grew fainter and fainter. He strained for the returning sound, the plane should be coming in for the approach. He waited and he waited but there was only the sound of his rasping lungs and the howl of the wind. He heard himself moan as the aloneness and pain once more imprisoned him. The hope that had so briefly kindled the possibility of rescue vanished with a quiet sigh.

Colin remembered his last promise to Suze, 'I'll bring her home.' Stubborn determination gripped him; he would not give in. The Twin Otter would be back. They had the position, and yet deep in his heart he knew that even the greatest of pilots cannot land in a blizzard in Antarctica. Once more he accepted that time for him had run out; once more he determined that he would do all he could for me.

Stiffly and painfully Colin pulled himself up on all fours once more. He had to find the tent, he had to get me into it. Only then could he rest. He didn't know how badly I was hurt, but he knew I was in shock and that in my state the body temperature sinks dramatically and that it was imperative to protect me from the cold and wind chill. In his random, painful, crawling search around the helicopter Colin found the life raft and considered, as a last resort, that he could inflate it – it had a canopy and would give us some protection, but he quickly discarded the idea when he realised it would be near impossible to secure it. The moment he pulled the emergency toggle, the raft would inflate and act like a sail, grabbed by the relentless winds, and be gone in a trice.

Debris and the contents of the helicopter were everywhere. Colin saw lightweight items airborne, playthings of the roaring winds, which prised them free and grabbed them, blowing them away and into the ether. Heavier items lay scattered among the snow – cans of oil, the spade, coiled rope, my computer bag, two duffle bags, but not the tent – at first he was angry that he couldn't find it, but quickly fury gave way to desperation. And then he found the other sleeping bag, still in its sack, ripped in two with much of the feathered contents already blown to the heavens. He looped the bag's drawstring around his arm and dragged it along with him as he continued his search. Finally, some 20 yards to the rear of the helicopter, he thought he could see the red, cylindrical shape of what he prayed would prove to be the tent bag. Colin was having difficulty with his vision, everything kept blurring. He wiped a gloved hand across his eyes, blinked repeatedly and for a short while things improved. He crawled closer and to his intense relief found that it was indeed the tent sticking up out of the snow at a 30-degree angle. He dragged himself over and lay hugging it while waiting for the pain to subside enough to nerve himself up for the next demands on his body.

Very carefully Colin pulled the hollow, collapsible aluminium poles with their elastic thread running through out of the bag. Every movement took a long time as he slowly, painfully clicked the three sections together, then reached once more into the bag for the pegs and the tent itself. First, he wrapped the guy ropes around his wrist to make sure the tent didn't blow away. Then to his dismay he realised there was no way the little pegs alone would hold the tent secure in the current blizzard conditions and in such light and powdery snow. He lay down in the snow, once more shutting his eyes. It was all too much. He needed to think, but thought was such an effort.

Patriot Hills 01.48GMT

Karl Z'Berg radioed through to Jason telling him that he'd located the site but conditions were too poor to risk landing the Twin Otter. The light was bad, the cloud was low and he was heavy with fuel. He said he had circled several times and had been able to catch glimpses of the site. He reported it was a heavy impact landing and that he could see no sign of life. It was agreed that he should return to Patriot Hills to offload the fuel he was carrying for the helicopter and the other Twin Otter waiting at Camp Bravo. Jason said that Doc Martin would be ready to return to the site with him. 'Estimate arrival 11.00 local,' Karl reported. They signed off.

Jason took off his headphones and swivelled round to face Mike seated next to him and Jaco on the other side of the tent. Mike had heard most of the conversation. Jason gave them the bad news that Karl had reported a heavy impact crash. Mike told Jason to keep his lines open to Karl and our satellite phone. He called Peter McDowell to update him and advise that it now looked fairly certain a Medivac would be required, if and when the Twin Otter could bring us out, and if we were still alive.

Jason asked Mike if South Pole and Rothera should be alerted. Mike thought for a moment, evaluating the weather, then, because of the rising wind and the possibility of the Ilyushin not being able to land at Patriot, he agreed they should be notified. Jason put through a call to both of them and advised that they had an 'incident'. Both offered assistance.

Patriot Hills had swung into emergency procedures. Everyone in camp checked in with Mike Sharp for duties and went quickly and efficiently to their allocated tasks. Mike told Fraser, the general camp assistant, 'Make sure Karl has enough fuel to mess around a bit. We'll also need to load camping equipment in case the Otter can't land close to the crash site and they are stuck there for some while.'

Next he told one of the DC3 engineers to take a skidoo to the fuel dump over by the ice runway. 'We'll almost certainly need a stretcher sledge, to transport either Colin or Jennifer from the Twin Otter to the medical tent. Bring back the heavy wooden sledge used for moving fuel drums around, collect a mattress from the underground cave and secure it to the sledge with bungee cords.' And so it went on…

Garry Middleton, who had done a first aid course, helped Doc Martin sort out medical equipment to take on the Twin Otter. Next they prepared a medical tent, getting it heated and putting two mattresses end to end so that there would be room to move around all sides. Garry would be accompanying Doc Martin on the flight back to the crash site.

Fran was on 'hot water duty'. First she shovelled up more snow to fill the snow tanks of the two stoves, then lined up all the thermoses she could find, some of which were to go in the Twin Otter. 'Time lost all meaning, hours passed like seconds, seconds seemed like hours, it was crazy,' Jason was to say later.

The Ronne Ice Shelf 01.50 GMT

'Colin, Colin,' I called his name desperately. Time went by and I called again. But the only reply was the sound of the empty wind and a strange whimpering, which I half registered was coming from me. I sat there doing nothing. I felt terribly alone. Colin was gone. Did I think he was dead? He never said that he was going to look for the tent – he said nothing. I believe at some stage I accepted that he was dead. It never entered my head that I might be able to go and look for him, that there was anything I could do – I had no heroic thoughts of being able to help him. I was more seriously hurt than him, wasn't I? Perhaps Jason saying 'Don't leave the helicopter' had influenced me. When Colin told me to get the satellite phone I had done so, but I had no constructive thought of my own and for the most part I felt disembodied. There was no self-pity, this wasn't me, this was someone else and I was looking at myself from the outside.

In a dispassionate way I wondered how long it would be before I lost consciousness. I could no longer feel my hands and feet. I remember illogically thinking that Simon would come and then, more logically, that in desperate situations people concentrated on loved ones. I willed myself to think about my family. 'I'll concentrate on them, I will see them again, I will live, it's just a question of hanging on, enduring the pain,' I repeated over and over to myself. Loving faces flickered through my mind and then I focused on my brand new grand-daughter, Talitha: 'I will live to see her, I will, I will, I will live to see her. I'm not going to die.' This felt like my dying mantra. I never prayed, I don't know why. Perhaps it was all part of the state of shock, I don't know. Instead I filled my mind with thoughts of love, but perhaps that was a sort of prayer. And if ever there was a time for prayer it was then.

London 01.55 GMT

Tamara and her fiancée, Ed, had been to the late showing of Lord of the Rings. They had then driven back to Hampstead for some early morning scrambled eggs and had just finished washing up when Tamara heard her mobile phone ringing in the bedroom next door. Quickly drying her hands she hurried to retrieve her phone saying, 'Gosh, who can be calling now?'

She had a message – she dialled 121. It was the worst message she had ever received.

Tamara logged the hours after that call:

> *I received a call on my mobile phone. 'Tamara, it's Peter McDowell of Antarctic Logistics at 22.00 local time, Punta Arenas. About 35 minutes ago while en route from Patriot Hills heading north we had advice from Jennifer that the helicopter had crashed. Jennifer is alive and speaking to our people. She believes she has a broken arm and Colin has chest injuries. We have an aircraft in the immediate vicinity and should learn more within 15 to 30 minutes. We are up and awake and will be for the rest of the night and are currently putting all of the necessary forward plans into place should they require a Medivac. Please don't call me, I'll call you.'*

Tamara staggered back into the kitchen, white as a sheet, saying, 'Oh my God, oh my God. The worst thing that could possibly have happened has happened – oh no, oh no, oh my God!' she gasped as she collapsed on the kitchen stool, grasping hold of Ed. Poor Ed had no idea what it was all about but he put his arms around her and gently asked what had happened.

Tamara blurted out the news – and then her phone rang again: 'I picked up the message at 1.56am and immediately after received another call from Peter McDowell (2.01am) to say they had flown over the crash site but could not land. I reported I would go straight to the office.'

The Ronne Ice Shelf 01.50 GMT

The plane had gone. The renewed knowledge that no one could reach us left Colin devoid of all hope. Defeat and despair encircled him – and the terrible pain, the only relief from which were the brief moments of oblivion. He said to himself, 'Stop being such a wimp, get on with the job,' and so, stealing himself for the next shafts of pain, he got back up onto his hands and knees. At that moment a particularly fierce gust of wind tore a section of cowling off the top of the helicopter – airborne it slammed into the back of Colin's head, knocking him flat into the snow once more. He lay there, momentarily stunned, confused about what had happened, his face buried in the loose snow. What was he doing? Why was he lying there – he felt the tent peg in his hand…the tent, he was trying to put up the tent, but the tent pegs were too short. He had to find something to secure the tent, he needed an anchor pin. Frustration gave way to anger and he was thinking 'Someone's really got it in for me.'

And it was then that fate took a more kindly turn. With his face still half-buried in the snow, he became aware of a new sound, a thrumming sound, the sound of fabric whipped by the wind. Slowly he looked around, and there, as if by some miracle, only a couple of yards away and sticking up out of the snow, was the Argentine flag that had been given to us. Only the top 12 inches were protruding. The sound was the slap, slapping of the wind catching a small amount of exposed fabric. The pale blue and white colours of the flag were just visible through the blowing snow – crucially, that flag was attached to a lifesaving three feet of sturdy bamboo pole. Colin pressed the tent back down into the snow to make sure it wouldn't blow away; then he crawled over to the flag and the pole and pulled it out of the snow; finally, inch by inch, he made his way back to where the tent lay. He untied the flag, slipped the sheath off the pole and released the fabric to the wind, free to blow where it willed, blessing the day that Colonel Rita of the Argentine Air Force had presented it to us all those weeks ago on our arrival in Buenos Aries.

Colin was then able to secure the tent; he had his anchor pin. He scooped snow around the windward edges before swinging the hooped aluminium poles upright. It did cross his mind, as he finally secured the tent, how tempers had flared at the South Pole over how to put up a tent and he thought with a wry inward smile that he hadn't done such a bad job on his own, and with a broken back.

Meanwhile, I think I must have drifted in and out of consciousness for I never heard the Twin Otter circling overhead. I had little recollection of time; time was suspended and yet endless. My system had shut down. Only disbelief and pain were there, interspersed with a few clear moments when I strangely remember looking down on myself, dispassionately regarding the situation, but even those moments were limited. I still had no constructive thoughts of seeing whether I could move or what I could do to help save the two of us. I believe most of my thoughts continued to be of my family, punctuated only by an awareness of pain, terrible loneliness and my constant calling 'Colin, Colin'...who never came.

And then, from beyond the cold black cocoon of the sleeping bag, unbelievably, Colin was there and he was saying, 'I've got the tent up, can you walk?' I was no longer alone, and the words on this page could never describe the emotions I felt. To hear a voice, Colin's voice, when I thought he was dead and there was no living soul within hundreds of miles was an indescribable feeling.

He asked me if I could move. Could I walk? I tried moving my legs – I could. I said, 'Yes,' nothing else, just 'yes'.

Colin was relieved to hear me say that. He'd been thinking of the impossibility of being able to take my weight and wondered whether he could drag me to the tent. I saw the base of the helicopter where my door should have been and thought how strange it was that the snow was nearly level with the opening. I don't remember undoing my safety harness; maybe Colin undid it.

I do remember saying, 'Don't touch my arm, don't touch my arm,' as I felt his hand guiding me up and out of the helicopter. With the sleeping bag still around my head and shoulders, my field of vision was limited to the small area by my feet. I never saw the destruction of the helicopter or the scattered debris. All I saw were my snow boots, moving across and through the snow, boots that didn't belong to me. I briefly glimpsed the bright green shape of the insulated bag in which I kept camera gear – the bag had been a freebie from my local friendly camera shop some years previously – and then once more it was only my boots and the snow as Colin guided me slowly towards the tent. We didn't speak. All our focus was on reaching the tent. And then I was on all fours crawling inside and Colin was telling me to get inside the sleeping bag and how difficult it was with my useless arm and my whole body shaking uncontrollably with the cold.

After getting me in the tent, Colin knew he had more journeys to make back to the helicopter before he could rest. He had to get the generator, the satellite phone, the stove and the can of fuel. He knew where everything was; he had seen them during his search for the tent. The generator was wedged up against the bulkhead in the helicopter, and the small fuel can for the stove was lying in the snow not far from where Colin had been sitting. On his way to get the generator Colin found several packets of the 'expedition food' half-covered in the snow and he stuffed them inside his jacket. He needed to charge the satellite phone. The phone should have been charging in flight, but the connector point was delicate and several times the charge hadn't functioned because we hadn't pushed it in securely enough; unfortunately that had proved to be the case during the flight from Patriot Hills.

Colin crawled back to the helicopter and hauled himself up into a standing position beside the only window left intact in the helicopter, the one in front of the generator. The door was immovable. Plexi-glass is immensely strong and under normal circumstances it would be near impossible for a reasonably strong man to break it by punching it out. Broken back and all, Colin gave it one great shattering punch, lifted all 17 kilos of generator out and collapsed on the ground – he had totally lost all feeling in his legs. For several minutes he lay in the snow, telling himself that soon he could rest, soon it would all be over.

He rolled the generator onto its side, that way it would slide more easily through the snow, and he hoped that it would not flood the engine. Digging his elbows into the snow Colin managed to pull himself forward a few feet at a time, his legs dragging uselessly behind him. He then reached back with his left hand and hauled the generator forward. Slowly, slowly, inch by agonising inch he made his way back to the tent.

He made two more journeys, one for the satellite phone and stove, the other for the fuel. On the last journey he found some more packets of expedition food and another packet with my contact lenses in – he stuffed them all into his jacket. Colin wanted everything to be in place for me once he was gone. I don't know why he thought I was going to last longer than him, for I was still behaving as though I was more seriously injured. But it was merely a hope that my injuries were not as serious as his. We had spoken so little.

Colin believed that the only way for me to survive was to try and warm me up, to give me a hot drink, to get something warm inside me. He could see that I was desperately cold, even though I had more clothes on than he did and I was in a sleeping bag. All he wanted to do was crawl inside the tent and collapse, but he was hell bent on giving me that drink. He had the cooker bag with its small accompanying billycan. He got it out, packed it full of snow, then shoved it, the stove and the fuel can inside the tent.

After that, all Colin had left to do outside the tent was to start up the generator. He lay down on his side and, clenching his teeth in anticipation of the pain, he gave a sharp tug to the generator cord to start it up – it must have been hell, but mercifully it coughed into life with the very first pull. He then dragged himself half into the tent, plugged in the satellite phone and pressed the recall button. Jason answered immediately – infinitely relieved to hear from Colin, although he had difficulty making out what he was saying as Colin's normally quiet voice was even quieter. The noise of the wind on the tent walls drowned out much of what he was saying, but at least Jason knew we were still alive and understood Colin had got the tent up. He also thought Colin was telling him his back was broken and we were very cold.

Jason explained that Karl had circled the site, but had been unable to land and was on his way back to Patriot: 'The Otter will be back here in half an hour. They'll be on the ground for another half an hour, refuelling and unloading your fuel, then they will return with the doctor and make another attempt to land. They should be overhead in two and a half hours.'

Colin's first reaction on hearing that the plane would be returning was a surge of hope, but then, knowing the weather conditions, his habitual pessimism and calm reasoning convinced him that there was no way anyone could land a plane in the prevailing conditions – he didn't dare to hope. He must have told me what Jason said, as all my conscious thought was on the fact that the Otter was coming and would be with us in two and a half hours. All we had to do was wait.

Colin got the stove going and melted the snow; feathers from his torn jacket and my torn sleeping bag were blowing all over the place and many had fallen into the water. He asked me if I minded the feathers and apparently I said I didn't. The strange thing is, I have absolutely no recollection of any of this, neither the feathers nor the drink, which I gulped down scalding hot, feathers and all.

Having given me the drink, Colin placed the satellite phone beside me and then lay down. He had done all he could and with that realisation the adrenalin, the iron will that had kept his body in motion over the last hours, slipped away, his legs and his torso paralysed. His legs were still outside the tent and he said later that if you had paid him a million pounds he couldn't have hauled himself further inside the tent. He only had on the one pair of medium-weight trousers. Now for the first time he realised how cold his feet were, but the rest of Colin felt warm, too warm, as fever was slowly engulfing him.

The only further movement he made was to raise his arm and pump the small stove from time to time to ensure the flow of fuel. Even that small chore was agonising and an immense effort as he slowly lost the power of all movement.

I was lying on the right-hand side of the tent on my right side, protecting my bad left arm. Colin's head was somewhere near my waist. I could feel his forehead – it was burning hot. Time crept by. Occasionally one of us would say, 'Are you OK?' and the other would reply that they were OK. The only sound was of the wind, beating against the walls of the tent and the hiss of the stove.

London, Tamara's Log 02.43 GMT

> *Peter called to say the crash site is known but they had still been unable to land. Colin was speaking to them on half-hour updates. He had been able to erect a tent but is talking of back and stomach pains. Jennifer has a broken arm and facial abrasions. They are not certain of her consciousness – she is reported to be very cold. The light conditions in the area are very poor – low light and low cloud. In an hour they will try to go to the site again. I agreed that I would inform the insurance company.*

What Tamara was not aware of was that news of the crash had gone out on the wire services – family and friends were already picking up news that a helicopter had gone down in Antarctica.

After receiving the text message and phone call from Peter McDowell, Tamara and Ed jumped in their car and headed out across the deserted streets of London to my home in South Kensington where Tamara and I have our office. It was 2.30am. On arrival Tamara quickly got her computer up and running and felt slightly more in control with two telephone lines – three counting her mobile – and the computer for emails. First, she phoned Punta Arenas to let them know she was in the office and available. Next she made a wake-up call to Airika Coutu, our insurance broker in the USA. And then she sat there, wondering who she should be contacting. The dilemma was that we had never discussed who she should contact first in a situation like this. She felt helpless: everyone was sleeping. What could she do? She still did not know that all the wire services had the news. She decided to wait and hope that she would get some positive news before having to call our families.

Patriot Hills 02.45 GMT

At 23.50 local time, the Twin Otter touched down at Patriot Hills. Everyone knew what to do. The drums of fuel were quickly offloaded and the Twin Otter's tanks filled. Karl repeated to Mike what he had said to Jason over the radio, that he could see no sign of life, how bad the conditions were at the crash site and that debris was scattered over a wide area. 'Having the definition of the helicopter and all the scattered pieces, I can calculate pretty much where the ground is even though it's impossible to see it. The risk of landing with all that fuel on board in those conditions was too great. Now we need the weather to ease off a little and hope those two can hold out till we get there,' he said.

Mike nodded his head and pointed to the kit being loaded into the Twin Otter: 'Got your camping gear and provisions. Let's hope though it doesn't come to a camping situation.'

In less than half an hour the Twin Otter was once again airborne with Karl Z'Berg and John Lekitch at the controls. Doc Martin and Garry Middleton were seated in the back quietly discussing events and what they might find, if and when they were able to land.

The Ronne Ice Shelf 04.15 GMT

The remembered sensations were a jumble of the intense cold, the ice beneath my body, the pain, the waiting and desperate hoping that the Twin Otter would be able to land – and then, for the first time I believe, I felt a real concern for Colin when he said weakly, 'I'm fading.'

Perhaps it was a selfish concern, the fear of being left alone, but I remember thinking, 'You can't do this to me.' Perhaps I was coming out of the deeper level of shock and yet I said nothing. I think we were listening, listening for the sound of the return of the Otter. I drifted in and out of awareness. There were gaps, and yet the pain was ever constant, the pain, the cold, and the total disbelief. But I was no longer 'outside myself'. I was me and I was hurting and just holding on, suspended, waiting, waiting – no thought beyond the pain. I listened to the incessant noise of the wildly slapping four walls of our tent and thought 'I can't cope with this pain', never appreciating how much worse Colin's condition was than mine. I had no room for his pain, but I needed him. God, how I needed him, he couldn't leave me all alone, and when he said, 'I'm fading', my whole being cried 'no, no you cannot go'. All selfish thoughts. The waiting seemed to go on for ever.

And then, in the distance, at first almost indistinguishable from the wind, we heard the drone of the Twin Otter's engines and in a rasping whisper Colin said, 'They've come.'

Thank God he was still hanging in there.

Karl was overhead and for the first time I was offering up a prayer, a prayer that he would be able to land. I remember clearly saying to myself, 'Dear God, please let them be able to land, please let them be able to land safely.' It was a moment of great clarity, thinking these men were risking their lives to save us. The Twin Otter circled and circled, neither of us spoke.

Inside the plane Karl was on the radio to Jason reporting that they were overhead; he could make out the crash site and the helicopter. 'No sign of life, but expect they are both inside the tent.'

The plane continued to circle. Karl next reported to Jason, 'I'm going in.' He then glanced over at John Lekitch and said he'd make one low pass, just skimming the snow to assess the sastrugi. Visibility was still appalling.

The sound of the engines grew louder and louder, only to once more fade away, we could no longer hear them, we listened – only the wind. I said, 'They've gone away.' Colin said nothing. There was nothing to say, we were alone again. Colin was fading. I was engulfed by loneliness, pain and despair, the flat despair that comes after brief hope has gone, the empty knowledge and acceptance that it was not to be, a numbing blankness, my mind emptied. It was over.

And then, in that great emptiness we heard voices and the crunch of footsteps – the most beautiful sound I have ever heard. Karl Z'Berg was talking to Doc Martin, saying, 'I'm sorry, I can't go in there.'

And then Doc Martin must have been in the entrance of the tent and he was asking; 'Who should I look at first?'

I said, 'Colin' and Colin said 'Jennifer'.

But Colin was the one by the entrance, so he looked at Colin first. Doc Martin quickly assessed us and got on the satellite phone to Patriot Hills. He told Mike that we would almost certainly need a Medivac, but that he wouldn't be able to do a full appraisal until he got us back to Patriot Hills. He signed off and once more turned his attention to us. He said, 'I'm afraid I will have to cut the tent open to get the stretcher in.' He had quickly assessed that Colin's condition was critical and mine less so. They needed to get him into the Twin Otter as quickly as possible and to stabilise him before returning for me. I heard Colin's half-stifled moans of pain as they tried to move him as gently as possible onto the stretcher. Doc Martin said they would be back as fast as they could.

Having cut the tent open and extinguished our stove, it became desperately cold. The snow was once more blowing all around me and I was aware of my whole body shaking. I could hear myself whimpering and could do nothing to stop it. But help had arrived; we were no longer on our own. I was in greater pain and colder than I had ever been in all my life, but hope had returned, I just had to hang on a little longer.

Doc Martin was back and he asked me if I could walk. I said I could. I tried to sit up – and failed. Every movement hurt and I seemed to have no strength, or maybe it was stiffness from the cold. They put me on a stretcher, too, and then I was inside the plane with sleeping bags being piled on top of me and Doc Martin was giving me a blissful shot of morphine.

The engines revved, the plane moved faster and faster over the snow, I could feel it getting lighter and lighter on its skis and then we were airborne. My last thought before the morphine took over was of overwhelming relief at being in safe hands and safely off the ground.

London 04.30 GMT

Peter McDowell called from Punta Arenas to tell Tamara that they had landed a doctor at the site and that he would update her on our conditions as soon as possible.

In Thailand it was 11.30 in the morning. Tamara called Phuket. My son-in-law Nick answered the phone. Tamara's opening words were, 'Do you have Suze and Chris with you?' Nick, a little puzzled, said that they were both there. Then she said, 'Please don't worry, Jennifer and Colin are alive, but the helicopter has crashed!' Tamara then updated him on all she knew and asked if they would tell my son Justin in Korea and my mother back in England. She felt it would come better from them. Nick said he wouldn't wake my mother until later.

Tamara's journal entry read:

> *Peter called to say that both Jennifer and Colin were stable, however, Colin has potentially life-threatening injuries consistent with a high impact. Given the nature of a high impact crash the internal injuries are of concern and he cannot be fully assessed on site. They will be flown to Patriot Hills and then on to Punta Arenas as soon as weather permits. They are in a plane with the doctor and expected to reach Patriot Hills in an hour.*
>
> *I called Colin's friend Henry Cressey to ask if he was the most appropriate person to call Colin's wife. He and Michael Starkey, another good friend of Colin and Michelle's, were going to see her in person.*
>
> *I spoke to Nick Powell in Thailand, Jennifer's son-in-law, who would tell her 3 children. I asked Nick to also call Jennifer's mother, perhaps via her brother. Simon's 'Ground Support' person in London, Simon Harris, rang to say he had had news of the crash. Simon Harris sent a text message to Pen asking him to call in first thing – it is thought that Pen should break the news to Simon.*

It wasn't until 8am that Tamara was aware that anyone else knew about our crash. Her mother called her saying that she had heard it on BBC Radio 4. The World Service had been announcing it since 01.50 GMT.

Tamara was shaking as she hung up the phone – nothing in her life had prepared her for having to handle the events of the last few hours.

Patriot Hills 06.30 GMT

The Twin Otter landed safely back at Patriot Hills where weather conditions were still good although the wind was strengthening. Colin and I were transferred to the medical tent.

I have no recollection of landing, no doubt thanks to the morphine, but as it began to wear off I started to register my surroundings and my discomfort. I was lying on a mattress in the medical tent with Fran sitting on a chair beside me. I think I was surprised to see her up. She said that no one had slept – that they would not be going to bed until we were on our way.

She had been asked to look after me. Many months later she told me how helpless she felt, not knowing how best to comfort me. She said that I appeared stunned and in a vacuum. But her mere presence was a comfort – I remember her going out of the tent at one point and not wanting her to go and how relieved I felt when she returned.

I tried to sit up and with Fran's help I managed it. I sat huddled on the edge of my mattress, wrapped in several sleeping bags, for although there was a small heater in the tent, the temperature was near freezing. For a while I felt more comfortable. I could see Colin lying, heavily sedated, a few feet away. He had an oxygen mask on and was on a saline drip. Doc Martin was hovering on one side of him and Garry on the other. 'How is he?' I asked.

'He's doing OK, but the sooner we can get him to a hospital the better. There's no way I can check out the full extent of his injuries, they're all internal,' he said as he once more bent down over Colin.

I continued to sit there, taking in the scene. I guess I was slowly emerging from my near catatonic state. I understood that Colin was in worse shape than I was, that his situation was critical. I didn't particularly analyse my own condition, I only knew I hurt and that we were alive and our dreams were shattered. I didn't or couldn't or refused to think too far beyond that, it was all so unacceptable and incomprehensible.

Mike Sharp came in, along with the usual blast of freezing air and snow. He took off his gloves and gave me a quick smile, 'Good to see you sitting up. Managing OK?'

I nodded and said, 'Yes, yes thanks.'

Mike turned to Doc Martin and asked how Colin was doing. The Doc sat back on his heels and reported that he appeared to be reasonably stable. 'What's the latest with the Ilyushin?' he asked.

Mike said it had taken off from Punta Arenas and we could expect it in about four hours and that they had 'Plan A', 'B' and 'C' in place. Everything was dependent on the winds and whether or not the Ilyushin would be able to land at Patriot Hills. Plan A was for a landing at Patriot Hills, but if the wind increased much more it would have to turn around and return to Punta Arenas.

Turning to me he explained, 'Under normal flight conditions with winds already gusting up to 27 knots, the Ilyushin wouldn't have taken off from Punta Arenas, but this is a Medivac flight – they have taken off all cargo and have kept the plane as light as possible, that will help in a high cross-wind landing.' He continued, 'Plan B is that if the Ilyushin can't land here we'll try and fly you to the South Pole in the Otter. If it's 'no fly' weather to the South Pole, well then we'll attempt Plan C to get you to Rothera.'

Plans B and C didn't sound great. It would be more a question of days rather than hours before we could hope to be back in civilisation and in a hospital. With mixed emotions I prayed the Ilyushin would be able to land, desperately hoping they would be able to, but equally anxious that they shouldn't take too big a risk on our account. 'What do you think the chances are of the plane landing here?' I asked.

'Well,' Mike said, giving a small smile of encouragement, 'they're Russian,' which said it all. Russians are good and brave pilots, conditioned to unorthodox flying, and they fly old machines into old airfields with few of the modern safety features we are used to in the west.

South Pole's medical facilities are better than at Patriot Hills, mostly because they are in a room rather than a tent. Also their C130 planes are able to operate more frequently as the winds are seldom severe at the earth's pivotal point – the average wind speed is 12 mph and the highest wind ever recorded was 55 mph back in 1989. Rothera is also able to operate more frequently. They have a Dash 7 aircraft that comes in from the Falklands but had advised Mike that they didn't have a schedule with the aircraft until morning and would be unable to contact their pilots before daybreak.

My mind was functioning slowly. I was in a world encompassed by shock and pain and I was thinking about the wind and the Russians when I realised Mike was talking to me again. 'We haven't been able to get through to Simon and Pen yet, they don't know about the crash. As you know, they only turn their sat. phone on for a short spell around their breakfast time. I've sent Pen a text message asking him to call in as soon as possible, but it's unlikely he will pick it up for some hours. They'll be sound asleep now. Hopefully you will be well on your way to Punta Arenas by the time they get the news.'

Simon, I would have given anything to have had him there with me. He was so close and yet he might as well have been on the moon. I began to worry that he would halt his expedition on our account and I told Mike that he must tell him to continue, that we were in good hands and that it would be terrible to have both journeys end: 'Please, please tell him that I insist they go on, it will make it all doubly sad if they too don't finish.'

He told me not to worry and said he would say just that, agreeing there was little Simon could do. He then asked if I had had a cup of tea and would I like one? Tea sounded wonderful. Fran volunteered to get it – perhaps that was when she went out. Shortly afterwards Doc Martin gave me another shot of morphine.

Cheshire, UK 07.00 GMT

My niece, Fiona Fontes was already dressed. There was much to do with the family wedding later that day. She had her eleven- and nine-year-old daughters, Sophie and Flora, to organise and give breakfast to before heading up to my mother's house for a 10am departure and the two-hour drive south for the wedding. Having woken the girls Fiona went into the kitchen, filled the kettle and turned on the radio to hear the news presenter reporting that a helicopter had gone down in Antarctica and that the signal had come from a British registered emergency location beacon.

With a feeling of utter disbelief she rushed upstairs and told the girls the appalling news, urging them to dress as fast as possible. She didn't want to break the news to everyone at my mother's house over the phone; she wanted to tell my sister (her mother), first. They all piled into the car and drove the short 500 yards to my mother's house.

My sister Gillian was laying the table for breakfast when Fiona and the girls burst in with the news. Gillian let out a little cry and promptly sat down on a chair giving little cries of 'Oh no, no, no!' Her son and daughter in law, John and Sasha came in. They too were told. Everyone sat in stunned, disbelieving silence.

They were all undecided whether to go and wake my mother, arguing that if they delayed, maybe there would be more news, maybe, just maybe we were alive? John shook his head and said that the chances of anyone surviving a crash in Antarctica couldn't be good. Then Gillian said that Mum might turn on her radio and that it would be better coming from them.

My mother was told. They all sat in the kitchen, holding hands, praying and making cups of tea. All thoughts of preparing for the wedding were on hold. At 9am they heard on the radio that we were alive! Ten minutes later Suze phoned them from Thailand.

Patriot Hills 11.00 GMT

Time passed. The morphine helped. Mike came in and asked if there was anyone I would like to call on his satellite phone. Until he said that I hadn't thought beyond speaking to Simon. I had no thought of a world beyond Antarctica, that people might know we had gone down, that loved ones would be worried. Whose phone number did I know? I thought of my daughters in Thailand and my son in Korea. I didn't know any of their numbers off by heart. I would call my mother.

I never thought about whether they knew or didn't know. Clumsily I pressed in the numbers, I got the answering machine. My brother Peter had left a message saying, 'If anyone is calling about Jennifer and Colin, they are alive!' How strange, how familiar. I had a momentary flash of my late father's study, with the telephone/fax machine sitting on top of the filing cabinet beside his cluttered desk, where nothing much had changed in the four short years since he had passed away. I left a brief message, probably rather garbled, and punched the 'end' button. I sat there, I was so tired, it was all too much effort and every little movement brought pain. I didn't want to think. In thinking I would have to face the truth that the helicopter was gone, that our dreams had ended. I needed to block it out. I wasn't even particularly thinking, 'Thank God we are alive.'

I thought I'd try just once more, maybe they didn't want to speak to anyone but maybe by now they had picked up my message. I pressed in the number again, it was the answering machine again, but Peter was giving his mobile phone number, which I had missed the first time. Perhaps I had missed it due to the noise of the fabric of the tent being whipped by the wind making it very difficult to hear anything. Or maybe I had hung up too soon. I read out the numbers and Mike Sharp scribbled them down.

I called his mobile number, Peter answered immediately with whoops of incredulous joy. We talked for a couple of minutes; they were on their way to the wedding and my mother was in another car. More numbers were written down, and then I was talking to her. Mum was wonderful, so full of love and overwhelming relief and so very, very happy to hear my voice and the reassurance that we were in good hands and soon to be on our way to Punta Arenas. I didn't tell her how critical Colin's condition was or that there was a possibility the Ilyushin might not be able to land. I told her I would call again as soon as I could.

For a few beautiful minutes I was with them. I was home, back in England and the green English countryside. I shut my eyes and listened to the sound of my mother's voice, to the love and relief and concern…and then they were gone and I was sitting in a tent in the middle of Antarctica and Colin was lying immobile at the other end of the tent with tubes and oxygen – and we should have been at Carvajal.

All Colin ever saw there was the roof of the tent as his neck was in the brace, but he tells me he heard everything. I gave Mike back his phone and he headed off to check in at the radio tent on the wind status and Ilyushin. The waiting continued and the hours passed.

Later, Martin Hartley poked his head in to say that the Ilyushin was 10 minutes out and was going to attempt a landing. The winds had strengthened and our tent looked as though it was about to take off, and it sounded as though an express train were about to burst through it. I had to shout to make myself heard. Martin said he thought it was gusting up to 65 knots. He said that Jason was talking to Rachit Saitov, the Ilyushin captain, and that Rachit had said he would make a low pass, that he might attempt a landing first time, but more likely he would go around once. Then if he thought it possible, then he would come in again and attempt to land. Martin hurried off to watch.

Doc Martin remained with us all the time. He appeared to be constantly checking on Colin. I sat on the edge of my mattress, wrapped in my sleeping bag, listening for the plane, but heard nothing above the sound of the wind and then, after what seemed an eternity, Mike came hurrying in with the glorious words that the Ilyushin had landed safely! 'They went around once,' he said, 'then came in and made a near perfect touch-down with 37 knots of crosswind.' Insane bravery, but such wonderful news. Mike added that two doctors and a nurse had come in on the flight from the Punta Arenas Clinic and that they would be looking after us on the flight back. Doc Martin would not be coming with us. Mike also said that Martin Hartley would be on board the flight. Having one familiar face with us was a real comfort.

A short while later I was helped out and onto the back of a snowmobile and we started the long, slow drive to the Ilyushin. which was parked half a mile away beside the ice runway. It took a long time as the snowmobile towing the wooden sledge with Colin on was driving at about two miles an hour, taking infinite care of Colin's neck and back. I have a vivid picture of him lying there, wrapped in several sleeping bags with a doctor poised at either end of his sledge, the one at the front holding the saline drip while the snowmobile inched across the hard-packed snow to the waiting Ilyushin.

The interior of the Ilyushin was a vast, empty, windowless cavern with metal bucket seats lining the two walls, where random assorted items were strapped. It looked more like the inside of an old warehouse than an operative plane. Two mattresses had been placed in the middle of the floor for Colin and me to lie on.

Many hands gently lifted Colin's stretcher off the sledge and carried him up the ramp, placing him on the forward mattress behind a large pile of goods secured under netting. I was told it was all emergency survival gear in the event of an unscheduled landing. I think Martin Hartley and Fran gave me a helping hand. People were saying goodbye. I think I thanked them. They walked away, back down the ramp. Slowly the great ramp closed and with it a last fleeting glimpse of sun on dazzling snow.

And so we left Patriot Hills and Antarctica in the belly of the Ilyushin.

Later

At the clinic in Punta Arenas, the doctors assessed Colin's situation and deemed it too dangerous to Medivac him elsewhere. Happily Dr Rebolledo, one of Chile's leading neurosurgeons, has his practice in Punta Arenas and patients from the capital city, Santiago, often fly south to be operated on by him.

Colin had immediate keyhole surgery on his ruptured insides. Two days later and when his condition had stabilised, he underwent a seven-and-a-half-hour operation on his back. Dr Rebolledo said it was a miracle not only that he had survived but that he was not paralysed. He believed the intense cold must have saved him, slowing down all his systems. He had to delicately remove slithers of Colin's crushed vertebra that were sticking into his spinal cord. He then constructed a metal framework around the shattered vertebra to support his back.

I was able to see Colin shortly after the operation and felt reassured that he was on the road to recovery. He sounded much like his old self, with lots of indignant complaints about the cleanliness of the hospital that he had been transferred to for the operation, and he appeared to be more concerned about his swollen, off-centre nose than his back! Having lain on his stomach for seven hours with his nose pressed into the operating bed, it was not its normal self and he was convinced they had broken it. Happily it wasn't broken and it regained its natural central position within a couple of days. The doctors told Colin he would have to spend two months in the hospital; he walked, or rather hobbled, out after two weeks, insisting that we should find another helicopter immediately so that we could finish the journey.

I was operated on for my dislocated elbow. The relief was overwhelming, although my whole body felt bruised and battered and my ribs and the cast on my arm made life difficult, and sleep more so, for some time.

We were far from home in a country where neither of us spoke the language and although we received a great deal of support from many people, it was a grey and difficult time. Gonzalo Campos, who had handled many of our logistics for Antarctica, came in every day, as did the acting British Consul John Rees. Martin Hartley dropped in several times before catching his flight back to England, and Peter McDowell and Rachel came by when they were able. I was suffering from post-traumatic stress, but I needed to be strong for Colin. After all I was the 'well' one. However, I felt shaky at the prospect of leaving the hospital and fending for myself in an alien town, so when my daughters, Suze and Chris, phoned me from Thailand and said that my son Justin was on his way south from Seoul to be with me for a few days after I left hospital, I wept.

I needed family and a shoulder to lean on and I wished Michelle could come and be with Colin. But we both knew that that was an impossibility as there was no way she could leave their young son Peter, who needed 24-hour care, and besides it was only a few days to Christmas and Colin, typically Colin, lay there saying, 'Don't mind me, I'm fine. I'm just concentrating on getting better.' Although, like most men, he wasn't the perfect patient; he had plenty of complaints. First it was the endless chattering of the nurses at night time while he was in the intensive care section, and then it was 'crying babies' when he was transferred to a private room. The hospital was primarily a maternity clinic.

I felt badly that Justin wasn't with his family for Christmas but he helped me through the worst of emotional times. I was in hospital for five days and then when Justin arrived we went to stay in a boarding house recommended by Gonzalo. The owner didn't speak a word of English but we managed fairly well with sign language and our very limited Spanish. My Lonely Planet phrase book would have stood us in good stead, but it never made it out of Antarctica. The boarding house was decorated inside and out with Christmas decorations and I even had a Santa Claus hand towel. In one sense it was lovely and a joy not to be in a sterile hotel, but we were reminded of Christmas at every turn.

On Christmas morning Justin and I went to the hospital to be with Colin. I had found him a pair of soft, fleece-lined leather slippers for the day when he was able to get out of bed. In the evening Justin and I celebrated Christmas with Peter McDowell and all at ALE. They laid on a lovely Christmas dinner in the hotel where, in happier times, we had met the climbers who had been waiting to fly in to Patriot Hills. Captain Rashit Saitov and his crew of the Ilyushin were also there. I was able to thank them and told them all how much we appreciated the risk they had taken on our behalf. Rashit replied simply, 'Jennifer, you and Colin are fellow pilots, we had to come.' But I know they would have done that for anyone.

It was all so difficult to handle. The crash, the suddenness of the end, the adjustment to the present. It was too recent, too raw. Perhaps that's what post-traumatic stress is, but I found it difficult to be strong for Colin and when Justin left after five days I felt desperately alone, weepy and rather sorry for myself. All I wanted to do was sit with Colin in the hospital where I felt secure, but that just made him feel guilty. He kept urging me to leave, to go and join my daughters. 'I don't need anything, I'm just focusing on getting out of here. I'll feel far better knowing you aren't alone out there, that you're with your family.' The final and deciding straw was hearing that the Russian crew were giving a New Year's Eve Party but had decided not to invite me as they though I might be shocked by possible drunken revelry. I couldn't face sitting all alone on New Year's

Eve, so I finally flew to my family in Thailand.

I left Colin there in the clinic, and I still feel guilty that I did. I joined him again three weeks later in Los Angeles where he was convalescing with our good friends Jay and Susan Smith. Colin had a thorough check-up at the Los Angeles Clinic and the doctor there confirmed that Dr Rebolledo in Punta Arenas had done a brilliant job and that there was no way he would be walking if it had been otherwise. They too marvelled at the fact that he hadn't been paralysed.

Had I ever really doubted we would be saved? I don't know. There was terrible loneliness when I thought Colin had died, there was the pain and there was the cold, but I believe I always thought we would be rescued. After all, I had spoken to Jason, I had given him our coordinates, not knowing of course that they were wrong – and I'm an optimist.

I have been asked if I was frightened, but for me, the true definition of fear is when you can almost see your heart pounding; fear is when adrenalin is pumping, when your limbs go weak, when you can see danger ahead. We had gone beyond that, we had gone beyond fear.

Thanks to the bravery, courage and expertise of all those who played a part in our rescue, Colin and I were safely in the Clinica Magallanes in Punta Arenas less than 22 hours after our dreams ended on the Ronne Ice Shelf. What can one say about the brave pilots who risked all for us? Karl Z'Berg in the Twin Otter, who managed to land on the second attempt in near whiteout conditions, the Ilyushin crew who landed with 37 knots of cross-wind, and the highly professional organisation of everyone at Patriot Hills. They were all heros and so many people were involved. Every one of them played a part – simply never to be forgotten.

But it would all have been too late if it hadn't have been for Colin.

RADIO CALL
N44EA
TRQ
MGT
FUEL
NG
FUEL QTY
FWD TANK
FADEC
TEST
TEST
THIS HELICOPTER MUST BE OPERATED IN COMPLIANCE WITH THE OPERATING LIMITATIONS SPECIFIED IN THE APPROVED FLIGHT MANUAL
VENT
FLOAT ARM
LDG LTS
BOTH
OFF
FWD
START
XPNDR IDENT
DISENG

Epilogue

'The air up there in the clouds is very pure and fine, bracing and delicious. And why shouldn't it be? – it is the same as the angels breathe.'
Mark Twain

Left: N44EA

Simon and Pen had waited two days on hearing the news to make sure we were OK before proceeding on their journey. They reached the South Pole on 28 January 2004, a journey of 58 days. Simon is the oldest man by some 10 years to walk unsupported from the coast of Antarctica to the South Pole – and Pen the first man to have walked unsupported to both poles.

Months late I tracked down Karl and over the telephone was able to thank him personally for the brave part he played in saving our lives. He was at his home in Canada, near the small airfield of Carp, some distance to the west of Montreal, and I was in London. I asked him if he would tell me how events unfurled from his side and of the rescue.

'Well,' he said in that quiet way of his, 'it was a standard pick-up.'

And for him, that was really all it was – just part of a day's work and what he had been doing for 30 years.

Then, briefly, he described that night on the Ronne Ice Shelf. 'The first time I couldn't land, the visibility was poor, I was heavy with fuel and I saw it was a heavy impact. I wanted to get the doctor. When we came back, the visibility was maybe no better, but the plane was lighter and I had the doctor. I had to rely on your helicopter for definition, I couldn't see the ground. I circled several times, then I did a low pass, just touching the sastrugi to check how firm it was. It was very soft. Next time I landed. The Doc and Garry went to your tent. John and I had to check the snow for my take-off, make sure there were no obstacles. We paced out the distance and then put some markers in the snow – we always carry some weighted plastic bags for this purpose.' He went on to say that you have to be extremely careful in the polar regions, the supply of Search and Rescue aircraft are limited and so is the fuel. 'If I had crashed it would have been a real mess.' But, as he said, it was just part of a day's work.

It wasn't until a month after our accident and just before the end of the short summer season that the insurance company would allow anyone in to the crash site, although a British Antarctic Survey plane, en route from Rothera to Patriot Hills, did go in – theirs was an unscheduled and unauthorised landing. Thoughtfully, they brought out the memory chip to my Canon camera and handed it in to Mike Sharp, who sent it on to me. I don't know what happened to the camera itself, I can only imagine it was smashed beyond repair having been in the bulkhead opening behind my head. They also brought out the WWF flag that we had flown at the Pole. It has some engine oil on it but is otherwise none the worse for wear.

The insurance brokers were anxious to salvage the helicopter. It took some convincing for them to realise just how inaccessible Antarctica is and that no large aircraft could land anywhere nearby. The only machine that could land close to the site was a ski-equipped, small light aircraft – or a helicopter with long range auxiliary fuel tanks, neither of which would be capable of bringing the machine out without sawing it up. Later the engineers who finally cut it up confirmed that it was indeed irreparable.

ALE was able to make one journey in before the end of the season to collect all that they could find of our personal effects, along with the engine and transmission. It was also obligatory to clean up the site as per the IEE document to which both ALE and we were signatories. ALE took several drum containers in the Twin Otter to the site and scooped up all the contaminated snow and emptied the fuel tanks. I wish the dry carcass of the helicopter could have remained there on the Ronne Ice Shelf, a dignified burial site for a noble machine, for within two years it would have been buried forever beneath the eternal ice. Instead, during this last summer season of 2005, ALE returned to the site, to find that only the tip of the rotor head was still visible above the snow. They had to dig it out, before sawing it up and carrying it out by Twin Otter. Then it was loaded into the Ilyushin and finally dumped in a landfill site in Punta Arenas. A sad end to a beautiful bird.

Keeping Antarctica clean has become a high priority – it wasn't always so, as we saw with our own eyes when we were at Carvajal where those thousands upon thousands of fuel drums lie rusting in a great heap up near the skiway and where the comparative warmth of the summer season ensures that the snows will never cover them.

Peter McDowell said that when he saw the state of the engine and the forces necessary to have caused that sort of damage, he appreciated what a miracle it was that our frail flesh and blood had survived, and what a testament it was to the design of the helicopter.

Mike Sharp commented that, looking on the positive side, 'You have shown that if an expedition is properly organised, that if you have Search and Rescue and all the necessary equipment on board, then even in somewhere as hostile and remote as Antarctica you have a fighting chance.' He added with a grin, 'It's good for us, too, we've shown that we have the crews, the structure and organisation to look after our expeditions.'

Many months later, when talking to members of ALE and getting their side of the story, I received this postscript from Jaco:

Dear Jennifer.

It was good to speak to you this morning. I often scramble what I want to say when not talking in my first language (Afrikaans). Easier to organise the thoughts when writing like now! Anyway if you feel we've covered all the necessary bases this morning, that's good, but I think I did not do justice to Karl Z'Berg when I omitted him from my list of 'heroes' that fateful night. I mentioned Jason and Doc Martin as persons whom I thought did some outstanding work. Jason, not for having made any decisions or whatever, but just for his professional handling of all the communication channels during a time of crisis. It may look like an easy job but it's not. Doc Martin for his medical expertise in the field. I'm no doctor but I'm sure had you and Colin been in less capable hands, the injuries and eventual physical conditions of especially Colin might have been a lot worse. However, it would be most unfair not to mention the superb flying skills of Karl Z'Berg in the same context. I was not there but according to the other 3 who were in the Twin Otter when they arrived to pick you up, he did an amazing job under very dodgy light and poor visibility. From my point of view, everybody did a truly fine job in camp as well, no matter the level of involvement. This includes the Ilyushin-pilots who managed to control the plane on the blue-ice with a crosswind factor of around 37 knots – luckily it was a steady strong wind and not very gusty – but still, I felt humbled to see such true professionals at work. Mike Sharp also could not have done a better job, and with the calm way he directed procedures, he definitely managed to get the best out of everybody when the chips were down. We all have tremendous respect for Colin, too, having managed to fix the tent up under what must have been excruciating pain, discomfort and cold. Yet focusing only on the heroics and forgetting the rest doesn't complete the picture though. I think in the back of everybody's mind, and most definitely yours and Colin's, we all wish it never happened, wishing it was just another uneventful night in the Antarctic, wishing that we would never have had to dig so deep to act professionally under so much pressure. Then again, in such a situation one doesn't think of these things, we all had only one purpose and that was to help you get out alive safely but also as quickly as was humanly possible. Evaluation only happens once it's all over. Still, I'd like to salute everybody – and not the least: Antarctica herself, whom we serve and not control...which is why many of us are so fascinated with the continent. All the best Jaco.

ALE finished the 2003/4 season without further mishap.

At the end of the 2003/4 season the engineers did manage to repair the damaged DC3 that had blown over the previous season at Patriot Hills and were able to fly it out successfully.

During the 2004/5 season the Cessna hangar was dug out and relocated on the surface near the ice runway.

Cerpolex traded some Russian icebreaker time in 2005 for American help in rescuing their Antonov 3 biplane that was stuck at the South Pole for two years.

Jonathon and Roxanna Selby have bought a plot of land in Ushuaia. Jonathon's business is flourishing.

Polly Vacher made it safely back to the UK to a hero's welcome.

Polly gave her fuel at Scott base to the Australian pilot, so he was able to fly back to Australia instead of abandoning his aircraft in Antarctica.

Tamara and Ed got married in July 2004. They now have a baby daughter.

Karl Z'Berg retired in January 2006 after 36 years and 22,000 hours of flying.

My husband Simon has no further cold weather plans.

Colin received The Royal Humane Society's bronze medal for bravery and the UK Gold Hero's Award. He still has back pain but is living a full life with plenty of time in the air.

In December 2006 Colin and I will once more set off in a Bell 407 helicopter in an attempt to fly round the globe via the South and North Poles.

Technical information

The Bell 407 Helicopter N44EA

Optional extra fitted equipment

19 US gallons aux tank in luggage compartment
83 US gallons aux tank fitted on seats in rear
ELT on 121.5 mhz
GPS Garmain 530
GPS HGarmin 430
Blue Sky Network D1000 Tracker Box with fixed aerial, linked to Iridium satellite phone
Trimble radar altimeter
Snow baffles

Other equipment

115 volt remote generator
24 volt battery charger
115 volt electric fuel pump
Snow picket loaned by Darrel Day
Extra heavy duty ratchet straps
Prist anti-freeze fuel additive
Tool kit
Snow picket loaned by Darrel Day

Survival kit

2 handheld H R Smith held EPIRB 406
1 Handheld Garmin 130 GPS
Six-man life raft
Life jackets
Survival suits
Three-minute emergency air supply units
Two-man Hilleberg tent
Multi-fuel burning stove with hose attachment for heating engine
Three-week supply of dehydrated food

The standard tank carried 110 gallons and the small optional auxiliary fuel tank in the luggage compartment held a further 19 gallons. The 83 gallon fitted auxiliary tank on the three forward facing rear seats was specially certified by the FAA. ELT on 121.5 mhz (fixed installation).

The helicopter was furbished and completed at Edwards & Associates, a wholly owned subsidiary of Bell Helicopter.

Route 2003

Day	Date	From	To	Nights	N Miles	Cumulative Miles
Wed	22 Oct	West 30thst, NYC	Washington, USA	1	180	180
Thur	23 Oct	Washington	Kitty Hawk, USA	0	182	362
Thur	23 Oct	Kitty Hawk	Charleston, USA	1	293	655
Fri	24 Oct	Charleston	Fort Lauderdale, USA	0	415	1070
Fri	24 Oct	Fort Lauderdale	Nassau, Bahamas	2	160	123
Sun	26 Oct	Nassau	Turks & Cacos	0	352	1582
Sun	26 Oct	Turks & Cacos	La Romana, Dom Rep	3	275	1857
Wed	29 Oct	La Romana	St Maarten, Antilles	0	211	2068
Wed	29 Oct	St Maarten	Le Lamertin, Martinique	1	232	2300
Thur	30 Oct	Le Lamertin	Moustique, Moustique	3	344	2644
Sun	02 Nov	Moustique	St George, Granada	0	64	2708
Sun	02 Nov	St George	Ile Margarita, Venezuela	0	144	2852
Sun	02 Nov	Ile de Margarita	Caracas, Venezuela	2	173	3025
Tue	04 Nov	Caracas	Cd Guiana, Venezuela	1	277	3302
Wed	05 Nov	Cuidad Guiana	Paramaribo, Suriname	2	475	3777
Fri	07 Nov	Paramaribo	Cayenne, F.Guiana	0	366	4143
Fri	07 Nov	Cayenne	Belem, Brazil	2	439	4582
Sun	09 Nov	Belem	Santarem, Brazil	3	383	4965
Wed	12 Nov	Santarem	Jacareacanga, Brazil	0	290	5255
Wed	12 Nov	Jacareacanga	Vilhena, Brazil	1	410	5665
Thur	13 Nov	Vilhena	Cuiaba, Brazil	2	292	5957
Sat	15 Nov	Cuiaba	Baro do Garcas, Brazil	0	215	6172
Sat	15 Nov	Baro do Garcas	Brazilia, Brazil	2	259	6431
Mon	17 Nov	Brazilia	Araxa, Brazil	0	234	6665
Mon	17 Nov	Araxa	Rio de Janiero, Brazil	5	273	6938
Sat	22 Nov	Rio de Janiero	Sao Paulo, Brazil	3	181	7119
Mon	24 Nov	Sao Paulo	Iquazu, Argentina	2	447	7566

Day	Date	From	To	Nights	N Miles	Cumulative Miles
Wed	26 Nov	Iquazu	Corrientes, Argentina	1	314	7880
Thur	27 Nov	Corrientes	Buenos Aries, Argentina	3	423	8303
Sun	30 Nov	Buenos Aries	Viedma, Argentina	1	420	8723
Mon	01 Dec	Viedma	Trelew, Argentina	1	173	8896
Tue	02 Dec	Trelew	Comodoro R Argentina	1	181	9077
Wed	03 Dec	Comodoro R	Santa Cruz, Argentina	0	258	9335
Wed	03 Dec	Santa Cruz	Punta Arenas, Chile	4	198	9533
Sun	07 Dec	Punta Arenas	Ushuaia, Argentina	2	131	9664
Tue	09 Dec	Ushuaia	Marsh, Antarctica	1	452	10116
Wed	10 Dec	Marsh	Carvajal, Antarctica	1	417	10533
Thur	11 Dec	Carvajal	Fossil Bluff, Antarctica	1	214	10747
Fri	12 Dec	Fossil Bluff	Fowler, Antarctica	0	369	11116
Fri	12 Dec	Fowler	Patriot Hills, Antarctica	3	231	11347
Mon	15 Dec	Patriot Hills	Thiel Mtns Antarctica	1	270	11617
Tue	16 Dec	Thiel Mountains	SOUTH POLE	0	330	11947
Tue	16 Dec	SOUTH POLE	Thiel Mtns Antarctica	1	330	12277
Wed	17 Dec	Thiel Mountains	Patriot Hills, Antarctica	3	270	12547
Fri	19 Dec	Patriot Hills	Crash, Ronne Ice Shelf	0	121	12778